Superbrands®

Annual 2019

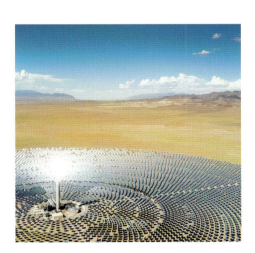

Vanity Nightmare
London Drag Queen

superbrands.uk.com

CHIEF EXECUTIVE, TCBA & CHAIRMAN, SUPERBRANDS UK
Stephen Cheliotis

DIRECTOR, SUPERBRANDS UK
Jessica Hall

BRAND LIAISON DIRECTORS
Anna Hyde
Daren Thomas
Rhiannon Harris

BRAND LIAISON MANAGER
Ashleigh Kelly

NEW BUSINESS DIRECTOR
Scott Thomson

EDITORIAL DIRECTOR
Angela Cooper

DESIGN DIRECTOR
Verity Burgess

To order further books, email brands@superbrands.uk.com
or call 020 7079 3310.

Published by
The Centre for Brand Analysis (TCBA) Ltd
5th Floor
Holden House
57 Rathbone Place
London
W1T 1JU

© 2019 Superbrands Ltd

FSC MIX
Paper from
responsible sources
FSC® C015829
www.fsc.org

Printed in Italy

ISBN 978-1-9997456-1-5

Contents

CONTENTS

BRAND STORIES

THOUGHT PIECES

APPENDIX

Key

B - Business Superbrands Qualifier

C - Consumer Superbrands Qualifier

About Superbrands

Superbrand status is awarded for quality, reliability and distinction by a combination of an expert council, and business executives or consumers voting on a comprehensive list of 3,200 consumer and business-to-business brands

---

The Superbrands Annual tells the story of many of these **successful brands, exploring their history, development and achievements**, showcasing why they are so well-regarded. These case studies provide **valuable insights into the strategies** and propositions of the brands that **consumers and business professionals trust and admire.**

The Superbrands organisation identifies and pays tribute to exceptional brands throughout the world.

The UK programme is run under license by The Centre for Brand Analysis (TCBA).

Endorsements

GRAHAM KEMP

Director
Marketing Agencies Action Group

The Superbrands Annual is always a welcome publication. For the marketing community it represents a valuable snapshot in time and for the brands that have achieved Superbrand status, a moment to reflect and celebrate.

They have built an enviable following through satisfying customer needs, through generating awareness, creating a trusting relationship and delivering their promise both physically and emotionally. However, celebrations must be brief because there is no room for complacency. Consumers face more options, choices and innovative solutions on an almost daily basis in markets that can be highly disrupted by new entrants in a world of digital transformation.

CATHERINE MASKELL

Managing Director
Content Marketing Association

The explosion of content over the past few years has made the creation, distribution and measurement of content one of the most vital marketing tasks for any brand – big or small. But these Superbrands have elevated the concept of content to an entirely new level, connecting with their customers in thrilling new ways and constantly striving to forge stronger and more creative bonds.

To achieve Superbrand status you need a powerful marketing strategy that fires the imagination and holds the attention, fusing high quality content with rock solid planning, and we are delighted to be associated with Superbrands and heartily congratulate all the featured brands.

JOHN NOBLE

Director
British Brands Group

As you look through the Superbrands presented here and ponder what they mean to you and the relevance they have to the way you live your life, spare a thought for the framework that underpins them, the less glamorous side of branding.

How do companies make the huge investments needed to make an impression with individuals without competitors reaping the return? How can they be confident their shoppers are not being duped into buying others' products in the belief that they are buying the original? How do they make sure that competition is vigorous but fair? These questions play to intellectual property, consumer protection and competition policy, areas that may seem dry but which are fundamental to the success of the Superbrands you see here. The British Brands Group is proud to work for an effective framework for brands in the UK and takes great encouragement from the successes portrayed in these pages.

JENNIFER SPROUL

Chief Executive
Institute of Internal Communication

Brands, and particularly Superbrands, are ubiquitous in our modern lives, and as customers of such brands, we have high expectations. We expect them to enable us to think, feel and do what they promise, and in order to achieve this, it's the employees who must be central to their mission. The brands featured in Superbrands are recognised as organisations that are working to achieve this and we are delighted to see them showcased.

We live in a world where our opinions of brands are more widely influenced and we look to our peers, and particularly those people representing the brand – its employees – to demonstrate its purpose and values. For brands to be successful, they must work with their employees to not only be brand ambassadors but ensure the experience expected by the customer is driven from the inside out.

Superbrands Selection Process

Superbrands Selection Process

Superbrands UK Annual Volume 20, 2019

The annual Consumer Superbrands and Business Superbrands surveys are long-running brand sentiment studies that identify the UK's strongest consumer and business-to-business brands respectively.

Brands do not apply or pay to be considered for Superbrands status. In order to provide a broad review of the market and ascertain the stongest brands in each category, all the key players in each sector are evaluated through the voting process. Just shy of 3,200 brands across 141 categories were voted on in this year's surveys. These initial brand lists were compiled using a range of relevant data sources, such as market share, share of voice and industry league tables.

Since 2006 this has been independently managed by The Centre for Brand Analysis (TCBA), which undertakes brand research, evaluation and strategy projects. TCBA's audit and consultancy services help shape brand, marketing and business strategies, enhancing brand reputation and underlying business growth. In mid-2017, TCBA took over the UK licence for Superbrands and continues to run the process as follows:

Consumer Superbrands
A total of 2,500 British adults vote on a list of 1,596 brands across 78 different categories. The list is also ratified by the independent and voluntary Consumer Superbrands Council; 32 leading marketing experts, providing a secondary quality control mechanism. Brands not highly rated by the experts are effectively vetoed from attaining Consumer Superbrand status.

Business Superbrands
This list is jointly chosen by 2,500 British business professionals with purchasing or managerial responsibility, and the independent, voluntary Business Superbrands Council; 24 leading business-to-business marketing experts. Both audiences voted on 1,586 brands in 63 categories.

Definition of a Superbrand
All those involved in the voting process bear in mind the following definition:

'A Superbrand has established the finest reputation in its field. It offers customers significant emotional and/or tangible advantages over its competitors, which customers want and recognise.'

In addition, the voters are asked to judge brands against the following three factors:

- **Quality** – Does the brand provide quality products and services?

- **Reliability** – Can the brand be trusted to deliver consistently?

- **Distinction** – Is it well known in its sector and suitably different from its rivals?

Naturally, as a brand perception and sentiment survey individual opinions will be impacted by a number of additional factors, some of which are addressed in the 'Research and Results Overview 2019'.

Only the most highly-regarded brands from these surveys are awarded Superbrands status. These brands do not pay for this status and can proclaim their success to stakeholders. Member brands are also able to use the Superbrands seal (shown to the right) to showcase their award.

Please visit Superbrands.uk.com for full details of the research methodology or for more information about TCBA please visit www.tcba.co.uk

TCBA

To access the consumer and business professionals that vote in our surveys, TCBA has partnered with the global leader in digital research data Dynata.

Dynata is one of the world's leading providers of first-party data contributed by people who opt-in to member-based panels. With a reach that encompasses over 60 million people globally and an extensive library of individual profile attributes collected through surveys, Dynata is the cornerstone for precise, trustworthy quality data. Dynata serves nearly 6,000 market research agencies, media and advertising agencies, consulting and investment firms as well as healthcare and corporate customers.

dynata.com

Introducing the Experts

Superbrands Councils 2019

The Business Superbrands (B) and Consumer Superbrands
(C) Expert Councils are chaired by Stephen Cheliotis,
Chief Executive at The Centre for Brand Analysis (TCBA)

Business Superbrands Council

Rob Alexander
Partner, Headland

Alex Bigg
CEO, MHP Communications

Darren Bolton
Executive Creative Director
OgilvyOne Business

Kate Cox
CEO, Bray Leino

Kirsty Dawe
Co-Founder & Director
Really B2B

Steve Dyer
Managing Director
Oil the Wheels

James Farmer
Publisher & Founder
B2B Marketing

Ian Haworth
Chief Creative Officer, EMEA
Wunderman

Nick Jefferson
Partner, Monticello

Steve Kemish
Managing Partner, Junction

Mark Lethbridge
CEO, Gravity Global

Claire Mason
Founder & CEO, Man Bites Dog

Stephen Meade
Chief Executive, McCann Enterprise

Vikki Mitchell
Director, Corporate Practice
KANTAR

Rob Morrice
CEO, Stein IAS

Michael Murphy
Senior Partner
Michael Murphy & Ltd

Rebecca Price
Partner, Frank Bright & Abel

Sandy Purewal
Founder, Superfied

Dave Roberts
Creative Partner, Superunion

Glenn Robertson
Owner & MD, Purechannels

Susanna Simpson
Founder, Limelight

Alan Vandermolen
President, International
WE Communications

David Willan
Co-Founder & Former Chairman
Circle Research (now Savanta)

Prof. Alan Wilson PhD
Professor of Marketing
University of Strathclyde

Consumer Superbrands Council

Andrew Bloch
Founder & Managing Partner
FRANK

Ed Bolton
Creative Director, BrandCap

Catherine Borowski
Founder & Artistic Director
PRODUCE UK

Rebecca Brennan
Managing Director, Cubo

Emma Brock
Founding Partner, Brock & Wilson

Vicky Bullen
CEO, Coley Porter Bell

Hugh Cameron
Chairman, PHD UK

Jackie Cooper
Senior Advisor, Edelman

Claire Cootes
Managing Director, LIDA

Christian Dubreuil
Managing Director
EMEA Ad & Audience
Dynata

Caroline Foster Kenny
CEO EMEA, IPG Mediabrands

Steve Gladdis
Chief Strategy Officer
MediaCom London

Vanella Jackson
Global CEO, Hall & Partners

Rob Kavanagh
Executive Creative Director
OLIVER UK

Owen Lee
Chief Creative Officer
FCB Inferno

Nick Liddell
Director of Consulting, The Clearing

Avra Lorrimer
Managing Director
Hill + Knowlton Strategies

Mick Mahoney
Partner & Chief Creative Officer
Harbour

Amy McCulloch
Co-Founder & Managing Director
eight&four

Nick Morris
Founding Partner, Canvas8

Richard Moss
Chief Executive, Good Relations

James Murphy
Founder & CEO, adam&eveDDB

Thom Newton
CEO & Managing Partner
Conran Design Group

Tim Perkins
Deputy Group Chairman
Design Bridge

Julian Pullan
Vice Chairman
& President International
Jack Morton Worldwide

Tom Roberts
CEO, Tribal Worldwide London

Gary Robinson
Creative Partner
Studio of Art and Commerce

Marta Swannie
Digital Creative Director
Superunion

Emma Thompson
Chair, Consumer Marketing
Weber Shandwick

Guy Wieynk
CEO, Publicis UK & Western Europe
Global Lead, Sapient Inside

Dylan Williams
Partner & Chief Strategy Officer
Droga5 London

Matt Willifer
Chief Strategy Officer, WCRS
Partner, Engine

Some council members may have changed roles since the time of voting and/or publication.

'Vorsprung durch Technik,' or 'Progress through Technology' – **three words that define Audi.** For more than three decades they have encapsulated the brand's **relentless desire to innovate,** and have been reflected in its **ground-breaking engineering and design** and distinctive tone of voice. **Always ahead, always exciting and always with a twinkle in the eye**

Market

2018 saw the total automotive market contract by -5.5%. For the first time in many years the Premium market also contracted, in part driven by new testing procedures that delayed car launches. Despite the market conditions, the Audi brand extended its lead in Brand Desirability and Consideration, earning more accolades for creativity and effectiveness than ever before, and also securing numerous coveted product awards, including Luxury SUV of the Year for the Q7 and Coupe of the Year for the A5 at the recent What Car? Awards.

The automotive industry is set to change more over the next 10 years than it has during the last 50, with drivetrain electrification and unprecedented automation of the driving experience being among the key disruptors. In its capacity as innovator and challenger to the status quo, Audi is in the vanguard of development in both fields. The first of its advanced autonomous systems will be available soon in the A8 luxury saloon, and it has embarked on a major electrification programme that will bring a total of 12 new fully electric Audi models to market by 2025, the first being the new e-tron SUV that is set to take to the road during 2019.

DID YOU KNOW?

An **Audi coat of paint** has **five layers** but is only **half as thick as a human hair**

Product

Audi offers an extensive range of models across a series of premium segments – from the A1, which was described by Autocar magazine as 'dripping with big car appeal', to the luxury class A8. Audi also offers a wide range of SUVs, from the compact, city-friendly Q2 through to the innovative, prestigious Q8, which joined the range during 2018 and, according to Auto Express Magazine, 'delivers as a luxurious flagship SUV'. In addition, its portfolio of high-performance Audi Sport models, including the RS range and iconic R8 supercar, has also attracted a sizeable following.

Achievements

Audi sold 143,717 cars in 2018. The UK remains the largest export market for Audi in Europe, and the fourth largest market globally. According to third-party brand tracking from Millward Brown, Audi leads the total and premium automotive market for Brand Desirability.

Audi won a raft of awards in 2018, including Luxury SUV of the Year for the Q7 and Coupe of the Year for the A5 at the recent What Car? Awards.

Furthermore, Audi won more than 23 awards for creativity and marketing effectiveness including the prestigious IPA Marketing Effectiveness Grand Prix and Gold Cannes Lion.

Recent Developments

Being 'Vorsprung' and embracing innovation is at the heart of everything Audi does. The A8, for example, is the first production vehicle in the world to have been developed for highly automated driving, and its highly efficient mild hybrid drivetrain, advanced all-wheel-steering and fully digital touchscreen cabin concept, are shared with the remarkable new Q8 SUV. Audi also launched the e-tron, which brings its world renowned flair for design, build quality and engineering to the fully electric vehicle sector for the first time in an SUV, delivering sub-six-second acceleration potential and a driving range of 248 miles. This spirit of innovation is not confined to its products but also infuses Audi business strategies and communications.

A 292 lightbulb moment
The new Audi A7 Sportback

The new Audi Q8.
It makes a
bit of an entrance.

⊙⊙⊙⊙

Official fuel consumption figures for the new Audi Q8 50 TDI quattro 8-speed tiptronic in mpg (l/100km): Urban 38.7 (7.3), Extra Urban 43.5 (6.5), Combined 41.5 (6.8). CO2 emissions: 178.

Brand History

1909 August Horch Automobilwerke GmbH is created in Germany. The eponymous founder uses the name 'Audi', Latin for listen and meaning 'hark' in German.

1932 Audi merges with Horch, DKW and Wanderer, to form Auto Union AG. The four rings of the Audi badge symbolise the four brands coming together.

1964 Volkswagenwerk AG acquires the majority of shares in Auto Union GmbH with Audi becoming a fully-owned VW subsidiary from the end of 1966.

1982 Audi employs BBH as its advertising agency. 'Vorsprung durch Technik' is born.

1990s Audi dominates British Touring Cars with its A4.

2000 Audi wins the Le Mans 24-hour race for three consecutive years and the brand becomes renowned as a premium brand with sporting and performance credentials.

2017 Audi launches an unprecedented number of new models. Audi's safety technology campaign 'Clowns' wins Campaign magazine's Film of The Year Award.

2018 Audi reveals the all-electric e-tron with the campaign manifesto of 'Electric has gone Audi'. Audi launches the Q8 – a new flagship in the SUV range, and is also awarded the IPA Marketing Effectiveness Grand Prix.

Promotion

First used by the advertising agency BBH for the brand in 1982, the line 'Vorsprung durch Technik', loosely translated as 'Advancement through Technology', is continuously being reinvented.

In 2018, Audi celebrated electrification with the e-tron campaign, reaching 23 million Britons in one day with with the 'Electric has gone Audi' message. The campaign led to 131,000 hits to audi.co.uk – the highest single day of traffic ever recorded. The Q8 was launched in great style with a unique live activation at the British Film Institute. A total of 6.9 million people watched the live reveal, crushing the target

DID YOU KNOW?

At 150kW stations, the Audi e-tron can charge faster than a smartphone

of 1.1m views. Audi partnered with Sky for niche targeting through AdSmart, using household data and understanding the specific packages they are subscribing to, in order to isolate the most appropriate households for each TV campaign.

Brand Values

'Vorsprung durch Technik' drives everything that Audi does. The brand always aims to deliver unforgettable experiences for its customers, not only through exciting, desirable cars that continue to push aesthetic and technological boundaries, but also at every physical and digital touchpoint on the purchase journey of those cars and beyond.

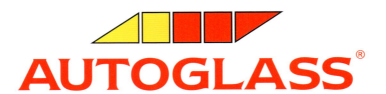

AUTOGLASS®

*Autoglass® is a **leading consumer and business automotive brand**, providing vehicle glass repair and replacement to more than one million motorists every year*

Market

Autoglass® is the UK's favourite vehicle glass repair and replacement specialist and is part of Belron® Group, which operates in 34 countries and served 16.5 million customers in 2017. Autoglass® has the widest reaching network in the UK with over 1,100 technicians providing a world class service to motorists.

Windscreens play an integral role in modern automotive design and the average car in the UK car parc uses 15% more glass than 10 years ago. The windscreen is important for vehicle safety – its correct fitting and bonding can save lives. Windscreens now incorporate complex technologies such as cameras and sensors to enable Advanced Driver Assistance Systems (ADAS) that form part of the journey to autonomous driving, such as Autonomous Emergency Braking and Lane Departure Warnings.

Autoglass® is exceptional in the vehicle glass repair and replacement market by having its own dedicated research and development team: Belron® Technical – a network of innovators and thinkers, all focused on driving technical standards and developing innovations that break new ground to improve the service provided to its customers.

Autoglass® works with insurance, fleet and lease companies – large and small – across the full spectrum of industries. Autoglass® handles the vehicle glass claims for seven of the top 10 motor insurance companies in the UK, providing a world-class service to policyholders demonstrated by its NPS score of 73 in 2017. The company has a dedicated specialist glazing division, Autoglass® Specials, which repairs and replaces glass on everything from trains to combine harvesters, and a sister company, Autoglass® BodyRepair, which offers a mobile bodyshop repair service.

Product

Autoglass® exists to make a difference by solving people's problems with real care. By providing exceptional customer service at every touch point and being an ambassador for road safety, Autoglass® has become one of the UK's most trusted service brands.

30% OF A VEHICLE'S STRUCTURAL STRENGTH IS PROVIDED BY THE WINDSCREEN

The company operates a 'Repair First' philosophy, ensuring that, wherever possible, it will repair a chipped windscreen rather than replace it, a safe solution that saves time and money, and is better for the environment. If the damage is beyond repair, Autoglass® will replace the glass. It only uses Original Equipment Manufacturer (OEM) standard glass, ensuring that each replacement windscreen is as good as the original.

Autoglass® is an industry leader in safety and champions the role that ADAS technology plays in improving driver safety. The calibration service provided by Autoglass® delivers a seamless customer journey with the glass replacement and

calibration happening at the same appointment. As well as being a far better customer journey, this eliminates any risk that may exist between the time of glass replacement and subsequent calibration – including on-board diagnostic checks prior to the windscreen removal to understand if there are any existing faults to the vehicle.

Achievements

Autoglass® has more than 70,000 customer reviews online with an average score of 4.4 out of 5, the highest number of reviews from any UK-based vehicle glass repair and replacement specialist.

Autoglass® is proud of being a trusted and respected company in the eyes of its people, customers and partners. Its work for charity is extensive and in 2018, through the annual Spirit of Belron® Challenge, Autoglass®, Belron® and associated brands raised £970,000 for Afrika Tikkun, equating to £8.6m in 17 years of support for the charity.

Autoglass® is committed to achieving continual improvement in environmental as well as Health and Safety management. It is certified to ISO 14001, ISO 9001 and OHSAS 18001 standards and constantly strives to reduce its relative use of non-renewable fuel and CO_2.

Brand History

1972 Autoglass Supplies Ltd is launched, providing mobile vehicle glass replacement.

1982 Autoglass Ltd becomes part of Belron®, the world's largest vehicle glass repair and replacement company.

1983 Autoglass Ltd merges with Windshields Ltd to become Autoglass Windshields, rebranding to Autoglass® in 1987.

1990 The windscreen repair service is launched. Autoglass® becomes a registered trademark.

1994 Autoglass® launches the 'Heroes' advertising campaign.

2007 Autoglass® becomes the first vehicle glass repair and replacement company to offer online booking.

2009 The Autoglass® Specials brand is launched.

2015 Autoglass® leads the industry with its Advanced Driver Assistance Systems (ADAS) calibration investment, and it is rolled out nationally in 2016.

2017 AutoRestore® rebrands to become Autoglass® BodyRepair.

2018 Autoglass® launches Rain Repel – the Advanced Windscreen Kit as well as the industry's first skill for the Amazon Echo, enabling customers to book an appointment using voice commands. Autoglass® expands its ADAS expertise to 70 centres offering calibration.

Autoglass® is also committed to embracing new technologies to provide a smoother customer journey and has utilised Artificial Intelligence (AI) technology to allow customers to take a photo of their car's damage, upload it to the website and receive a quote instantaneously – choosing this option means a quote is calculated 70% quicker than through the previous method.

Recent Developments

Proudly being at the forefront of innovation in the automotive after-market, Autoglass® invested heavily in understanding the implications of ADAS technologies and was the first to offer a nationwide ADAS calibration service in 2016.

By the end of 2018, Autoglass® had 315 trained ADAS technicians and 70 centres offering calibration across the UK and will continue to invest as the adoption of this technology grows.

Autoglass® has also spearheaded the creation of an industry standard ADAS training accreditation in collaboration with the Institute of the Motor

Industry (IMI). The new accreditation will ensure technicians can identify and interpret information relating to a specific vehicle and its ADAS features, in order to determine which method of calibration is required and then calibrate correctly – significantly reducing the completion time. In 2018, Autoglass® calibrated over 100,000 motorists' ADAS sensors, double the number performed in the previous year.

Throughout 2018, Autoglass® has expanded its partnership with a range of prestigious fleet companies, signing new contracts with Wincanton and Bibby Distribution.

Promotion

Autoglass® became a household name in the 1990s after signing as the main sponsor of Chelsea Football Club. Since then, it has invested in several high-profile brand campaigns to ensure it remains at the forefront of motorists' minds, cementing its position as a great British brand.

In 2005, its 'Heroes' advertising campaign was launched, featuring real technicians. Autoglass® firmly believes its people are 'everyday heroes' that deliver its brand promise consistently to customers. This format has been extended throughout the company's brand communications, with employees appearing on vans and online. Sonic branding, in the form of the famous 'Autoglass® Repair, Autoglass® Replace' jingle, is one of the most recognisable assets of the brand.

In 2018, Autoglass® participated in the tenth biennial Best of Belron® competition, to find the world's best vehicle glass technician. Representing the UK was Ryan Millar from Nairn in Scotland, who qualified for the global final by winning the UK stage in 2017.

Brand Values

Autoglass® makes a difference by solving people's problems with real care.

With over **325 years of history and expertise in banking**, Barclays is a transatlantic consumer and wholesale bank. Offering products and services across **personal, corporate and investment banking**, credit cards and wealth management, it is **united by a common set of Values and a single guiding Purpose: Creating opportunities to rise**

Market

Barclays has three clearly defined divisions, Barclays UK, Barclays International and Barclays Execution Services, which provide diversification by business line, geography and customer; enhancing financial resilience and contributing to the delivery of consistent returns through the business cycle. Its strong core business is well positioned to deliver long-term value for Barclays' shareholders.

Product

Barclays operates in over 40 countries and employs 82,000 people. It moves, lends, invests and protects money for customers and clients worldwide.

Achievements

Barclays is a company of opportunity makers, working together to 'help people rise' – customers, clients, colleagues and society.

It is a long-standing industry leader in championing diversity and inclusion both within the workplace and in delivering services. It was the first bank to employ a female branch manager back in 1958 and consistently appears in The Times Top 50 Employers for Women as well as ranking highly on the Bloomberg Gender Equality Index.

Barclays was also the first bank to roll out 'talking' ATMs and high visibility debit cards in the UK, assisting those with visual impairments. It is also recognised as a Disability Confident Leader by the UK Government and actively works to promote the scheme to other colleagues.

Always aiming to improve its colleagues' work-life balance, Barclays launched its Dynamic Working campaign in 2015 and now over 63% of colleagues work flexibly. Externally, it has been recognised as Best for Embedded Flexibility and as a Top 10 Employer for Working Families. Furthermore, the bank recently became one of the first signatories to the UK Government's Race at Work Charter.

Another reflection of Barclays' social responsibility is its pioneering credentials in green finance. It has

DID YOU KNOW?

In 2017, Barclays celebrated **50 years since launching** the world's first ATM

successfully launched an inaugural green bond, green mortgage, asset finance facilities, trade loans, corporate and innovation loans as well as corporate deposits.

Recent Developments

Barclays consistently plays a part in driving economic growth and social progress by supporting access into employment. It is committed to upskilling millions of people, providing them with the vital skills needed to thrive within the modern workplace. It also supports entrepreneurs with high-growth, high-impact companies not only to facilitate access to job opportunities but to create broader opportunities for growth, which in turn helps to build long-term demand for banking services.

Barclays began working with the Unreasonable Group in 2016, launching Unreasonable Impact – the world's first international network of accelerators focused on scaling up entrepreneurial solutions that will help employ thousands worldwide, while solving

some of our most pressing societal challenges. With advice and guidance from a community of world-class mentors and industry specialists, including experts from across Barclays, the programme has supported growth-stage ventures to collectively create 7,000 new jobs and positively impact over 100 million people.

LifeSkills, created with Barclays, is an employability programme that has inspired more than 6.7 million young people over the last five years. It raises their aspirations and equips them with the core, transferable skills and the work experience needed to move forward into the workplace. Over 10,000 colleagues have volunteered for the programme.

Barclays Connect with Work is another innovative employability programme that provides people from often overlooked communities with the specific skills they need to get a meaningful job with organisations that are hiring. The programme makes the connection for them with companies looking for new employees, including Barclays clients and suppliers. Globally, Connect with Work has already supported thousands of people into work and is providing a pipeline of new, diverse talent.

Barclays also has a banking service for armed forces customers, with a range of products to specifically suit the needs of military personnel. Products include bank accounts, mortgages and credit cards, enabling customers to use garrison addresses when applying for new accounts. This builds on Barclays' longstanding support for armed forces personnel including programmes which help them transition back into civilian life after service and improve employment outcomes.

Promotion

In 2018, Barclays' advertising continued to promote its LifeSkills programme for young people. It also broadened its DigiSafe initiative by lifting the lid on unequal data exchanges as well as showcasing helpful money management features within the Barclays Mobile Banking app. Barclays has helped

Brand History

1690 John Freame and Thomas Gould start trading as goldsmith bankers in London.

1728 Freame and Gould move to 54 Lombard Street, beneath the sign of the Black Spread Eagle.

1920 William Morris is invested in, helping him become the biggest car manufacturer in the UK.

1958 Barclays appoints the UK's first ever female branch manager, Hilda Harding.

1966 Barclaycard, the UK's first credit card, is launched.

1967 The world's first ATM is unveiled by Barclays.

1987 Barclays launches the UK's first debit card.

2007 Barclays launches the UK's first contactless payment card.

2012 Pingit launches, the first payment service allowing customers to transfer money via a mobile phone.

2014 bPay wearable payment devices are launched.

2015 Barclays launches Rise, a community for Fintech startups to connect, co-create and scale innovative ideas.

2016 Voice Security is launched to UK retail customers.

2017 The first solution for corporate clients combining biometric technology with advanced digital signing is launched.

2018 Barclays completes one of the biggest ever restructurings of a bank – the closure of Non-Core, exiting Africa, launching Barclays Services Limited and standing up the first UK ring-fenced bank. Barclays also launches its Purpose, 'Creating opportunities to rise'.

over five million people take positive action to become more digitally safe as part of its DigiSafe work.

Barclays Eagle Labs are in more than 20 locations nationwide to help businesses and communities create, innovate and grow. Advice and digital skills have been provided to more than 100,000 individuals and Eagle Labs is currently home to more than 400 businesses.

Barclays has been the headline sponsor of Pride in London since 2014. In addition to this, thousands of Barclays colleagues take part in over 25 other Prides across the UK. In 2018, Barclays unified this activity under the creative identity of 'Love Goes the Distance'. The campaign reimagined Pride as a march towards the end of injustice, fuelled by 'what will get us there – love'. The campaign ran across social media,

press, colleague communications, and the Barclays branch network.

Barclays C-Suite and institutional investor audiences are highly competitive and zealous because their time is at such a premium. They are, however, naturally curious and hungry for information. Barclays engages this group in long-term strategic dialogue, through ideas and video-based storytelling. With the aim of delivering the Investment Bank's deep understanding across sectors, asset classes and economies, thought-leading insights provide a transparent view into the way Barclays works with clients and the real impact its services can have on their businesses.

In 2017, to prevent malware and remote access Trojan fraud, the first solution for corporate clients that combines biometric technology with advanced digital signing was launched. This solution

biometrically ties a transaction to an individual as well as introducing Behavioural Biometrics across digital channels.

Brand Values

Barclays' strategy is underpinned by the energy, commitment and passion of its people who deliver its purpose – 'Creating opportunities to rise'. This concept spans customers, clients, colleagues and society as a whole. Everything that the bank does is underpinned by five Values: Respect, Integrity, Service, Excellence and Stewardship.

For more than a century **BP has provided heat, light and mobility to help society grow and prosper.** Operating across six continents, its products and services are **delivered to customers in more than 70 countries** through a range of internationally respected brands

Market

From the deep sea to the desert, from rigs to retail, BP delivers energy products and services to people around the world. It finds and produces oil and gas on land and offshore and is one of the largest renewable energy operators amongst its peers. BP provides customers with fuel for transport, energy for heat and light, lubricants to keep engines moving and the petrochemicals products used to make items such as paints, clothes and packaging.

BP employs 74,000 people. In 2017 it produced 3.6 million barrels of oil equivalent per day, 1,432MW from wind farms and 776 million litres of ethanol equivalent, from its biofuels sites.

Product

BP has a diverse energy portfolio, producing energy resources for people on the road, at home or for business. BP leads the field in a series of specialist energy technologies. This includes seismic imaging that enables it to 'see' underground and find new oil and gas reservoirs.

BP has been investing in renewables for many years and is one of the top wind energy producers in the US, currently operating 10 farms. BP believes that biofuels also offer one of the

DID YOU KNOW?

Each year BP **is investing $500m** in low carbon businesses

best large-scale solutions to reduce emissions in the transportation system and has three biofuels sites in Brazil.

BP has over 1,200 service stations in the UK, which provide trusted quality fuels and everyday convenience items, while Wild Bean Cafés provide food and coffee for on-the-go motorists. In addition to its own offering, BP has partnered with Marks & Spencer Simply Food at selected locations across the UK to provide customers with an even greater choice.

Achievements

In 2017 BP joined forces with Lightsource, Europe's largest solar developer. The goal was to accelerate growth of worldwide solar. By 2018, the Lightsource BP partnership had doubled its footprint, with a presence in 10 countries.

In 2018 BP acquired the UK's largest electric vehicle charging company. BP Chargemaster operates more than 6,500 charging points across the country, with ultra-fast charging points due to start appearing on BP forecourts from spring 2019.

BP's support for the arts and culture in the UK goes back more than 50 years. Today it is focused on long-term partnerships with the Royal Opera House, National Portrait Gallery, British Museum and Royal Shakespeare Company. BP estimates that over this period some 53 million people have benefited from BP's sponsorship.

BP is the principal funder of the Science Museum Group Academy, which launched in October 2018. It will reach up to 600 teacher and museum educators and 250 scientists / STEM professionals each year, training them in approaches to build science capital. It is being delivered in partnership with the UK-wide Association of Science and Discovery Centres (ASDC).

Recent Developments

The energy transition the world is facing over the next decades is defined by the 'dual challenge' –

The world demands more energy.

The world demands less carbon.

Can the world have both?

We see possibilities everywhere.

keep advancing

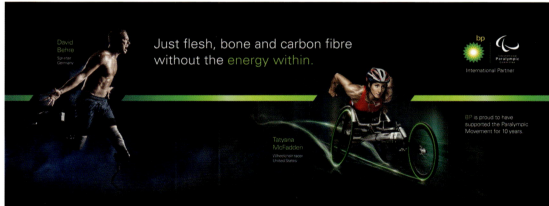

Brand History

1909 The Anglo-Persian Oil Company, as BP was first known, is formed.

1940s BP's sales, profits, capital expenditure and employment all surge upwards as post-war Europe restructures.

1975 BP pumps the first oil from the North Sea's UK sector ashore after purchasing the Forties field – financed by a bank loan of £370m.

1990s BP merges with US giant Amoco, and the acquisitions of ARCO, Burmah Castrol and Veba Oil turn the British oil company into one of the world's largest energy companies.

2000 The brand relaunches, unveiling the new 'Helios' brand mark.

2005 BP Alternative Energy is launched, a new business dedicated to the development, wholesale marketing and trading of low carbon power.

2012 BP supports Britain in staging the world's biggest sporting event – the London 2012 Olympic and Paralympic Games – as an Official Partner.

2017 BP and Lightsource agree to form a strategic partnership, bringing Lightsource's solar development and management expertise together with BP's global scale. The company is renamed Lightsource BP.

2018 BP announces it is to buy the UK's largest electric vehicle charging company, Chargemaster, which operates more than 6,500 charging points across the country. The company is renamed BP Chargemaster.

---

the need to meet the world's demand for more energy, whilst also lowering carbon emissions.

In 2018 BP set itself some ambitious targets to reduce carbon in its traditional energy operations, improve its products so its customers can reduce their emissions, and create new low carbon businesses.

In fact, BP introduced an Advancing Low Carbon (ALC) accreditation programme in 2018 to shine a light on some of its successes and help further drive low carbon actions across the company.

Promotion
At the start of 2019, BP launched its first global advertising campaign in a decade. The campaign's optimistic adverts feature a range of activities from across BP's broad portfolio, including natural gas, wind, solar, advanced fuels, electric vehicle charging and venture partnerships. Together, the campaign stories illustrate how BP 'sees possibilities' in making all forms of energy cleaner and better, and is committed to delivering the energy the world needs, while advancing a low carbon future.

The campaign launched in the UK, US, Berlin and Brussels, as well as in some of the world's busiest airports. Media included TV, print, digital, out-of-home and social content. The advertising reinforces BP's brand essence – 'Keep Advancing' – signalling that the energy BP provides truly helps advance human progress.

Brand Values
BP is committed to values of safety, respect, excellence, courage and one team. In a fast-changing world, these values provide continuity and a shared point of reference for every action taken and every decision made.

BP's goal is to create an environment of inclusion and acceptance. BP believes that for its employees to be motivated and to perform to their full potential, they need to be treated with respect, dignity and without discrimination.

BP has been supporting the Paralympic Movement since July 2008 when it became the Official Oil and Gas Partner for the London 2012 Paralympic Games. Not only is the continued growth of the Paralympic Movement something that BP is proud to be a part of, its Paralympic partnerships in more than 10 countries around the world are a strong cultural fit as they share similar values, particularly courage, respect and excellence.

bp.com

Throughout its 100-year history, **British Airways has been at the forefront of innovation in aviation. Its pioneering spirit has led to numerous industry and world firsts.** 2019 marks **British Airways' centenary year,** with an **ongoing commitment to putting the customer at the heart of everything it does,** and a star-studded new brand campaign

Market

British Airways, part of International Airlines Group, is one of the world's leading global premium airlines and the largest international carrier in the UK. With its home base at London Heathrow, British Airways flies to more than 200 destinations in more than 80 different countries. British Airways carries more than 123,000 customers every day and has a fleet of more than 280 aircraft.

Product

British Airways offers a range of flights to UK domestic, short-haul and long-haul destinations. It offers a range of travel classes, with something for every taste and budget, from First, Club World, World Traveller Plus and World Traveller in long haul, to Club World and Club Europe, which operate on short haul routes.

Achievements

British Airways recently unveiled the details of its 2019 investment programme, which sees £6.5bn being invested across new aircraft, cabin enhancements, lounge refurbishments and new digital technology, designed to improve the customer experience. 2019 also sees the launch of new routes to Charleston, Pittsburgh, Osaka, Kos, Corsica, Ljubljana and Montpellier among others, showcasing the airline's biggest route network in more than a decade.

Over the next five years the airline will take delivery of 72 new aircraft, including four new types for the British Airways fleet: the Airbus A350 and Boeing 787-10, which will operate on its long-haul routes. Over the last five years it has taken delivery of 57 new, fuel efficient and quieter aircraft, including A380s and Boeing 787 Dreamliners. By 2020 British Airways will have received 100 new aircraft in less than a decade. British Airways is also fitting out 128 of its long-haul aircraft with new interiors.

All short-haul aircraft are to be fitted with wifi. In addition, more than 60 of British Airways' long-haul aircraft are now fitted

25m **CUPS OF TEA** ARE SERVED BY THE AIRLINE EACH YEAR

with full streaming capability, high-speed wifi. The system will be installed in 90% of long-haul aircraft by the end of 2019.

On the ground, new lounges are also being unveiled for customers to relax in and enjoy ahead of their flight, in San Francisco, Johannesburg, Geneva and New York's JFK.

Furthermore, 18 months since it opened, British Airways' award-winning First Wing at Heathrow's T5 welcomed its one millionth passenger in 2018.

Recent Developments

In January 2019, British Airways announced a calendar of major events to celebrate its centenary year, a real milestone in aviation and British industrial history.

The airline can trace its origins back to the birth of civil aviation, when the world's first daily international scheduled air service between London and Paris was launched by British Airways' forerunner company, Aircraft Transport and Travel Limited (AT&T).

The celebratory plans are centered around three main areas: its heritage, looking forward to what the future of flying might hold, and celebrating its landmark birthday with customers and colleagues.

To honour its heritage, British Airways revealed plans to paint aircraft in popular heritage liveries, beginning with the painting of a Boeing 747 in the much-admired design of its predecessor, British Overseas Airways Corporation (BOAC). It is also digitising its archive so people can take a look through the rich history of the brand.

Later in the year, the strategy will shift to the future with a focus on the future of fuels, the future of the flying experience and future careers. This will culminate in a virtual reality experience that will enable people to see how flying has evolved and what it might look like in the next 100 years.

Brand History

1919 AT&T operates the first commercial scheduled flight.

1924 Imperial Airways is formed as the UK's first nationalised airline to operate UK air services.

1936 British Airways Limited is formed from United Airways, Hillman Airways and Spartan Airlines.

1974 BOAC and BEA merge to form British Airways.

1987 British Airways is privatised.

1988 Club World and Club Europe cabins are launched. British Caledonian joins British Airways.

1999 The oneworld® alliance launches with British Airways, American Airlines, Canadian Airlines, Iberia and Qantas as the founding members.

2010 A redesigned first class cabin is unveiled and a joint business with American Airlines and Iberia launches.

2011 British Airways and Iberia complete their merger to form the International Airline Group (IAG).

2012 IAG finalises the purchase of bmi in April. The brand sponsors the London 2012 Olympic and Paralympic Games.

2019 British Airways celebrates its 100-year anniversary on 25th August 2019.

The airline's Flying Start charity partnership with Comic Relief also hit a milestone in November 2018, reaching its £20m fundraising target. Flying Start began in 2010 with a goal to raise £20m by the end of 2020, and it has achieved its fundraising target more than a year ahead of schedule, thanks to generous donations from British Airways' customers and colleagues.

Promotion

In February 2019, British Airways launched a new brand campaign, which will run throughout its centenary year. The star-studded TV ad at the heart of the campaign features celebrities including Gary Oldman and Paloma Faith boarding a plane dubbed 'BA100' as cabin crew, pilots and engineers carry out their final touches in preparation for take-off. The stars

DID YOU KNOW?

The airline carries up to 123,000 customers every day and 45 million customers a year

of the ad are seen penning a love letter to Britain, and showing the people, ideas and values that make the very best of modern Britain.

To tie in with its centenary celebrations, British Airways also announced the return of its popular BA Magic campaign, committing to mark its 100th birthday with 100 acts of kindness.

Brand Values

The British Airways brand is built upon the belief that it is the flow of people and ideas around the world that make Britain great. The brand looks to embody four modern British values – open-minded, pioneering, creative and welcoming. It is a modern, forward-facing outlook, and one that evokes a feeling of pride, whilst confidently showcasing the best of modern Britain to the rest of the world.

British Airways' service ethos is built around delivering personalised, intuitive and friendly service that makes its customers feel cared for and excited about their next British Airways journey.

The **British Heart Foundation (BHF) promises to beat the heartbreak caused by the world's biggest killers**: heart and circulatory diseases. In **2018 it raised £136.4m** to fund **groundbreaking research**. Since the charity was formed, its research has **helped halve the number of people in the UK dying from heart and circulatory diseases**

Market

There are nearly 170,000 registered charities in the UK and the British Heart Foundation is number three in YouGov's Charity Brand Index.

The BHF is a medical research charity and for over 50 years has pioneered life saving research. However in the UK, more than seven million people are living with heart and circulatory diseases and more than 1 in 4 people still die from these conditions – that's one death every three minutes. Despite this, other diseases are often seen as more worrying and receive more generous funding.

The BHF currently funds over half of all the independent heart and circulatory research carried out in the UK, supporting around £100m of new, inventive research projects each year. In addition, BHF scientists have developed new technology that could predict people at risk of a heart attack years before it occurs, allowing them to be given preventative treatments.

In 2019, the BHF opened applications for its Big Beat Challenge – one of the world's largest research grants to bring together knowledge and talent from around the globe. The winning project will receive £30m, with the potential to revolutionise the prevention, diagnosis or treatment of any heart and circulatory conditions. The BHF's retail estate is the largest in the sector with around 730 shops across the UK, generating over £27.7m net profit annually. There are more than 3,350 paid staff, a network of over 20,000 volunteers and 18 million customers a year. The eBay store, which raises around £3m a year, was started by a few dedicated volunteers above a shop in 2006 – demonstrating the culture of innovation throughout the BHF.

The BHF holds numerous fundraising events including its flagship event, the annual London to Brighton Bike Ride, which has been running for 41 years.

DID YOU KNOW?

More than **1 in 4 of us die from heart and circulatory diseases** each year in the UK, that's **nearly 170,000 people**

Product

As well as investing over £100m – the majority of its income – into life saving research each year, the BHF also works with patients and the public to improve the nation's health. It supports people affected by heart and circulatory diseases and offers high-quality information to those affected. This includes providing online information and support on heart and circulatory diseases and their risk factors as well as distributing five million health resources in the UK each year.

Another key area is the development and implementation of programmes to improve cardiac arrest survival rates, which include supporting CPR training in schools and the development of a database to make public defibrillators easier to locate in the event of a cardiac arrest. The BHF has joined forces with Microsoft and the NHS to create a database of all UK public-access defibrillators, to significantly improve the survival chances of people who suffer an out-of-hospital cardiac arrest in the future.

The BHF also encourages people to know their blood pressure and cholesterol numbers and runs trials to take and apply their research findings into clinical settings.

Influencing government and healthcare systems to create policy and legislative change on issues such as pollution, salt and sugar levels in food is also of importance.

Achievements

2018 was a strong year for the BHF. YouGov named it as the UK's most popular entry in their list, which ranks the popularity of anything and everything in the UK. A total of 87% of people surveyed liked the BHF, putting it in joint top position alongside Sir David Attenborough. Also in 2018, Morar HPI released a new league table ranking UK charity brand values. This saw the British Heart Foundation valued at £1.2bn, the second most valuable charity brand.

The BHF is a passionate campaigner. Following years of lobbying, the Government announced plans to make CPR a compulsory part of the secondary school curriculum in England. Another example is the enforced change to cigarette packaging – they must now be sold in plain packaging with graphic health warning messages.

As a result of another tireless campaign, the Government announced its intention to establish Max and Keira's law – an opt-out system for organ donation in England in the name of heart transplant patient, campaigner and BHF advocate Max Johnson and the little girl whose heart saved him.

Recent Developments

Insight has shown that whilst many people in the UK recognised the BHF, not enough people knew what the charity does. Following an in-depth strategic brand review, the BHF launched a future-facing, outcome-led promise to 'Beat Heartbreak Forever'. This was developed to raise awareness of what the BHF is here to do: beat heartbreak

'It starts with your heart' 2018 brand campaign

Brand History

1961 Facing a national epidemic, with heart and circulatory diseases causing more than half of all deaths in the UK, concerned doctors joined forces with philanthropists to establish the British Heart Foundation.

1968 Surgeon Mr Donald Ross performs the first UK heart transplant following five years of BHF-funded research into transplant surgery techniques.

1976 BHF Professor Michael Davies proves that heart attacks are caused by blood clots in the coronary arteries, setting the stage for a revolution in life saving heart attack treatment.

1995 Two trials, led by BHF Professor Stuart Cobbe and Professor Sir Rory Collins respectively, show the life saving benefit of statins.

2011 BHF-funded Dr Paul Riley shows that heart cells can be activated to repair damage caused by a heart attack, demonstrating the transformative potential of regenerative medicine.

2017 The BHF celebrates 50 years since pioneering research funded by the BHF led to the first human heart transplant. In addition, approximately 14,000 cyclists take part in the iconic London to Brighton Bike Ride, together raising more than £2.8m for life saving BHF research.

2019 BHF-funded Professor Philip Bath is trying to find out whether a simple adhesive patch that delivers a drug through the skin improves the outcomes of people who have a stroke. It is applied to a patient's shoulder or back and administers a drug whilst a patient is travelling to hospital. The ability to start treating patients within an hour could revolutionise stroke treatment and lead to this technique being adopted worldwide.

for families and loved ones affected by these conditions, by funding research to identify preventions, diagnosis, treatments and cures. This gives supporters a clear understanding of what their support can achieve.

In addition, communications highlight the full scope of the BHF's research. Focus is placed not only on heart disease but more than 50 conditions including circulatory diseases like stroke and vascular dementia as well as risk factors such as diabetes. This broadens the BHF's appeal and enables the charity to engage on a more emotional level.

The BHF brought this new promise to life with a flexible, modern look and feel called 'Activate the Beat'. This creative idea drives everything that the BHF does, both emotionally and visually. It is activated by the Big Beat logo and design system that creates a dynamic, pulsing expression that beats with the pace of life. It also includes a unique typeface for headlines that takes inspiration from the logo, conveying a unique, warm and bespoke feel.

Promotion

There is a preconception that the BHF only funds heart research. Its work in other circulatory diseases such as vascular dementia or stroke and their risk factors such as diabetes often goes unrecognised. To help launch its new brand promise, the BHF released a campaign in 2018 that informed people of its broader remit, and explained that the conditions are all connected.

'It starts with your heart' highlighted that if your heart isn't beating and your blood isn't flowing properly then you're in trouble, which is why the BHF's research 'may start with your heart, but it doesn't stop there'. This campaign successfully informed people of the BHF's wider work, helped increase consideration to donate, and portrayed the BHF as a more modern, forward-facing organisation. It saw a departure from its previous communication strategy that aimed to raise awareness of the sudden and unexpected devastation that heart diseases can cause, to anyone at any time, which saw significant increases in urgency metrics.

Brand Values

Every day, BHF staff and volunteers live and breathe its values – compassionate, brave, informed and driven – to beat the heartbreak caused by heart and circulatory diseases. These values inspire staff to be fearless in their approach to everything they do; they are encouraged to try new things and innovate, inspired by the pioneering breakthroughs by BHF researchers.

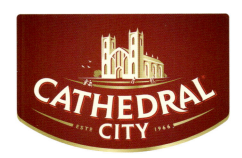

For over 50 years, **generations of expert cheesemakers have been making Cathedral City cheese** using only milk from dedicated farmers in the West Country, to create its **distinctively rich, smooth and creamy taste every time** and making it the nation's favourite

Market

Despite retail price inflation, cheese remains integral to the UK's shopping baskets, bought by 99% of all households (Source: Kantar Worldpanel, 52we 30th Dec 2018). No brand exemplifies this popularity more than Cathedral City, proudly the nation's favourite (Source: IRI SIG Grocers and Kantar Discounters & Bargain Stores, Prepacked Cheese, 52we 31st Dec 2018), present in more than 56% of the UK's fridges (Source: Kantar Worldpanel, 52we 30th Dec 2018) and the 23rd largest grocery brand in the UK, worth £267m RSV (Source: IRI SIG Grocery Outlets 52we 29th Dec 2018).

Whilst the UK remains Cathedral City's heartland, the past few years have seen the brand's presence grow overseas, with products available in international markets including Germany, Austria and Switzerland.

Product

Cathedral City exists to meet the needs of cheese lovers, whoever they are, whenever or wherever

DID YOU KNOW?

David Jason voiced Cathedral City's 2016 'Love Cheese? Welcome to the Club' campaign

they enjoy cheese, and to this end offers a broad range of products ranging from fridge staples like block and more convenient solutions like slices and grated, to kids and adult snacking ranges.

All Cathedral City's cheese is made at its award-winning creamery in Davidstow, Cornwall, by expert cheesemakers, generations of whom for more than 50 years have been making Cathedral City, using only milk sourced from dedicated farmers in the West Country, the richest milkfields in the UK, to make the distinctively rich, smooth and creamy taste of Cathedral City. Every batch of cheese made is checked to ensure consumers always get only the very best cheese.

Achievements

Cathedral City's focus on taste and quality is recognised not only by consumers but throughout the industry, having won numerous accolades including Gold awards at The British Cheese Awards, the prestigious Nantwich International Cheese Show and the Global Cheese Awards. The brand has also recently been rated 'Best Chilled / Frozen Brand' in the 2019 YouGov Brand Index (Source: 2018 YouGov BrandIndex Best Brand Rankings).

Recent Developments

Whilst Britain remains a nation of cheese lovers, consumption and shopping habits continue to evolve quickly. As a result of this, 2018 saw the launch of Cathedral City's first Lactose Free range of cheese, taking the brand into the fast-growing Free From sector.

The brand also renewed its focus on convenient product formats, responding to ever-increasing demand for solutions to fit consumers' time-starved lifestyles, with the launch of 'The Big Slice',

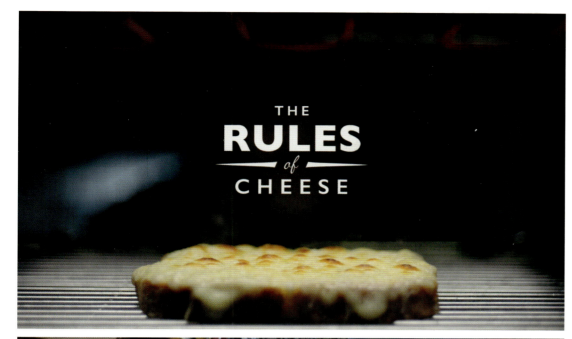

1966 Cathedral City is born at Mendip Foods Ltd.

1981 The Milk Marketing Board creates a division called Dairy Crest, the buyer of last resort for all surplus raw milk, ensuring all milk producers in the country have a buyer for their milk.

1987 Dairy Crest becomes a limited company.

1995 Dairy Crest acquires Mendip Foods Ltd and Cathedral City.

2003 Cathedral City launches the first reclosable pack.

2004 Dairy Crest invests £50m into upgrading and creating a world-leading cheddar creamery at Davidstow and production of Cathedral City starts here.

2005 Cathedral City launches its first major campaign – 'See it, Want it'.

2007 Cathedral City creates Lighter cheese, smooth and mellow with all of the flavour but 30% less fat.

2011 Cathedral City extends into kids and adult snacking with the launch of a range of products for little ones including Nibbles. In addition, Selections, a post dinner evening treat, is launched.

2013 Cathedral City partners with Burton Biscuits to launch Baked Bites, a savoury biscuit snack.

2016 Cathedral City launches the 'Love Cheese? Welcome to the Club' campaign.

2017 Cathedral City launches a range of 100kcal Snack Bars.

2018 Cathedral City extends into Free From with the launch of a Lactose Free range of cheese.

designed to fit perfectly in a slice of bread for cheese in every bite.

The brand's adult snacking range continues to lead the way in what is a fast-growth sector driven by the launch of Cathedral City's range of 100kcal Snack Bars, available in Original Mature, Sweet Chilli and Caramelised Onion flavours, which can be found in both Food to Go and supermarket main fixtures.

In recent years the brand has also moved beyond the chiller with the launch of Baked Bites, a savoury biscuit snack.

In 2018, Cathedral City sought to reassure mums and engage kids with the refresh of its kids snacking range, moving to Mild Lighter Cheese – all the taste but 30% reduced fat – and an on-pack partnership with Nickelodeon featuring characters from Paw Patrol, SpongeBob SquarePants and Teenage Mutant Ninja Turtles.

Promotion

Britain is a nation of cheese lovers and so in 2016, Cathedral City launched 'Love Cheese? Welcome to the Club', a campaign looking to bring the nation together in this wonderful unsaid club. A love that manifests itself through habits or rules that are commonly unknowingly followed, like eating the last bit of grated cheese that's too hard to grate, eating the crispy bits off the lasagne before serving it or selecting the nacho with the most cheese – what Cathedral City has coined as 'the Rules of Cheese'.

The campaign has featured through the line from TV, BVOD, digital video, social media – including influencer activity and PR to in store with activity at point of purchase.

Brand Values

Cathedral City's purpose is to feed the nation's love for great cheese and meet the needs of cheese lovers, whoever they are, whenever or wherever they enjoy cheese through a commitment to the highest quality and craftsmanship. The brand's relationship with the countryside means reducing the impact of its supply chain on the environment are of utmost importance. Part of this is seeing Cathedral City actively working to reduce the amount of packaging it uses and to increase the proportion of recyclable packaging across its product range, with the brand on a mission to make all of its packaging recyclable by 2022.

106m PACKS OF CATHEDRAL CITY WERE BOUGHT IN 2018

As an **international tyre manufacturer and leading automotive supplier,** Continental develops technologies for transporting people safely, whatever the wheel. The corporation sets the future of motion with five strong divisions – **Chassis & Safety, Interior, Powertrain, Tyre and ContiTech**

Market

Continental is renowned as a leading premium tyre manufacturer, offering best in braking across all weather conditions. The German manufacturer is in fact much more than a tyre brand; also being one of the world's leading automotive suppliers, shaping the automotive landscape for a safer future leading to zero accidents, fatalities and injuries. Generating sales of €44bn in 2018 and currently employing 244,000 people in 61 countries, Continental has won four out of five independent tyre tests in Europe and its tyres are fitted to one in three new cars across Europe.

Product

Over the last 147 years, Continental has built a rich heritage of developing ground-breaking technologies and mobility solutions, offering a range of tyre fitments for all applications. Continental works with manufacturers to develop innovative solutions, whilst looking to the future with tyre innovations such as ContiSense and ContiAdapt, with the adjustable rim concept. It invests heavily across its ranges, with the latest EcoContact 6 offering a double AA EU tyre label rating across the majority of the range and increased mileage due to the new Green Chili™ 2.0 compound.

DID YOU KNOW?

To receive vehicle manufacturer approval, **original equipment tyres have to pass around 100 tyre tests,** this process can take up to four years

2018 saw Continental's first all season tyre for Europe, the AllSeasonContact, which in its tyre test debut won coveted titles not only across Europe but also in the UK's biggest selling car news weekly, AutoExpress.

Sustainability is at the heart of everything Continental does, which is why it has further developed Taraxagum dandelion rubber. The Taraxagum Lab officially opened in Anklam in 2018, designed as a research base for the farming and extraction of Russian dandelions as an alternative to rubber trees found in the tropics. With the opening of the new lab, Continental aims to bring Taraxagum into series production within the next 10 years, meeting the rising global demand for sustainable natural rubber sources.

Achievements

Continental's market-leading approach has been frequently recognised, with a range of UK tyre test wins and international awards. In 2018 Continental took the top spot in the AutoExpress summer, winter and all season tyre tests, the first tyre manufacturer to win all three tyre test awards in a single year. Continental's commitment to technical excellence and innovation ensures its tyres deliver superb braking, handling and performance. It is the only tyre manufacturer to have an automated braking test centre, enabling year-around testing. Continental completes

more than 700 million test miles annually and works with more than 200 rubber compounds daily. Continental is the leading tyre choice for many of the world's top car manufacturers, with over 500 current model approvals. If the manufacturer trusts the tyre brand's products, drivers can too.

Recent Developments

Over recent years, Continental has developed a range of partnerships to maximise its brand awareness across its audiences. Working closely with adidas, Continental has brought advanced tyre technology to the soles of trainers, creating rubber compounds with exceptional grip in both

wet and dry conditions. Continental showcases its partnership with adidas through the Conti Thunder Run event and the adidas City Run series.

The brand's commitment to safety and performance extends to its partnerships with leading cycling events such as Prudential RideLondon and the Tour de France, which provide a perfect engagement platform with keen cyclists, reflecting its positioning as safety experts 'whatever the wheel'.

In 2018, Continental partnered with the London Cycling Campaign to support the launch of the 'Stay Wider of the Rider' initiative. The campaign educated cyclists and drivers about the distance that should be left when overtaking and featured a short video, featuring the Brownlee

Brand History

1871 Continental-Caoutchouc-und Gutta-Percha Compagnie is founded in Hanover.

1904 Continental presents the world's first automobile tyre with a patterned tread.

1914 There is a triple victory for Daimlers fitted with Continental tyres at the French Grand Prix.

1979 The takeover of the European tyre operations of Uniroyal, Inc., USA, gives Continental a wider base in Europe.

1993 Continental has approximately 2,000 tyre retailers and franchises across 15 European countries.

1998 Continental adds sites in Argentina, Mexico, South Africa and Slovakia.

2001 Majority holdings are purchased in two Japanese companies.

2003 The world's first road tyre approved for speeds up to 360km/h, the ContiSportContact 2 Vmax, is unveiled.

2006 The automotive electronics business of Motorola, Inc. is acquired by Continental.

2017 Continental's PremiumContact 6 succeeds the award-winning PremiumContact 5.

2018 Recognition in UK tyre tests continues with Continental winning the Auto Express summer, winter and all season tests – the first time a manufacturer has won all tests in a single year.

brothers as well as a website where cyclists could log any close passes that they had experienced.

Continental continues to champion women's football and is a proud partner of the Lionesses on their quest to win the 2019 FIFA Women's World Cup™.

In addition, Continental is in its sixth year as a Partner in Excellence at Mercedes-Benz World, the pioneering brand experience centre, located at Brooklands motor racing circuit. In 2018 Continental again offered free driving experiences, demonstrating the benefits of premium tyres through a range of driving demonstrations, along with the latest safety systems, such as Autonomous Emergency Braking.

Promotion

Over recent years, its five strong divisions have helped establish Continental as one of the top automotive suppliers globally, with technologies contributing to zero accidents and fatalities in the future, known as Vision Zero. A partnership with the New Car Assessment Programme (NCAP) through its Stop the Crash campaign has further enhanced Continental as a leader in automotive technology and safety. As partners of Stop the Crash, Continental engaged consumers at the Coventry Motofest through demonstrations of the advanced safety systems and tyre technology currently available. As a proud corporate supporter of TyreSafe, Continental brought safety to the streets, educating motorists about the simple tyre safety checks all drivers should undertake.

To support the Vision Zero initiative, Continental hosted a series of Vision Zero Live driving events. These events took place in three locations across the UK and Ireland during which consumers and retailers were given the opportunity to experience advanced vehicle and tyre technologies through a series of live demonstrations.

Brand Values

With its tyre technologies, and automotive knowhow, Continental works towards its Vision Zero initiative of zero road accidents. Its contributions make not only for an exciting driving experience, but a safe one. Continental's pioneering safety technologies, paired with educating road users globally, reflects the company's commitment to road safety.

DeLaRue

De La Rue is not just an industry leader. **For more than 200 years it has defined the industries it leads, providing governments** and organisations with the secure products and **services that enable countries to trade, companies to sell, economies to grow** and people to move securely around an ever-more connected world

Market

De La Rue is a global business, with customers in more than 140 markets, seven manufacturing locations across four continents and products and services in use in every single country around the world.

A trusted partner of governments, central banks and commercial organisations, De La Rue delivers products and services that underpin the integrity of trade, personal identity and the movement of goods. It does this in the form of banknotes, passports and secure product identifiers.

Security is at the heart of De La Rue's work, constantly developing better tools, techniques and solutions to defend against the threat that counterfeit poses to society. De La Rue operates in three key markets: Currency – a sector growing at around 4-5% per annum and fundamental to financial inclusion, in which De La Rue is the recognised commercial market leader; Identity – in a world where more than 5,700 people board an international flight every 60 seconds, De La Rue is the largest commercial passport printer globally; Product authentication and traceability – the global counterfeit industry is worth an estimated US $1.7tn, equivalent to the 10th largest economy in the world by GDP – De La Rue is gaining an increasingly strong foothold, supporting both governments and brands alike.

Product

De La Rue doesn't just supply currency, passports and labels, it provides complete solutions which help countries trade, companies sell, economies grow, and people move securely around an ever-more connected world.

Its integrated banknote solutions provide central banks with control over the design, production, circulation and management of both paper and polymer banknotes, with DLR Analytics™ providing an in-depth understanding of how cash moves around a nation's economy.

De La Rue delivers passports and national identity services, eGovernment and complete identity data management solutions, tailored to each country's specific needs and individual requirements.

DE LA RUE EXPORTS TO OVER 140 COUNTRIES ACROSS THE GLOBE

De La Rue creates and delivers bespoke authentication and traceability solutions that support government revenue collection programmes – from secure physical identifiers in the form of tax stamps and product authentication labels to digital software solutions. It also provides solutions to commercial organisations that help to both enhance and protect their brands from counterfeit and illicit trade, securing revenues and safeguarding reputations.

All of these solutions are underpinned by design excellence and a sophisticated layering of security features; an integrated approach, unrivalled technical know-how and an absolute attention to detail, guiding and collaborating with its customers every step of the way.

De La Rue's list of customers includes the Bank of England, Government of Kenya, Microsoft, HSBC, FIFA, South African Reserve Bank, Brother Industries, Bahamas, Diageo, State of Qatar's Ministries of Interior and Foreign Affairs, Bank of Mauritius, Sveriges Riksbank and Note Printing Australia.

Achievements

De La Rue is a responsible business, working to the highest of ethical standards and standing firm in its fight against counterfeit and fraud. Signatories to the UNGC and a strict internal Code of Business Principles ensures its contribution to a safer, more secure and sustainable future. Alongside this, an unrivalled commitment to innovation ensures that it remains at the forefront of new developments in the delivery of security, integrity and trust.

De La Rue is honoured to be recognised for its many achievements. In recent years, the business has won 14 industry design awards, the Queen's Award for innovation on four separate occasions, two Central Banking Innovation awards for its DLR Analytics™ software platform, Currency Services Provider of the Year and, most recently, De La Rue has also been awarded Superbrand status.

De La Rue has a strong and long-standing relationship with the UK Government, Foreign Office and the Department of International Trade and is also an official partner of their GREAT Britain campaign under the 'Innovation is GREAT' banner. Through a unique collaborative activity in 2017 between De La Rue, GREAT and Disney, just 1,000 limited-edition Star Wars: The Last Jedi commemorative banknotes were produced and auctioned off to raise almost £186,000 for the children's charity, Together for

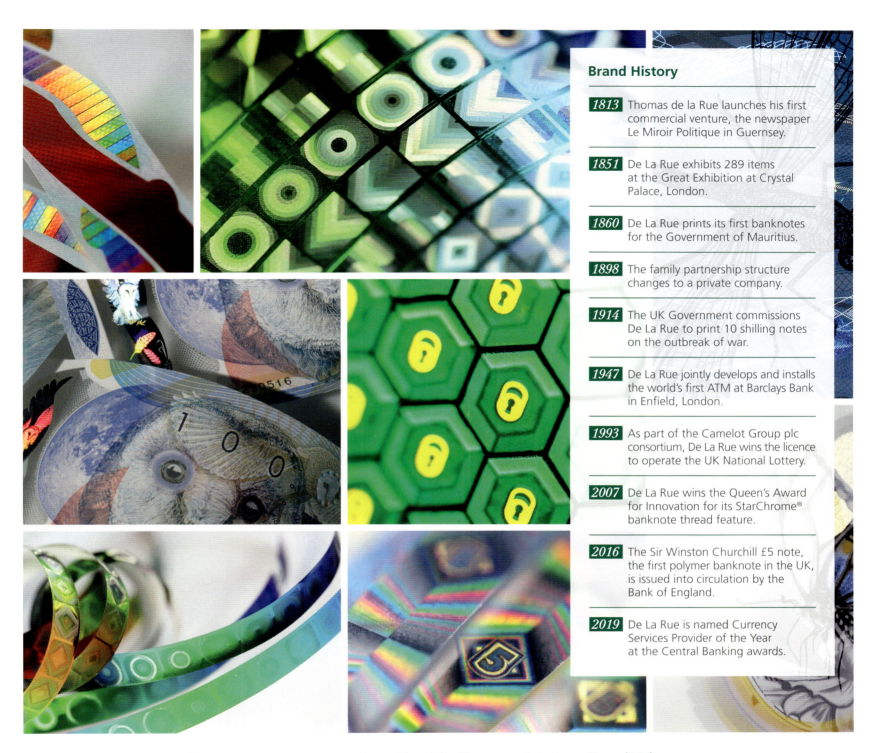

Brand History

1813 Thomas de la Rue launches his first commercial venture, the newspaper Le Miroir Politique in Guernsey.

1851 De La Rue exhibits 289 items at the Great Exhibition at Crystal Palace, London.

1860 De La Rue prints its first banknotes for the Government of Mauritius.

1898 The family partnership structure changes to a private company.

1914 The UK Government commissions De La Rue to print 10 shilling notes on the outbreak of war.

1947 De La Rue jointly develops and installs the world's first ATM at Barclays Bank in Enfield, London.

1993 As part of the Camelot Group plc consortium, De La Rue wins the licence to operate the UK National Lottery.

2007 De La Rue wins the Queen's Award for Innovation for its StarChrome® banknote thread feature.

2016 The Sir Winston Churchill £5 note, the first polymer banknote in the UK, is issued into circulation by the Bank of England.

2019 De La Rue is named Currency Services Provider of the Year at the Central Banking awards.

Short Lives. The campaign itself was also awarded a silver Clio Award for advertising in the international entertainment category for partnerships and collaborations.

Recent Developments
An inherent culture of innovation and integrity drives the organisation forwards and through the products and services it launches, ensures it always stays one step ahead of the counterfeiter.

De La Rue's polymer solution Safeguard® – the next generation banknote substrate – has helped it to win 57% of all paper banknote conversions with 31 new polymer denominations. De La Rue is number two in the polymer currency market and the only vertically integrated polymer banknote solution in the world.

DLR Analytics™, a sophisticated cloud-based software platform delivering data-driven insights into cash cycle management, has more than 40% of the world's central banks signed up to its service.

De La Rue has achieved significant growth in the tax stamp market and is looking to double the size of this business over the next three years through the delivery and implementation of integrated physical, digital and service contracts.

De La Rue is the world leader in holographic origination and recently launched Pure Image™ using the latest new digital techniques to deliver its brightest, most crisp hologram ever.

Promotion
De La Rue's marketing strategies are centred around maintaining and enhancing its reputation globally. Key messages focus on: global reach, deep partnerships with its customers, responsible and ethical practices, design excellence and a heritage of innovation; all of which are underpinned by video and online content. De La Rue uses thought leadership on the key issues that are affecting its customers and has successfully introduced a 200-year-old business to the rewards of digital marketing and social media.

Brand Values
The De La Rue brand is widely acknowledged as being one of its greatest assets. Its brand purpose – to enable everyone to participate securely in the global economy – is at the heart of everything it does. De La Rue achieves this by providing the tools and foundations needed to create trust in society and its institutions – supporting everything from financial inclusion through to secure free movement of people and goods.

As an organisation, the brand values are kept top of mind, with a thorough understanding of how this translates for De La Rue's customers: Drive Change & Innovate – leading the way; Act With Integrity – doing business ethically; Take Responsibility – being accountable; Excel In What We Do – delivering on promises; and Work Together – building long term partnerships.

The **original disruptor of the e-commerce world**, eBay has come of age –
but it's still shaking up traditional retail with a global marketplace that welcomes big brands,
empowers entrepreneurs and **serves 25 million customers a month in the UK alone**

Market

eBay was the first online marketplace. Today, it's a household name. A regular feature in lists of best-loved brands, it connects millions of buyers and sellers, helping customers to find the item they're looking for from its 1.2 billion listings.

With buyers in 190 markets, trade is fast. The 2018 World Cup had us bringing home a waistcoat a minute in July due to Southgate fever and eBay reported nearly two searches for 'Chesterfield Sofas' every minute following the debut of BBC One's hit TV show, McMafia. This incredible interest directly benefits the small businesses who trade on eBay, giving them access to an audience once unthinkable for a small shop on the high street. Unlike other online platforms, eBay does not compete with or undercut its sellers.

Product

Whether an item is new, luxurious or rare, fashionable or one-of-a-kind, it's probably for sale on eBay.co.uk. The brand's mission is to be the place where the world shops first and a continued focus on its powerful search gives strength to that promise.

While eBay remains true to its marketplace roots, 89% of the items for sale on eBay are now offered at a fixed price and 84% are brand new. The UK's big retail brands also continue to gravitate towards the marketplace, setting up their own eBay stores to be where British consumers are shopping.

All sellers on eBay benefit from one of the most popular mobile apps in the market – downloaded more than 440 million times and counting – along with a ready-made web presence that is fast, mobile and secure.

Achievements

Throughout its 24-year history, eBay has helped many thousands of small businesses to succeed. Small British firms regularly rank in the top five grossing sellers on eBay.co.uk's biggest trading days like Black Friday, and more than a thousand British sellers who started with a shop on eBay are now running million-pound businesses, providing jobs to people in their communities.

Each year eBay champions the best of its sellers through the eBay for Business Awards: a nationwide hunt for the best and brightest innovators on the marketplace. As a hub of retail in the UK, the marketplace also continues to welcome top brands to the site – including Joules, Currys, Halfords, Argos, BooHoo and more.

eBay also makes it easy for customers to give to charitable organisations. Using eBay for Charity, sellers can donate a portion of their sales and buyers can shop while supporting their favourite causes – adding to the £135m that eBay.co.uk has raised for UK charities to date.

In September 2018, eBay expanded its Retail Revival programme to the UK, partnering with the City of Wolverhampton to help local retailers make the most of the online opportunity. For 12 months, experts from eBay will be providing exclusive support to 64 businesses in the city, growing the local economy and demonstrating that online and high street retail can survive and thrive together.

Recent Developments

With a wealth of 'firsts' to its name, eBay remains at the forefront of online retail.

The marketplace created one of the first-ever mobile apps, and today over 60% of international buyers shop on eBay through their mobile device, putting the products of small businesses directly into the hands of consumers whenever they want to shop.

Thanks to the 200,000 small businesses who make ebay.co.uk unique.

And the 25m UK buyers who found just the right thing in 2018.

From small business to big.

It's happening on eBay.

ebay

Brand History

1995 eBay founder, Pierre Omidyar, launches AuctionWeb. By the following year, US $7.2m worth of merchandise is sold.

1997 Feedback is introduced, allowing members to rate their transactions – a first for the web that's now an industry staple.

2000 Buy It Now, allowing users to buy an item instantly at a set price, is introduced.

2002 eBay purchases PayPal, followed by Gumtree three years later.

2008 eBay is one of the first companies to launch an iPhone app, featuring in the Apple App Store launch.

2009 eBay receives a 100% rating from the Human Rights Campaign – and has received it every year since.

2016 In partnership with Myer, eBay launches the first-ever virtual reality department store as well as a smart, personal shopping assistant, powered by artificial intelligence.

2017 eBay's 22nd year in the UK sees Image Search and Find It On eBay launching, allowing shoppers to search using a picture.

2018 eBay's Retail Revival programme moves to the UK city of Wolverhampton. Small businesses involved in the programme reach £1m in sales in just three months of the scheme.

Fast-forward to 2018 and eBay is still driving new developments: embracing artificial intelligence and partnering with PayPoint, making its Collect+ parcel shop network available to use as eBay Click & Collect collection points.

eBay's social media presence was bigger than ever in 2018. Focusing on mobile-first creative bespoke to each social platform, eBay worked with over 100 influencers, from YouTuber Colin Furze to comedian Katherine Ryan, to shout about its brand offering and increase consideration.

Promotion
In 2018, eBay launched its latest brand proposition – 'It's Happening'. The campaign holds a mirror up to modern culture, positioning eBay's diverse, vibrant and dynamic marketplace as a reflection of modern mindsets and what customers are into.

For Christmas 2018, eBay brought the campaign to central London, using the Piccadilly Lights as an opportunity to exclusively promote

its best Cyber Monday deals. The brand used this opportunity to show how it empowers entrepreneurs, shining the spotlight on one of its SMB sellers, Velocity Electronics.

25m BRITS A MONTH ARE SERVED BY EBAY IN THE UK

eBay regularly partners with other high-profile brands who understand the power of the marketplace in bringing products to life. In November 2018, eBay teamed up with Warner Brothers for the release of Fantastic Beasts: The Crimes of Grindelwald, taking five Wizarding World superfans on a Wizarding Workshop, using wands and merchandise sold on eBay. eBay also partnered with YouTuber DanTDM, Disney and Make-A-Wish to place Dan in Disney's latest animation, Ralph Breaks the Internet. Dan's personalised Disney character was used on exclusive eBay merchandise, sold to raise money for Make-A-Wish.

Brand Values
eBay's vision for commerce is one that is enabled by people, powered by technology and open to everyone. eBay focuses on providing opportunity for all, allowing charities, businesses and individuals to participate in – and benefit from – global commerce. This is bolstered by eBay for Charity, allowing buyers and sellers to donate.

EDWARDIAN
HOTELS
LONDON

Offering a collection of individual hotels, inspired by London and rooted in the neighbourhoods the hotels inhabit, from **stylish boutiques through to luxury on the grandest scale**, each hotel boasts stunning interiors and exceptional comfort. With complimentary wifi throughout, chic bars and concept restaurants, **Edwardian Hotels London's service ethos delivers unforgettable experiences**

Market

Founded by Jasminder Singh OBE in 1977, Edwardian Hotels London is intrinsically linked to the landscape, with 11 of its 12 properties being in London and one in the heart of Manchester.

The group has been committed to establishing upscale hotels in the city for decades and is inimitably embedded within the London landscape. The luxury London hotel market is a highly competitive environment and Edwardian Hotels London is able to stand out from the crowd with stunning four and five-star properties in key London locations. What helps to distinguish the brand from other key players is its individuality. As a family business, the company offers top quality and unique design combined with a style of service that is genuine.

Product

Known for its presence in London's most sought after locations; Edwardian Hotels London has eight hotels in Zone One alone. With strong and sustained investment across the portfolio and a contemporary environment in each hotel, the properties are designed for comfort and convenience. Adorned with tactile furnishings and original art throughout, each hotel is distinct in its look and feel.

Staying in an Edwardian Hotels London property is an experience. From Kensington to Covent Garden or Bloomsbury to Mercer Street, each has a unique personality. The group's 'Yes I Can!' service philosophy means nothing is ever too much trouble.

Achievements

Edwardian Hotels London has been ranked as one of the best hotel groups in the UK in Which? Travel consumer magazine.

Focused on creating bespoke experiences, each hotel is a one-off, and strives to achieve the best in hospitality by creating exceptional memories. This ethos is further evident at its Manchester property, winner of The Beautiful

DID YOU KNOW?

The **Radisson Blu Edwardian, Vanderbilt** takes its name from the influential American family, **the Vanderbilts,** who converted the building from **ten 19th century town houses into a single hotel in the 1920s**

South Gold award, as well as Manchester Tourism's Hotel of the Year over consecutive years. Sustainability is also high on the agenda, with numerous awards cementing the brand's reputation as one of the UK's greenest hotel groups, including a Green Tourism Business Scheme Gold Award, Best Carbon Reduction in a Hotel Chain, and a Sustainable Restaurant Association Two Star badge. Edwardian Hotels London is the official corporate fundraising partner to Cancer Research UK, with funds raised by the wider company going to the Francis Crick Institute in London, a world-leading centre of biomedical research and innovation.

Digital innovation is at the forefront of the group's progression, with a number of new initiatives ensuring a seamless guest experience. Shortlisted for a Catey award and Best Multi-Channel Customer Service 2016, its virtual host 'EDWARD' has been a huge success. An automated, intelligent text-based interaction service, EDWARD responds to and executes guests' requests, enquiries and bookings via mobile phone. Online check-in and check-out has also become a popular feature, with guests given the freedom to choose their room prior to arrival, and check-out quickly and easily.

Recent Developments

Edwardian Hotels London remains part of one of the world's fastest growing upscale hotel groups, while retaining its individuality as a privately owned hotel collection. 2018 saw the company develop its offerings, with the newly refurbished At The Hampshire Penthouse delivering bespoke private dining experiences with enviable London skyline views; and a multimillion-pound renovation in Manchester, resulting in a stunning new lobby, with relaxed, social spaces, and the addition of a new restaurant and bar – Peter Street Kitchen. Showcasing an exquisite selection of Japanese and Mexican small plates, with fine wines, signature cocktails and sake, this new dining spot brings something new and exciting to the heart of the city. The latest exciting development in Leicester Square comes in the form of a new

Brand History

1977 Edwardian Hotels is established by Jasminder Singh OBE.

1992 A marketing agreement with Carlson is signed to increase global reach and the brand becomes Radisson Edwardian Hotels.

2004 The first hotel outside London opens in Manchester, a five-star hotel in the city's iconic Free Trade Hall.

2007 The company opens a brand new hotel opposite The O2 at New Providence Wharf in London.

2012 An agreement is signed with Radisson Hotel Group (originally Carlson) to become part of the global Radisson Blu brand portfolio and the brand becomes Radisson Blu Edwardian, London.

2013 Radisson Blu Edwardian, London launches Steak & Lobster as well as Scoff & Banter.

2016 May Fair Kitchen opens at The May Fair Hotel, followed by Monmouth and Leicester Square Kitchens at the Mercer Street and Hampshire hotels, respectively.

2017 Plans get underway for The Londoner in Leicester Square, opening in 2020.

2018 At The Hampshire Penthouse opens and Manchester welcomes a multimillion-pound refurbishment, new restaurant and bar.

hotel, The Londoner, which opens its doors to the public in 2020. The 350-room property will comprise a number of bars, restaurants, two Odeon cinemas and a banqueting suite as well as leisure facilities.

Promotion

The group's brand communications remain distinctive. Through cherry-picked partnerships and a cross-channel brand activation calendar, every hotel continues to weave itself into the fabric of the community in which it resides. In the capital, Radisson Blu Edwardian, London properties demonstrate their affinity with the arts through longstanding partnerships with the National Theatre, Royal Shakespeare Company, and The Donmar Warehouse,

DID YOU KNOW?

The May Fair Hotel was **launched in 1927,** with **King George V** presiding over the official opening

to name three of its extensive partnership portfolio. The May Fair Hotel continues its status as the Official Hotel Partner to London Fashion Week and the London Film Festival. Meanwhile in the north, Radisson Blu Edwardian, Manchester continues to cement

its place in the heart of Manchester through its title as the Official Hotel of Manchester Pride.

Brand Values

The essence of the Edwardian Hotels London brand is its core 'Yes I Can!' philosophy – an approach not only to service, but also to the way it does business. This positive attitude enables the delivery of a customer promise that makes people feel special with individual service aiming to build mutually beneficial relationships with a commitment to create business. Authenticity is at its core, the environment and experience guests enjoy at Edwardian Hotels London is uniquely cosmopolitan.

EQUINITI

Equiniti has been an **inventive and assuring presence** for the **UK's biggest names for nearly 200 years**. From mobile apps to virtual AGMs and augmented reality, it is **reimagining how companies look after their employees**, shareholders and pensioners

Market

With a history reaching back nearly 200 years to the early days of the Paymaster General, Equiniti is now a leading player in the UK's payment and share administration sector. In 2018, Equiniti managed over £160bn worth of payments by delivering technology-enabled solutions to some of the world's best-known brands and the UK's largest public-sector organisations.

Equiniti manages shares for the majority of FTSE 100 companies as well as many employee share plans. In addition, 15% of the NYSE rely on Equiniti to help them respond to the challenges of an increasingly complex and regulated world. From mobile apps to virtual AGMs and augmented reality, Equiniti is reimagining how companies look after and interact with their employees, shareholders and pensioners.

Through its services to both corporate clients and retail customers, Equiniti serves 28 million people in the UK and 120 countries around the world. With over 5,000 employees worldwide, it has quickly expanded and responded to the increasing demand for more streamlined, cost effective payment administration, and better customer experience.

Product

The core capabilities of Equiniti are focused in delivering specialist expertise and technology at scale to help large companies tackle digital

DID YOU KNOW?

Equiniti have been providing the **Armed Forces Veterans** with their **pensions since 1836**. The same year that London's first railway opened

transformation, complex regulation and payment administration. The Group is made up of four key divisions: EQ Boardroom – the UK's leading supplier of share registration and employee share plan administration for listed companies; EQ Paymaster – managing complex and regulated pension and payment administration for public and private sectors; EQ Invest – building the tools and platforms for millions of retail investors to access the stock market and invest cost effectively; EQ Digital – helping the UK's most recognised brands and government agencies to build their digital capability, enhance their customer management, combat financial crime and automate consumer and commercial lending.

Achievements

In 2018, Equiniti reached a market capitalisation of £1.2bn and was entered into the FTSE 250 index.

The Group is consistently recognised by the industry for its dedication to improve the way it blends financial technology services with great customer experience. In 2018 it was awarded 'Best Investor Education' by Shares Awards, the industry leading accreditation, for its work to provide retail customers with clear and unbiased educational content to ensure they were properly equipped to make sound and informed financial decisions.

In addition, Equiniti has recently received several awards which include Best Technology at the Excellence in Business Awards 2018; Best Technology Partner at the Lending Awards 2018; Customer Contact Association (CCA) Global Standard; Main Market Company of the Year at the UK Stock Market Awards 2018; and Learning and Development programme of the year at the Skillsoft India Innovation Awards 2018.

Equiniti plays a positive, proactive role in its local communities and empowers employees to support causes which matter most to them. It partners with local schools, charities, businesses and other interest groups to improve lives in the localities in which it operates. In 2018, over £82,000 was given to local charities as a result of colleague led fundraising.

Meticulous

When we say we'll do something, people know we'll do it properly. With a sharp eye for the detail, they know we'll deliver.

Inventive

We're constantly engineering new ways to do things, with our clients and each other. Testing and developing, discovering what works.

Real

We're grounded, supportive and encouraging. We invest in our relationships. Play our part and pull together when it matters.

Brand History

2007 The Equiniti name is established after being acquired by Advent International from Lloyds TSB.

2008 ProSearch asset reunification services is acquired, followed by David Venus Company Secretarial Services the following year.

2010 Xafinity Group Pension Solutions and Hazell Carr Regulatory Resources are acquired.

2011 Natwest Executive Dealing and 360 Clinical Medical Revalidation Platform and Services are acquired.

2012 Prism Cosec Company Secretarial Services and Peter Evans Financial Services Software are acquired.

2013 Killik Global and Executive Share Plans are acquired.

2014 Selftrade, Charter and Pancredit are acquired.

2015 Equiniti lists on the LSE and becomes Equiniti Group plc. In addition, Transglobal Payment Solutions, International Payments and KYCNET Know Your Customer technology and services in Amsterdam are acquired.

2017 Nostrum Group Loan Administration and Marketing Source Data Analytics and Cyber Security are acquired.

2018 Wells Fargo Shareowner Services in the US, Boudicca Proxy Limited Solicitation and Aquila Pension Platform 'Administrator' are acquired.

Recent Developments

2018 saw the completion of Equiniti's acquisition of Wells Fargo's Shareowner Services business in the US, a significant milestone in the Group's strategy to expand its services globally. The expansion allowed Equiniti to acquire 15 new US corporate accounts in less than six months.

One of the Group's core strategies for 2018 was to concentrate on improving customer experience and gain a deeper understanding of its customer base. This led to the creation of a Chief Customer Officer and a group-wide team focused on ensuring the interaction and experience of its customers is outstanding across all channels. This not only seeks to improve the experience Equiniti has with its clients but also to improve the experience its clients have with its end customers, leading to higher customer satisfaction rates and reduced costs for inbound contact and complaint management.

Promotion

A number of divisional marketing and communication strategies have heightened the exposure of the Equiniti name and brand. This has been aided by the use of the latest in digital technology, such as Augmented Reality, which Employee Share Plan clients are increasingly taking advantage of to boost awareness and engagement amongst their employees, leading to increased participation rates.

With the recent introduction of GDPR regulations and the concerns over cyber security, the EQ Paymaster division launched a major integrated marketing campaign in 2018, looking to leverage how the quality of its data analysis capabilities can help pension providers ensure their member's data is safe and robust. The campaign reinforced Equiniti's authority to talk about personal data in the fintech sector and created the opportunity to cross-sell its EQ Digital technology into the EQ Paymaster division client base.

Brand Values

The Equiniti brand is positioned on its three strongest personality traits – Meticulous, Inventive and Real – that were discovered through a process that explored what its people are like

when they are operating at their best. The three traits form the foundation of the brand and underpin everything that the company creates to tell people its story.

At Equiniti, Corporate Social Responsibility (CSR) is based on a philosophy of carrying out all its business activities in an ethical and responsible way. It is committed to caring for the environment and society in all regions in which it operates through the responsible performance of its business activities.

Equiniti's overall business strategy has been developed with sustainability at its heart, prioritising organic growth with a focus on maintaining strong client relationships.

Its three CSR pillars are: People – to provide a safe and supportive working environment where all colleagues can develop and succeed, regardless of difference; Community – to play a positive, proactive role in the local community and empower employees to support causes which matter to them; Environment – to constantly seek ways to minimise its impact on the planet.

An ADNEC Group Company

ExCeL LONDON

*Bringing people together, face-to-face, is a proven way of doing business. It is ExCeL's vision to be 'The Home of World Leading Events'. By continuously investing in the **experience and providing the best facilities**, the venue brings people together to share ideas, **showcase new technologies, solve problems and do business***

Market

ExCeL has two key commercial divisions, representing the markets that it operates in, namely Exhibitions and Conferences & Events (C&E).

Each year, the venue welcomes four million people to more than 400 events, including global brand showcases, world-leading exhibitions and international association meetings. With over one million visitors travelling from outside of the UK, ExCeL is responsible for driving 25% of London's inbound business tourists. What happens at ExCeL generates £4.5bn in economic impact for London and supports 37,600 jobs, every year.

The global exhibitions industry is responsible for driving £11.5bn of economic impact annually, attracting and engaging 13 million visitors each year. The international conference and events market is highly complex and competitive, with venues and destinations competing for what is now a £1tn global business.

ExCeL's Exhibition customers are mainly based in the UK. With C& E, half of clients are from the UK alongside 25% based in Europe and 25% in North America.

EACH HALL AT EXCEL COULD FIT 742 DOUBLE DECKER BUSES AND 2,047 MINIS STACKED INSIDE

The ICC hosts globally recognised brands and associations and includes a fully flexible auditorium, catering and exhibition space, as well as a variety of meeting rooms, from a 10-person boardroom to a 1,000-delegate theatre-style set-up. In 2016, a dedicated meetings and training venue, CentrEd at ExCeL, opened with views overlooking Royal Victoria Dock and Canary Wharf.

ExCeL's event space is complemented by a wide variety of services including catering, IT, branding opportunities, AV and rigging, providing everything required for a tailor-made event experience.

Achievements

During the past 10 years, ExCeL has won more than over 35 national and international leading industry awards, including The World's Leading Meetings & Conference Centre from the World Travel Awards; Venue of the Year at the AEO Excellence Awards; and the Carbon Saver Gold Standard Award. In 2018 it was re-certified to both the ISO 14001 and ISO 20121 environmental standards, which set sustainability management benchmarks in the events industry.

Recent Developments

The success of ExCeL is inextricably tied to that of its customers and constant innovation and investment is essential. Every year, ExCeL has a significant budget for capital expenditure, which has enabled the venue to listen to clients' feedback and make the necessary changes to maintain its position as an internationally competitive venue.

In 2018, investment took place across several areas with the aim of delivering the best possible experience for guests.

Product

Located in London's Royal Docks, ExCeL is the capital's largest events venue and home to the city's International Convention Centre (ICC). The space encompasses multi-purpose event halls and state-of-the-art conference facilities, as well as smaller meeting rooms.

ExCeL sits within a 100-acre site, with a variety of hotels, bars and restaurants, within walking distance and London City Airport five minutes away. In addition, three onsite stations link directly to London Underground, providing access to London's key stations and major airports.

In food and drink, new retail concessions Urban Garden and Brilliant Punjabi were launched to expand on the already extensive food and drink offering. This builds on ADNEC's £15m investment in the catering experience at ExCeL, which took place in 2015 – a redevelopment that saw more than

Brand History

2000 ExCeL London opens in November.

2008 ADNEC acquires ExCeL and phase two construction begins.

2010 Phase two opens following a £165m investment by ADNEC, creating an additional 35,000m² of event space.

2011 Following ADNEC's further £50m investment, the Aloft Hotel opens, bringing ExCeL's total onsite hotel capacity to 1,400 rooms (2,722 rooms by 2018).

2012 ExCeL is named as the most complex venue in the history of the Olympic Games. As the host venue for seven Olympic and six Paralympic sports, it welcomes 1.5 million visitors and is the only venue to host daily events during the Games.

2013 ExCeL sees the acceleration of world-leading events, including ICE Totally Gaming and Bett, as well as corporate events for global brands including Salesforce, Microsoft and Adobe.

2014 ExCeL London welcomes its 20 millionth visitor.

2015 ExCeL hosts Europe's largest medical association meeting and the world's largest cardiovascular event, with over 32,000 delegates. It also hosts one of Europe's largest corporate events, HPE Discover London.

2016 CentrEd at ExCeL, a £1.5m, state-of-the-art meeting and training venue, located onsite, opens overlooking Royal Victoria Dock.

2017 London moves to fifth in the global International Congress and Convention Association rankings, rising from 19th since 2010.

2019 ExCeL continues preparations for the opening of its onsite Elizabeth line station at Custom House. It is set to transform travel across London, allowing ExCeL to welcome an extra 18,000 visitors per hour.

20 new retail units being opened, catering for a multitude of palates and dietary requirements.

The technology infrastructure has also been invested in with Ruckus wifi increasing the performance and capacity of the venue's wifi as well as the resiliency of internet provision.

Furthermore, a new Content Management System now supports the future vision for the digital media estate at ExCeL. The new system will provide greater flexibility to clients, allowing them to display more creative content, and benefit from functionality, including day parting.

Finally, to help combat single-use plastics, ExCeL has launched a 'No Plastic' campaign to outline its commitment to tackling this global issue. Steps taken to date include the removal of plastic straws from point-of-sale, the installation of water fountains and discounts for guests using reusable coffee cups.

Promotion
At the beginning of 2018, Marketing and Communications was restructured to create a central team. This resulted in the ability to share resources, unify planning and consolidate communications.

In 2019, the ambition is to build on the progress made last year, creating a more streamlined approach to communications and focusing on ExCeL's key audiences – organisers, exhibitors and visitors – to maximise budgets and resources, generating a bigger impact for ExCeL.

To communicate its key messages effectively, PR, client and guest HTMLs as well as social media will all be used. All key events taking place at ExCeL have been scheduled to ensure that the opportunity each brings, in terms of PR, photography and case studies, is maximised.

PR forms an important part of ExCeL's marketing strategy. In 2018, 156 features were placed with the industry press, representing a reach of 1.23 million views. In 2019, PR will continue to support disseminating key messages to customer audiences in the UK, Europe and North America.

The Marketing and Communications plan is also designed to support the commercial ambitions of both sales teams across Exhibitions and C&E. Whilst there is a desire to centralise marketing, it is recognised that the wide variety of clients that ExCeL has, do at times, have different needs. The marketing plan therefore includes activities for distinct audiences.

Brand Values
ExCeL's vision is to be the home of world-leading events, hosting the very best in the industry, from global brand showcases and exhibitions to international association meetings and everything in between.

Everyone at ExCeL is united by a common purpose, working together to deliver the best experience for everyone who comes to the venue and, using its knowledge and expertise, help all clients achieve their goals.

ExCeL is also mindful of tackling the challenges of sustainable development and operating as a responsible corporate business, ensuring that it has a positive impact on the local community and beyond.

FedEx Express provides rapid, time-sensitive delivery to more than 220 countries and territories, linking more than 99% of the world's GDP. Unmatched air route authorities and transportation infrastructure, combined with leading-edge information technologies, make FedEx Express the world's largest express transportation company

Market

FedEx Corporation provides customers and businesses worldwide with a broad portfolio of transportation, e-commerce, and business services. With annual revenues of US $65.5bn, the company offers integrated business applications through operating companies competing collectively and managed collaboratively, under the respected FedEx brand. Consistently ranked among the world's most admired and trusted employers, FedEx inspires its more than 425,000 team members to remain 'absolutely, positively' focused on safety, the highest ethical and professional standards, and the needs of its customers and communities.

Product

FedEx Express offers time-definite, door-to-door, customs-cleared international delivery solutions, using a global air-and-ground network to speed delivery. It can deliver a wide range of time-sensitive shipments, from urgent medical

DID YOU KNOW?

FedEx is **investing US $200m** in more than **200 global communities** by 2020 to **create opportunities** and **deliver positive change** around the world

supplies, last-minute gifts and fragile scientific equipment, to bulky freight and dangerous goods. Each shipment sent with FedEx Express is scanned 17 times on average, to ensure that customers can track its location online 24 hours a day.

In addition to the international product range offered by FedEx Express, FedEx UK provides

customers with a wide range of options for domestic shipping. Within the UK this includes time-definite, next-day and Saturday delivery services. All services are supported by free and easy-to-use automation tools, allowing customers to schedule pick-ups and track their packages online.

Achievements

FedEx Express started life in 1973 as the brainchild of its founder Frederick W. Smith, CEO of FedEx Corp. Over the years it has amassed a long list of 'firsts'. FedEx Express originated the overnight letter, was the first express transportation company dedicated to overnight package delivery, and the first to offer next-day delivery by 10.30am. It was also the first express company to offer a time-definite service for freight and the first in the industry to offer money-back guarantees and free proof of delivery. In 1983 Federal Express (as it was then known) made business history as the first US company to reach the US $1bn revenue landmark inside 10 years of start-up, unaided by mergers or acquisitions.

In 1994 FedEx Express received ISO 9001 certification for all its worldwide operations, making it the first global express transportation company to receive simultaneous system-wide certification. This accreditation is still valid today. In January 2019, for the 19th consecutive year, FedEx was once again ranked among the most admired companies in the world, according to a survey published in FORTUNE magazine.

Recent Developments

Further to the FedEx acquisition of TNT in 2016, FedEx Express and TNT are now making good progress in coming together to offer new opportunities, a better service and stronger support. Integrating the world's largest air express network and an unparalleled European road network will take time, but significant progress has already been made.

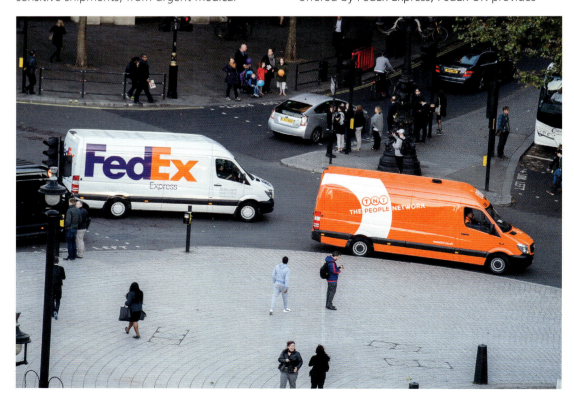

Brand History

1973 Federal Express establishes operations.

1980s Regular scheduled flights to Europe begin and direct operations in Dubai and the United Arab Emirates are established.

2006 FedEx Corp. acquires UK-based ANC, to be run as a wholly owned subsidiary of FedEx Express EMEA.

2010 FedEx Express launches an important new connection between Asia and Europe.

2016 FedEx Corp. acquires TNT Express – the largest acquisition in FedEx history – expanding access in Europe, the Middle East and Africa, Asia Pacific, and the Americas.

2018 FedEx Corp. acquires P2P Mailing Limited, a leading provider of worldwide e-commerce transportation solutions, including unique last-mile delivery options.

As the company moves forward, its teams are committed to delivering the same exceptional service customers would expect from both companies.

Through the integration process, customers will start to see better coverage and greater global connectivity, as well as a broader selection of service options.

Promotion
Passion, commitment and excellence. FedEx believes that these are the factors that create success in sport and are also a winning formula in business. FedEx also believes that a connected world is a better world, and this belief guides everything it does, connecting even more people and possibilities, 'one game-changing delivery at a time'.

It's this harmony between sport and FedEx that makes it a proud sponsor of the UEFA Europa League and the ATP World Tour, associations that are dedicated to the achievement of excellence.

Brand Values
FedEx's team members have the can-do spirit that has made it one of the most admired and reputable companies in the world. That common culture is what makes FedEx uncommon. FedEx empowers team members to create innovative solutions that its customers depend on, support the communities in which it operates, and help FedEx work smarter and more sustainably. Throughout FedEx's global operating companies, the first priority is a safe, inclusive and rewarding employee environment. One where its people have opportunities to grow and succeed. One that puts its team members first. One that strengthens its commitment to connect people and possibilities around the world.

As a major player in the Fintech space, with **90 of the world's top 100 banks using its solutions**, the company has seen strong adoption of its new brand in 2018. With firm foundations now in place, **Finastra is well positioned to play a leading role in shaping the future of financial services**

Market

In an era of increasing choice and regulation, all customers – corporate, institutional and retail – are demanding greater value from financial services. They expect greater agility, innovation, integration and security than ever before.

Finastra helps its customers to break the shackles of closed, legacy systems that limit transparency, block innovation and ignore vast amounts of data. Its scale and geographic reach mean that Finastra is able to serve customers, regardless of their size or geographic location – from global banks to community banks and credit unions. Unlocking this potential today means that financial institutions can embrace the future with confidence and assure their position in the banking world of tomorrow.

Product

Finastra's goal is to be the number one open platform for innovation in the world of financial services with FusionFabric.cloud which utilises the latest technology and standards. It is a 'platform-as-a-service' solution built on open architecture and technology that embraces a wide ecosystem of customers, partners, system integrators and co-innovators. This unique strategy sees the

175m+ RETAIL ACCOUNTS ARE POWERED BY FINASTRA

company opening its technology platform and core systems to third parties, who can leverage the platform to build, sell and consume their own apps.

Achievements

From award-winning products to award-winning training and development programmes, Finastra has solidified its name in the Fintech world. Continuing its success from previous years, Finastra added several awards to its name in 2018. Finastra won the Global Finance, FStech and Handelsblatt Diamond Star awards for Fusion LenderComm, its innovative blockchain-based solution which streamlines information exchange between agent banks and lenders, driving transparency and efficiency in the syndicated loan market.

In the Asia Pacific market, the company has been awarded the SBR International Business Award for its work with Yoma Bank. With the help

of Finastra's core banking solution, Fusion Essence, Yoma bank has been able to restructure its processes, systems and channels completely around its customers across its 74 branches over the last few years.

As an employer, Finastra has been awarded in the Princess Royal Training Awards, which are delivered to UK companies for outstanding training and development programmes. The win brings recognition to Finastra's investment in its people and its ability to successfully link skills development to business performance.

Furthermore, Finastra has been positioned as a category leader in the Chartis RiskTech Quadrants, ranked in the top 10 of the Risk Tech top 100 as well as being placed 13th in the IDC Fintech 100. With many opportunities to collaborate and innovate in the finance industry, Finastra is in a strong position to continue being a leader in the field and a significant Fintech force.

Recent Developments

Under Finastra's commitment to open architecture and collaboration, its focus in 2018 was to accelerate brand awareness, drawing on the strong attributes associated with its two legacy brands and positioning the company for the future. 2018 also saw the launch of FusionFabric.cloud, its open technology platform, with Finastra embarking on its journey to becoming a platform company.

Promotion

Finastra believes that the future of finance is open, and that collaboration and co-innovation are key to its future success, and that of its customers. To amplify this 'Open' message, a comprehensive marketing strategy has guided Finastra's product and communication efforts in this area. As part of its digital approach, an advertising campaign went online in the first quarter of 2018 targeting the business decision maker audience in banks and financial institutions, to further increase Finastra's brand reach and awareness as well as drive deeper engagement with customers.

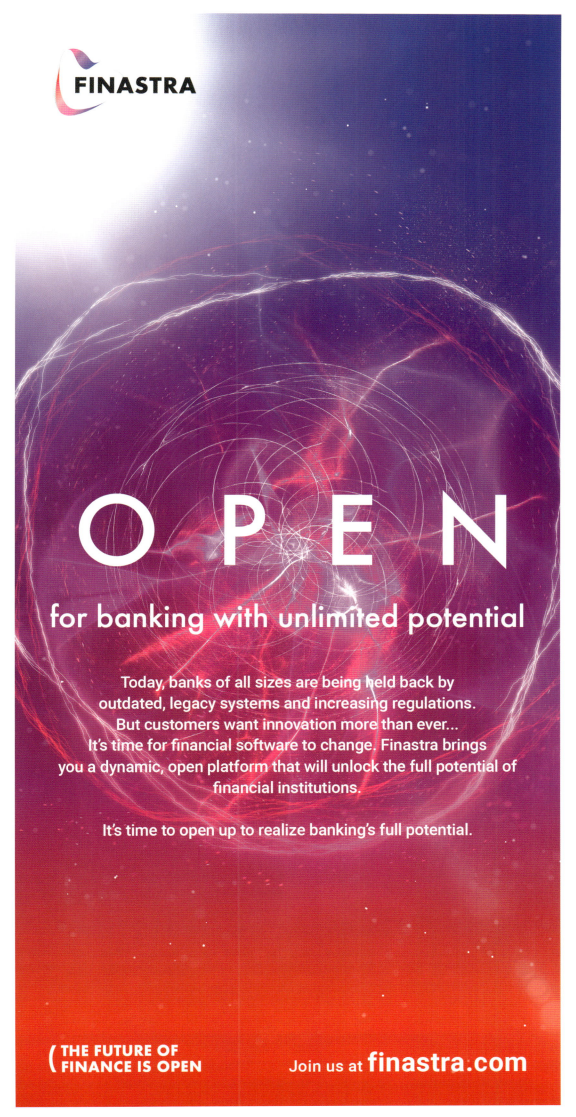

Brand History

1875 D+H is founded.

1979 Misys is founded and supplies computer systems to UK insurance brokers.

1994-1996 Misys acquires Kapiti and ACT, followed by Summit Systems.

2010 Misys acquires Sophis.

2012 Misys is acquired by Vista Equity Partners and merges with Turaz – treasury and risk management software.

2014 Misys acquires IND Group – as well as Custom Credit Systems – all-in-one lending and Misys Fusion software portfolio is launched.

2015 D+H acquires Fundtech.

2016 Misys unveils its PaaS strategy.

2017 Vista Equity Partners acquires D+H and Finastra is formed through the combination of Misys and D+H.

2018 Finastra acquires Malauzai and Olfa Soft.

Throughout 2018, Finastra attended not only the usual industry trade show events, but for the first time the brand had an impactful presence at Money2020, both in Europe and in the US, to engage with the Fintech community that is an integral part of Finastra's platform strategy.

Brand Values

The name – derived from FIN for Finance and ASTRA meaning star in Latin – embodies the expertise and strength through which Finastra will unlock the potential in finance. The following unique attributes enable Finastra to lead customers into the open future of finance:

Comprehensive – With a large global footprint and deep domain expertise, Finastra serves clients of all sizes spanning retail and corporate banking, lending, treasury, capital markets, investment management and enterprise risk.

Innovative – Finastra is leading the way in which financial software is written, deployed and consumed in the world of financial services. As a pioneer in SaaS and cloud, Finastra delivers next-generation financial software – open, reliable, secure, agile – either on premise or in the cloud.

Collaborative – Its architecture and open platform approach stimulate co-operation and co-innovation.

Since inventing the hover mower more than 50 years ago, Flymo has become a market leader in effective and affordable garden care products. Its range now encompasses everything from grass trimmers to robotic lawnmowers. With constant design and technological innovations being at the heart of Flymo, the brand is continually revolutionising its range

Market

Flymo is part of the Husqvarna Group, which is a leading global producer of outdoor power products including lawnmowers, robotic mowers, garden tractors, chainsaws and trimmers. In the UK, Flymo is a leading lawnmower brand as well as being at the forefront of design and innovation across a wealth of other gardening equipment segments.

Over the years, Flymo has built a very close relationship with UK gardeners, learning about what they need and what problems they have in the garden, then using its 'Easier by Design' philosophy to create and develop new products to make gardening easier. Customer satisfaction and support is a key priority, Flymo research has found that over 70% of people who have bought from the brand would purchase a Flymo lawnmower again. The company therefore works hard to retain these high levels of brand loyalty.

Product

Flymo's consistent drive to make products 'Easier by Design' stems from its invention of the hover mower, back in 1963. The traditional heavy petrol lawnmower was transformed into a significantly lighter and easy to use product, literally floating on a cushion of air and easy to manoeuvre in any direction. Since then, Flymo has set the pace by producing high performance hover mowers alongside other gardening power tools.

83% OF DIY CONSUMERS RECOGNISE THAT FLYMO IS THE UK'S LEADING LAWNMOWER BRAND*

*Source: Survey Sampling International (SSI)

In 2019 Flymo will launch two new Hover lawnmowers. The first being an update on the classic hover mover, the Turbo Lite 250 is the smallest non-grass collecting hover within the range with a 25cm cutting width and a metal blade. Designed for efficient mowing of small lawns, this hover has first-time buyers and novice gardeners in mind. It is lightweight and easy to use and if used regularly, doesn't require grass to be collected.

The slimline Hover Vac 250 is another new light and easy to use addition. Suited to small gardens, it features a 25cm cutting width and a metal blade, ensuring a clean cut every time. The 15L grass basket is accessed from the top of the mower, for easy emptying.

Both of these compact, lightweight models feature handles that fold down for easy storage.

Since launching the 1200R robotic lawnmower in 2013, when robotic lawnmowers were almost unknown in the UK, Flymo has helped grow the market segment by making robotic lawnmowers more available and affordable, now taking a significant share of the UK market. These lawnmowers leave no visible grass on the lawn because they cut such a small amount at a time. By cutting little and often, the lawn always looks healthy. The robotic lawnmower works within a set boundary in the garden, it will mow in the rain and will automatically return to its charging station.

In addition to its comprehensive lawnmower range, Flymo's garden power tool range has seen the launch of the Contour Cordless 20V Li, EasiCut

Cordless 20V Li and SabreCut XT Cordless 20V Li, which tackle a variety of trimming jobs. All these products are available in 2019 with a new powerful 20V Lithium-Ion rechargeable battery, eliminating the need for a power cord.

Achievements

Over the 55 years that Flymo has been in business it has become an established and iconic sight in UK gardens. It has consistently held high market shares in the UK, at its peak taking over 50% share of the UK lawnmower market.

In the 1980s, Flymo gained the Queen's Award for Technological Achievement as well as receiving royal recognition for its ability to export – taking its lawnmower to over 60 countries worldwide. Heavy investment and research has seen Flymo introduce an automation programme, making it the first company in Britain to fully assemble and test its products using robots.

Recent Developments

Flymo has recently turned its attention to battery-powered products as they can solve some of the problems consumers face when using electric products that have power cables. Battery technology has rapidly advanced, becoming a more powerful and reliable power source.

Brand History

1963 The Air Cushion mower is invented by Karl Dahlman, taking inspiration from the newly launched Hovercraft.

1964 Flymo Ltd is formed and manufacturing begins at Aycliffe, in the north of England.

1970 Flymo's first electric model launches.

1981 The first grass collecting air cushion mower is introduced. The following year, Flymo receives a Queen's Award for export achievement.

1988 The launch of the Multi Trim electric trimmer is the most successful in Flymo's history.

1993 Flymo GardenVac is successfully launched, going on to create a new market segment all over Europe.

1999 Flymo launches its first cordless, battery powered mower for small gardens.

2013 The 1200R Robotic Lawnmower is launched.

2014 Flymo launches a new hover collect lawnmower with unique twin chamber hovering deck for a cleaner neater cut and closer cutting up to edges.

2017 The first Flymo Lithium-Ion battery lawnmower, Mighti-Mo 300 Li, launches.

2019 Flymo celebrates its 55th birthday and the first Flymo Lithium-Ion interchangeable battery range, C-LiNK is launched together with a complimentary range of C-LiNK compatible products.

Flymo launched its first Lithium-Ion battery lawnmower, ideal for the typically small UK lawns, the Mighti-Mo 300 Li, in 2017. Powered by a 40V battery, it is lightweight and compact, whilst being a surprisingly powerful small lawnmower.

Following on from this success, 2019 sees the launch of a cordless, interchangeable battery system, C-LiNK. This lightweight power head connects to three interchangeable gardening tools – a hedge trimmer, grass trimmer and blower. All three products within the range use a powerful 20V Lithium-Ion battery, the first of its kind for handheld Flymo tools. The new C-LiNK range is complimented by three C-LiNK compatible products, which use the same battery and charger system. These are a lightweight trimmer with a specially designed, innovative, in line edging wheel to make lawn edging easy, the Contour Cordless 20V Li; a lightweight hedge trimmer, the EasiCut Cordless 20V Li; and the SabreCut XT 20V Li, which is a versatile, long reach hedge trimmer, to tackle taller awkward hedges.

Promotion

Flymo supports its products and innovations with multi-channel promotions. Over the years it has run many national TV advertising campaigns alongside national media press campaigns. Going forward, a leading focus for 2019 and beyond will be to strengthen its digital and online presence to support the consumer shift from in-store to online shopping behaviour. Indeed, Flymo estimate that over 40% of all its sales are now online via one form or another. Enhancing the customer experience online is now a major priority for Flymo at every stage of the customer journey. The Flymo website acts as a hub for the latest information about the brand, gives the opportunity to register products as well as keep up to date with the Flymo newsletter and enter special member competitions.

Brand Values

Flymo was founded on innovation and in its 55th year in the UK, its thirst for design and technological development continues. Its aim is to create products that are 'Easier by Design', suited to today's modern lifestyle in order to help consumers maintain impeccable gardens.

With over 45 years' experience, Green Flag provides breakdown cover 24 hours a day, 365 days a year. It has revolutionised the breakdown market by **utilising a network of service providers throughout the country.** This innovative and efficient model provides a **high-quality service and better value for customers**

Market

Green Flag is the UK's third largest breakdown brand in a market dominated by only three key players. Together, the RAC, AA and Green Flag accounted for an estimated 84% of breakdown membership in 2018, with Mintel valuing the market at £1.78bn in 2018 (Source: Vehicle Recovery UK, September 2018).

In a typically inert market, 67% of people automatically renew their AA or RAC cover each year (Source: Vehicle Recovery UK, September 2018) with membership either being bought directly by the consumer (39%) or indirectly through an intermediary (61%).

The market has seen steady growth in recent years but is increasingly under pressure from smaller players. Whilst the AA and RAC use a traditional fleet of branded vans, Green Flag operates differently, working with a flexible, nationwide network of local garages, providing a high-quality service at significantly lower prices.

Product

Green Flag is a disruptor in the market. Its purpose is to rescue customers and develop mobility solutions that meet their needs in a smart and innovative way. Its point

of differentiation is based on the revolutionary idea of partnering with a smart network of specialist local mechanics and garages up and down the country and in Europe, rather than relying on a fleet of owned vans. This allows Green Flag to provide a more agile and adaptable service.

Green Flag believes that by not operating a fleet of owned vans also creates an efficient business model, eliminating costs, and allowing savings to be passed on to customers. In fact, Green Flag beats AA or RAC renewal quotes by 50% (for vehicles 10 years and under on its closest equivalent UK vehicle cover).

DID YOU KNOW?

Nationwide, **1,900 rescues a day** are attended to by **Green Flag**

By not deploying a one size fits all model, Green Flag's network is flexible and adaptable. It also means that vans are not kept on the road when they aren't needed and Green Flag can partner with whoever is best placed to give the customer what they need to get moving again. This can include the provision of hire cars and taxi services.

Achievements

Customer satisfaction is key to Green Flag's success – 89% of Green Flag's customers rated the technicians 8/10 or above between Nov 17 and Nov 18 – and its Recovery Plus product has received a five star Defaqto rating. Furthermore, Green Flag ranks highly in a range of UK Customer Satisfaction surveys, results that are supported by its strong Reevoo scores. Green Flag has also won Best Direct Breakdown Insurance Provider at the Your Money Awards in 2018 and has a Net Promoter Score (NPS) of +64.

Recent Developments

The beginning of a new era for Green Flag was marked in 2017 with new leadership. Green Flag's transformation began and the 'Common Sense to the Rescue' concept was created.

This reaffirmed a commitment by Green Flag's leadership team to continue to develop its service and product, rescuing customers in a 'Smart, Connected' way.

Alongside building the brand, investment began in core systems and processes to create enhanced control of customers' journeys, enabling Green Flag to build on its growing NPS performance.

Green Flag also developed the first Rescue Telematics product, Green Flag Alert Me, which connects the customer's car to the Green Flag app and notifies the customer of impending Battery Failure and Engine Management System faults. The Green Flag app has become a vitally innovative part of the rescue experience as consumer behaviour changes. Through the app, customers can also register a call for help and track their technician. This helps Green Flag keep connected to broken down drivers and ensures that the customer is kept informed and in control.

Brand History

1971 Green Flag is established under the name National Breakdown Recovery Club (NBRC).

1984 NBRC is acquired by National Car Parks (NCP).

1994 The company is renamed Green Flag and begins sponsoring the England football team.

1999 Green Flag becomes part of RBS Group, which is then acquired by Direct Line.

2008 Green Flag branded vans launch across the network.

2014 Green Flag sponsors Premiership Rugby.

2015 Green Flag begins sponsoring ITV National Weather.

2017 Green Flag is named as Your Money, Best Online Breakdown Insurance Provider.

2017 Green Flag reboots its brand and marketing strategy.

2018 The company launches a new smart network of service providers and wins Best Automotive campaign at the PRCA Awards.

2019 The brand celebrates its 25th anniversary as 'Green Flag'.

As the world of motoring changes with the rapid development of vehicle technology and ownership preference, Green Flag continues to innovate its products and challenge the industry norm through its challenger brand approach.

Promotion

Thinking differently has always been Green Flag's approach since its beginning in 1971, built on the ambition to revolutionise the breakdown market. In 1994, it became the first ever brand to sponsor the England football team, a partnership that ran until the 1998 FIFA World Cup.

Being bold and challenging, whilst showing a smarter way of doing things, carried through to the brand review in 2017. Strengthening Green Flag's position in the market and the 'Common Sense to the Rescue' concept aimed

to boldly contrast the shortcomings and inefficiencies that the brand had pinpointed within the AA and RAC offerings. A fresh TV campaign connected with drivers across the UK, demonstrating that Green Flag is a smart, credible alternative and 50% cheaper at renewal. 'Common Sense' being shorthand for a smarter approach to the category, a service that is more agile and adaptable to current and future breakdown needs. 'To the Rescue' has two meanings: it represents the quality of service as well as the customers' position, namely rescuing them from the inefficiencies and shortcomings of the competition. The reinvigoration of the brand was brought to life through TV, radio, OOH and digital channels. In March 2018, to cement Green Flag's status as a market challenger and innovative thinker, that isn't afraid to be disruptive, Mud & Motors – the world's first common

sense obstacle course for cars – was launched. Alongside TV star Chris Hughes, drivers competed in a muddy course using their common sense, with the reward being a cash prize. The campaign went on to win Best Automotive campaign in the 2018 PRCA Awards.

Brand Values

Built on 'Common Sense to the Rescue', everything Green Flag does is aimed at providing an efficient service to meet its customers' needs. Its innovative model enables customers to take ownership of their mobility and gets them back on the road as soon as possible, in a smart and connected way. Green Flag is passionate about providing an alternative to automatically renewing car breakdown membership with other companies.

GROUPON

Groupon is building the **daily habit in local commerce, offering a vast mobile and online marketplace.** By enabling **real-time commerce across local businesses, travel destinations, consumer products and live events,** shoppers can find the best a city has to offer, at their fingertips

Market

With an international online and mobile presence, Groupon is redefining how small businesses attract and retain customers by providing them with customisable and scalable marketing tools and services to profitably grow their businesses. In turn, it is providing customers with a central online destination where they can discover and save on things to do, see, eat and buy. As the business develops, Groupon's vision remains clear – to become the global marketplace for local services, experiences, goods and travel.

Product

The idea for Groupon was born from The Point, a website for organising group actions. Its goal was to help people congregate around the issues they care about and combine forces to make things happen. Only once a critical mass of people have committed to the cause, the combined force will 'tip' the issue to push for change.

In 2008, an offshoot company developed, leveraging people's collective bargaining power to purchase, and this became Groupon. A combination of Group and Coupon, Groupon's belief was that pooling consumers' buying power together, could achieve the very best savings with local businesses.

Groupon's first deal was a half-price offer for pizza at the restaurant on the first floor of its building in Chicago. By November 2018, the business had celebrated its 10th anniversary, worked with more than one million merchants, had nearly 50 million active customers worldwide, sold nearly 1.5 billion Groupons and was operating in 15 countries. Since that first deal went live, Groupon has sold more than 85 million pizza slices.

Groupon's incredible sales record doesn't end there. To date it has sold tickets for 47 million hours of live music and been responsible for 65 million ounces of steak being served, 15 million fitness classes survived and 240 million ounces of coffee brewed.

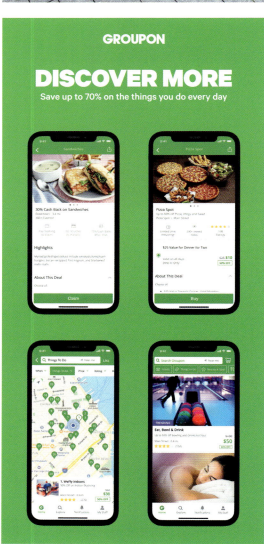

Achievements

Over its lifetime, Groupon has been consistently recognised for its work. In 2011, it won the Webby Breakout of the Year award when it was still in its infancy. Then, in 2012, it received an Employees' Choice, 50 Best Places to Work award. 2015 saw Groupon receive a Mobile Commerce Award in the Internet Retailer Excellence Awards. The following year, it was recognised as one of the Best Places to Work for LGBT in Equality and Human Rights Campaign's (HRC) Corporate Equality Index. More recently, in 2018 Groupon received the Best Marketing Innovation award from Button-Performance Marketing; Best YouTube Bumper Ad from YouTube and The Webby Awards; and was also rated as the Top Six Ranked App of All Time on iOS by App Store users.

Recent Developments

In 2016, the one billionth Groupon was sold, putting the company amongst Apple, McDonald's, Elvis and the Beatles as other brands that have achieved the billion-sold milestone. Amazingly, the billionth deal sold was for a local family-owned Pizzeria in St Louis, very similar to the first Groupon ever sold when the business started.

This doesn't include the national merchants, who lend household names and broad geographic coverage to the marketplace.

As the marketplace has grown, so too has the Groupon app. Its 2018 'Top Six Ranked App of All Time on iOS' by App Store users milestone shows the shift that the business has taken from a discounted deal email model, to a thriving marketplace where more than 80% of user traffic is on mobile. Groupon mobile apps have been downloaded 197 million times.

Promotion

Groupon's recent Discover More campaign encourages people to explore their local areas and seek out new and exciting experiences all around them. The campaign was rolled out throughout Europe across television, radio, billboards, taxis and trams, showcasing quality

Brand History

2007 The Point is launched, a tipping point-based collective action website dedicated to getting people together to accomplish a goal.

2008 An offshoot of the business, named Groupon, is formed, a site dedicated to advertising local businesses by offering deals for a limited time. The world's first Groupon was a pizza deal for Motel Bar, located downstairs from Groupon headquarters in Chicago.

2009 Groupon sees rapid expansion across the US and around the world, now serving over 150 markets domestically and 100 more worldwide.

2010 Groupon launches its mobile app to enable the discovery of local experiences on the go.

2011 Groupon Goods and Groupon Getaways are launched, adding products and travel to the ever-growing Groupon business.

2012 Groupon moves away from the daily deal model and relaunches as a full global marketplace.

2016 Groupon hits a huge milestone – the sale of its one billionth Groupon.

2018 Groupon celebrates its 10th anniversary.

THE GIN SAUNA

things to do and putting quality businesses at the very forefront. The campaign served to remind people that no matter where they are, there is always a Groupon waiting for them to discover.

Humour is firmly embedded in Groupon's DNA, which provides great scope for quirky, fun communications. With an approach that is bold, witty and often tongue-in-cheek, Groupon likes to go against the grain to excite and inspire with refreshing stories and themes that encourage its customers to try new things.

Groupon's creative stories have included the making of the world's most expensive burger, the first ever Gin Sauna, a portable lawn – allowing you to sunbathe anytime, anywhere – and the creation of a nail varnish infused with fizz.

DID YOU KNOW?

Nearly 1.5 billion Groupons have been sold, pumping over US $20bn into local businesses around the world

During the summer of 2018, Groupon focused on one of its key audiences – parents – who were looking for exciting, fun and pocket-friendly ways to keep their children entertained. The brand showcased messy, fun, chaotic and imperfectly perfect family summers through its #SummerUnfiltered social campaign.

Brand Values

The Groupon brand is built around the belief in great communities, specifically the belief that successful local businesses are the backbone of vibrant spaces and great neighbourhoods. It is the combination of interesting and thriving businesses coupled with people who visit frequently.

Groupon celebrates experiences, everyday things that it believes makes life more meaningful. It is all about discovering new places, new products and new things to do. Groupon wants to give its customers the extra nudge that they might need to try something new whilst knowing they are supporting their local community.

Heathrow

Heathrow is the **UK's gateway to the world**. Last year the airport helped
80 million passengers travel across the globe, more than any other airport in Europe.
Providing **world-class shopping** and a wide range of services is key to Heathrow's
success with **passengers choosing it for travel, adventure, business and leisure**

Market

Heathrow welcomed over 80 million passengers through the course of 2018, the first time this milestone has been achieved. July proved to be the busiest month with 262,000 passengers travelling through the airport on one day.

As the UK's Global airport hub, Heathrow flies to more destinations than any other European airport. The most popular destinations range from New York to Hong Kong as it hosts more than 80 airlines. Heathrow is also one of the largest employers in the UK, with 76,500 employees working together to make every journey better.

Product

Heathrow is focused on providing passengers with a smooth and memorable journey from the moment they leave home. Heathrow is within easy reach of London on public transport and has parking options ranging from Short Stay to Valet Parking in order to ease passenger journeys. The Heathrow Express service provides travellers with the fastest route to Heathrow, getting them from London Paddington to Terminals 2 & 3 in just 15 minutes.

Heathrow also prides itself on the quality and variety of its retail, offering exciting experiences from The Harry Potter Shop to Chanel, as well as restaurants including Spuntino, a new American-Italian inspired eatery. Its online service, Heathrow Boutique, enables travellers to explore a premium retail offering online, with the option to Reserve and Collect when passengers fly.

Achievements

Last year, passengers voted Heathrow's Terminal 2 the 'World's Best Airport Terminal' in the 2018 Skytrax World Airport Awards, with Terminal 5 coming in fourth place. In addition, Heathrow was awarded 'Best Airport in Western Europe' for the fourth year running, and 'Best Airport for Shopping' for the ninth year in a row. In recognition of Heathrow's brand and marketing performance, the airport was awarded 'Travel Brand of the Year' by the Travel Marketing Awards.

DID YOU KNOW?

700 pairs of sunglasses are sold each day at Heathrow whilst the **London red bus fridge magnet** is the **most popular souvenir**

Recent Developments

In 2018, the UK Government passed a vote for Heathrow's expansion, which will pave the way for 180,000 new jobs as well as delivering economic growth benefits across the country.

Heathrow has unveiled plans for carbon neutral growth. The vision is to build on technological changes within the aviation industry to make travel more sustainable, treating environmental performance as a key consideration for new flight allocations. Heathrow has also offered to waive landing fees for the first commercially viable electric flight.

Heathrow has partnered with the UK Government's GREAT initiative to promote tourism to the UK, installing 12 3D frames in-terminal to provide passengers with immersive experiences of the UK's most spectacular destinations; from Glencoe to the Royal Pavilion, an initiative designed to drive tourism and growth to all corners of the UK.

To coincide with Christmas 2018, Heathrow welcomed back Edward & Doris Bair to the airport with its third Christmas television advert. The ad was voted as one of the leading Christmas adverts, topping numerous polls and warming the hearts of the nation, as the two loveable bears were seen flying home to loved ones for the festive season.

Heathrow also created a scaled gingerbread model of the airport, featuring all four terminals, a runway and control tower, all made from the delicious festive treat. The festive creation was brought to life by Michelle Wibowo in partnership with Great British Bake Off winner, Candice Brown.

Heathrow oversaw a year of aviation progress in 2018, with Qantas flying non-stop flights from Heathrow to Perth for the first time. Heathrow also doubled its direct connections to China, growing the network from five destinations at the start of the year to 11 by year end, showing Heathrow to be a vital link between China and the UK.

#HeathrowPride
Pride in London 7th July 2018

DIGITALPRIDE

Welcome

Vanity Nightmare
London Drag Queen

Heathrow

Brand History

1946 London Airport opens on the current site.

1966 The British Airports Authority is created and London Airport is renamed Heathrow Airport.

1977 The London Underground reaches Heathrow.

1977 The Terminal 5 public planning inquiry – the longest in UK history – comes to an end.

1998 The Heathrow Express rail service begins.

2008 Terminal 5 opens and the first commercial A380 flight arrives at Heathrow.

2010 Terminal 2 is demolished and works starts on its £1bn replacement.

2012 Heathrow welcomes the world as Host Airport for the Olympic and Paralympic Games.

2014 Terminal 2: The Queen's Terminal opens in June.

2015 Expansion of Heathrow is recommended by the Airports Commission.

2016 Heathrow celebrates its 70th birthday.

2017 With younger travellers in mind, Mr. Adventure is joined by the new exclusive character, Little Miss Explorer.

2018 Heathrow commits to sustainability plans for carbon neutral growth, in an effort to make travel more sustainable within the aviation industry.

Promotion

Heathrow's communications teams look to present the world through the eyes of its passengers, showing the importance of travellers being at the heart of everything it does. In recognition of the heightened emotions that are so tightly and uniquely linked to travel, the communications strategy remains to keep passengers emotionally engaged, building warmth and love for the brand and all it means to them.

The emotional stories that unfold every day at Heathrow are evident in the latest summer and Christmas campaigns. Whilst summer dramatised the beautiful moment a mum switches off from work and shifts her focus to enjoying time with her two kids, Christmas saw the return of the Heathrow bears; a symbol of reunion at this important time of homecoming.

Heathrow also further highlighted its support for passengers during Pride week, creating a unique flag made up of colourful kisses from passengers and colleagues that flew proudly on the flag pole above Terminal 2. The campaign also saw the airport unveil the LGBTI faces of its Welcome Campaign adverts, featuring five members of the community – including three Gay Star News competition winners and two airport colleagues. This brought passengers and colleagues together to demonstrate the importance of inclusivity and diversity.

HEATHROW SERVES 204 DESTINATIONS IN 85 COUNTRIES

The airport's work on sustainability demonstrated Heathrow's continued commitment to reduce the impact of its business on the environment and improve the lives of employees. A series of animations communicated its commitment to 100% renewable electricity, reduced plastic and create more electric vehicle charging points.

Brand Values

Heathrow wants to make passengers feel welcome and 'give passengers the best airport service in the world'. As a gateway connecting the United Kingdom to over 80 long-haul destinations, Heathrow believes that the airport brings people closer. Over 250,000 passengers get closer to their loved ones, dream jobs or new adventures every day as Heathrow continues to be driven by the stories of its passengers.

HOLLAND & BARRETT

With nearly **150 years of experience**, Holland & Barrett aims to **enhance the wellbeing of its customers** around the world by delivering the **highest quality and best value** nutritional supplements and wellness products

Market

Holland & Barrett is one of the world's leading health and wellness retailers and the largest in Europe. The brand competes very successfully against a range of specialists and established grocers, as well as more recent online giants. With nearly 150 years of experience in the industry, the Holland & Barrett name is a familiar sight in almost every major city and town across the UK and is becoming increasingly visible further afield, in markets as diverse as the Netherlands, Belgium, Sweden, Singapore and China.

Product

Holland & Barrett offers a range of more than 6,500 individual products across vitamins and supplements, food, sports nutrition and 'clean beauty', which can be bought either online or in any of its 1,000-plus stores. The brand prides itself on offering the latest developments in health and wellness, most recently demonstrated by being the first retailer to bring CBD beauty products to the market.

Customers come to Holland & Barrett for its advice as well as for its products. The brand is particularly proud of its extensive specialist-training programme that is unparalleled in the health and wellness market. Under its own unique 'Hive' training programme, associates are able to gain qualifications in the provision of health advice to an 'A-level' equivalent standard and are officially recognised by the UK Government's 'Education Development International' programme. This is the first recognised training scheme to cover health on the high street, and means customers can confidently have access to useful advice to help them make informed product and lifestyle choices that match their health and wellness needs.

HOLLAND & BARRETT WAS THE FIRST RETAILER TO BAN MICROBEADS

Achievements

Being ranked sixth in The Sunday Times Grant Thornton Top Track 250 is testament to the strength of Holland & Barrett's business performance, with nine years of consecutive growth proving that the brand can continue to prosper, even in challenging times for retail.

The company was also granted the prestigious Queen's Awards for Enterprise: International Trade, in recognition of its achievements in building an international proposition, which now covers more than 16 territories, demonstrating that consumers around the world value British expertise and trust the quality of British-made products.

Closer to home, Holland & Barrett's award collection includes Retail Week's Speciality Retail of the Year, Natural & Organic Products Europe's award for Best Retail Chain, Natural Beauty Retail Awards and numerous other awards for customer service, business performance and investment in technology. Most recently, in November 2018, the editor of the brand's popular in-store magazine, Healthy, won Editor of the Year for Branded Content at the British Society of Magazine Editors Awards. Holland & Barrett is also proud to have won first prize in TFL's 'The Women

Me.No.Pause.

Supporting women through menopause, naturally.

HOLLAND & BARRETT

Brand History

1870 Holland & Barrett is formed by Major William Holland and Alfred Slapps Barrett, who establishes a store in Bishop's Stortford selling groceries and clothing.

1920 Holland & Barrett is acquired by Albert Button & Sons.

1970 Booker acquires the business.

1992 Holland & Barrett is bought by Lloyds Pharmacy.

1997 NBTY Inc. acquires Holland & Barrett.

2010 The Carlyle Group acquires Holland & Barrett and NBTY.

2017 The business is bought by Letter 1 Retail Group.

2019 Holland & Barrett has more than 6,500 individual products across vitamins and supplements, food, sports nutrition and 'clean beauty'.

or treating a minor ailment. The most recent mission-led campaign, Me.No.Pause, takes the lid off what may be considered the last taboo around women's health, the menopause. The campaign urges women and men to talk openly about what is a very natural stage in life, and to seek help and advice should they need to. Developed and produced by Holland & Barrett's creative agency Pablo, the campaign features five natural women talking about their experiences and how they are 'not taking a pause during menopause'.

DID YOU KNOW?

Holland & Barrett offers free nutritional education to all its employees

We See' competition, which promotes diversity in advertising. The win reflects the the brand's commitment to diversity and raising awareness of important issues such as menopause.

Recent Developments
Holland & Barrett is currently focused on further building upon its ethical values and driving forward its digital first strategy to make every health and wellness journey easy and enjoyable for its customers.

Ethics has always been close to its heart, being the very first high street retailer in the UK to ban plastic bags and microbeads from all products, some six years before the Government decided to legislate. It's a brand that isn't scared to take action, even if this means delisting products and has, amongst other examples, worked closely

with Greenpeace to ban krill oil products to safeguard marine life and protect fish stocks. The brand's extensive network of owned and franchised stores overseas has grown fast and a series of initiatives are in progress to consolidate that growth. This includes a proposed new hub in Singapore and a range of new and innovative partnerships either recently implemented or under development in other parts of the world such as China, as well as initiatives closer to home including an in-store partnership with Tesco.

Promotion
Holland & Barrett realises that health and wellness are not just about taking a pill or using a product, which is why it takes such a holistic approach to serving its customers' needs, looking at the full 'customer mission' – whether that be preventative, such as eating an increasingly plant based diet,

Brand Values
Holland & Barrett is a brand with both a deep-rooted heritage and a modern, opinion-leading approach. It has been on British high streets since 1870 and is a much-trusted alternative supplements retailer that, at the same time, keeps leading the very latest health and wellness trends.

Its well-trained, 'qualified to advise' staff offer support on whatever health and wellness journey they are presented with. They also provide advice about the latest products and hold the highest ethical standards.

hollandandbarrett.com

The Hoover brand has innovation in its DNA; with a desire to challenge the status quo and push boundaries using disruptive technologies designed to improve daily life. Its comprehensive product portfolio includes laundry, cooling, dishwashing and a range of built-in cooking appliances

Market

Since creating the world's first vacuum cleaner more than a century ago, Hoover has been in continual pursuit of innovation and excellence, developing stylish home appliances that enhance modern life.

Operating across major domestic appliances and small domestic appliances, Hoover produces everything from cordless vacuum cleaners to the most advanced wifi-controlled ovens.

Market penetration in the UK for major domestic appliances is extremely high and exceeds 90% for cooking, refrigeration and laundry appliances (Source: Mintel, Major Domestic Appliances, UK, April 2018).

Hoover Candy Group is one of Europe's fastest growing domestic appliance companies and 21% of the Group's turnover is achieved within the UK.

Product

Hoover UK offers a full range of domestic appliances, from floorcare products through to large kitchen appliances, both freestanding and built-in.

Its comprehensive product portfolio comprises state-of-the-art laundry, cooling and cooking appliance. Its range spans washing machines, washer dryers, tumble dryers, dishwashers, fridges and freezers, ovens, microwaves, hobs and hoods. It also produces an extensive range of innovative vacuum cleaners, steam cleaners and irons.

Hoover was the first manufacturer in the UK to launch a range of fully connected wifi kitchen appliances back in 2015 and has since made it a number one mission to lead the way with smart models of high-quality, stylish design.

DID YOU KNOW?

Hoover was the UK's first manufacturer to launch a full collection of wifi-connected kitchen appliances in June 2015

In 2018, Hoover launched its most innovative and groundbreaking products yet, the AXI collection. This range spans laundry, dishwashing and cooling appliances complete with artificial intelligence.

Achievements

Globally, the Hoover Candy Group is a market leader in innovation, particularly in the washing machine sector, where it holds a 61% market share in Europe.

In the UK, Hoover's products have received many awards and accolades such as Best Appliance Innovation – Gold Award – Designer Kitchen & Bathroom Award 2018 for the Hoover AXI Washing Machine; Electrical Safety First / Safety Innovation Award, Highly Commended, for the Hoover HHV67SLX WiFi Hood; Sirius' Manufacturer of the Year 2018, a title the brand has secured seven times; and an Appliance Innovation Award, EK&BBusiness Awards 2017, for the Hoover Vision Oven.

Recent Developments

Hoover has been a market leader in smart tech domestic appliances since 2015 and has made it its mission to continually lead the way with a comprehensive range of smart models.

Mid-2018 saw the brand launch a collection of ultra-smart appliances equipped with innovative artificial intelligence (AI). The manufacturer's AXI collection includes washing machines, washer dryers, dishwashers and fridge freezers. AXI is the first full

collection of AI kitchen appliances that are compatible with Amazon Alexa and Google Home.

Hoover has also launched a collection of premium cooking models, in its Vogue and Vogue Premium Collections. These high-end stylish ranges aim to provide premium, restaurant-quality results in domestic settings, with products such as steam ovens, sous vide systems as well as warming and vacuum sealer drawers.

Another recent landmark launch from the brand was the Hoover Vision Oven. Users can watch cooking video tutorials on the glass oven door, access selected websites, generate, save and amend favourite recipes, create a personal library of cooking

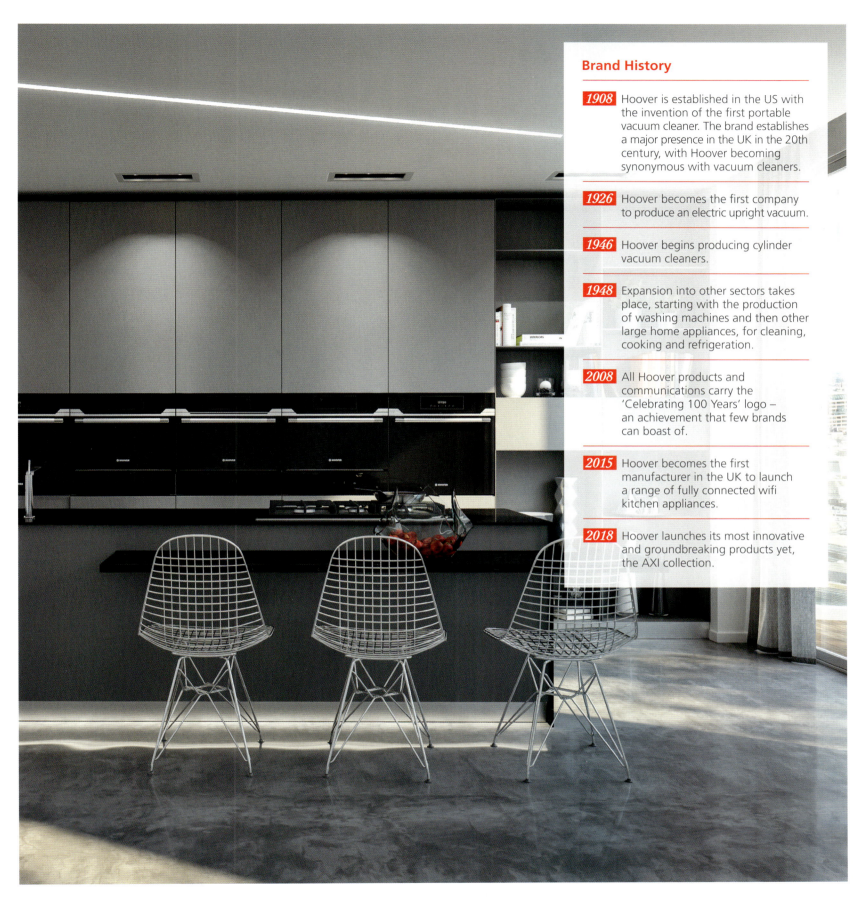

Brand History

1908 Hoover is established in the US with the invention of the first portable vacuum cleaner. The brand establishes a major presence in the UK in the 20th century, with Hoover becoming synonymous with vacuum cleaners.

1926 Hoover becomes the first company to produce an electric upright vacuum.

1946 Hoover begins producing cylinder vacuum cleaners.

1948 Expansion into other sectors takes place, starting with the production of washing machines and then other large home appliances, for cleaning, cooking and refrigeration.

2008 All Hoover products and communications carry the 'Celebrating 100 Years' logo – an achievement that few brands can boast of.

2015 Hoover becomes the first manufacturer in the UK to launch a range of fully connected wifi kitchen appliances.

2018 Hoover launches its most innovative and groundbreaking products yet, the AXI collection.

programmes, as well as check the temperature and cooking time remaining. The in-cavity camera is another key feature, allowing users to get a close-up of cooking progress via the Hoover Wizard app on a smartphone or tablet.

Promotion

The brand's 'Hoover, That's Who' promotional campaign, which began with a TV launch in 2017, has the aim of highlighting the brand's smart and innovative credentials. The campaign has since been utilised across OOH, social media, mobile and digital channels.

The stylish creative aims to reaffirm Hoover's position as an innovative manufacturer and demonstrate how the brand understands customer needs, developing products that consistently exceed customer expectations; something it has championed since its inception in 1908.

Brand Values

James M. Spangler, the inventor of the first portable vacuum cleaner, marked the start of Hoover's journey with this groundbreaking product. His creation put innovation at the heart of the brand's DNA.

Hoover strives to meet the needs of all its customers with a commitment based on style, innovation and care. It's not always about designing something new, but a drive to imagine what could be a better solution. It's about exploring new opportunities through bespoke care, style and innovation, keeping its founder's future-facing vision alive.

hoover.co.uk

INVESTORS IN PEOPLE

Investors in People is a community interest company and an agent of change, calling for a movement that puts people first – for the benefit of every person in every workplace, for increased productivity across organisations, and for a stronger, healthier and happier society

Market

Investors in People was launched in 1991 to raise the performance of UK businesses relative to international competitors. Having started out as a UK Government project, Investors in People is now an independent, not-for-profit company that helps thousands of organisations to successfully lead, support and engage people for sustainable results.

In today's world of uncertainty and exciting opportunity, more is expected from employers than ever before, with a desire for constant improvement. Individuals, employees and customers are increasingly wanting to work with sustainable, ethical organisations that align societal, individual and business objectives.

Investors in People believes that by putting people first 'we can create more together'. Others focus on leadership and support capabilities, only Investors in People focuses on the whole picture for whole success – for individuals, organisations and society.

Investors in People has a bold and worthy purpose: to make people, workplaces and society stronger, happier and more productive as a whole.

Product

In an age of job uncertainty, growing competition and rising workplace stress and anxiety, people expect more from their employers, not just a job and a workplace. Investors in People has been working hard on expanding and diversifying its product offering by developing several additional solutions to further support and equip organisations of all shapes and sizes.

Jumpstart was developed as part of Investors in People's broader mission to help organisations enhance business success through empowering their people. A digital platform, launched in late 2018, it is designed for start-ups and small organisations who want to take the first step in analysing their people practices and understanding how they can improve, in a bid to unlock the potential of their team.

Investors in People wellbeing accreditation has been revamped to ensure it includes the latest data-gathering approach, insights and technology to support and evaluate organisations' commitment to wellbeing. The accreditation evaluates and focuses on three areas – physical, psychological and social wellbeing. An organisation undergoing the accreditation can expect a robust analysis of its culture, work-life balance and how its health and wellbeing workplace practices stack up.

Achievements

As a brand, Investors in People has maintained significant awareness amongst UK businesses, and retained its position as the dominant B2B people management accreditation provider for a fifth consecutive year.

Currently, 2.7 million employees work for an Investors in People accredited organisation, impacting communities of all shapes and sizes in more than 50 countries, from the UK to the Philippines.

Investors in People has been awarded the Social Enterprise Mark, an achievement reserved for

organisations whose primary purpose is to make improvements for people and for the planet. The social benefit that it provides to workplace communities is threefold, creating happy people, competent managers and productive businesses.

DID YOU KNOW?

Since 1991, more than 11 million people have worked in organisations recognised by Investors in People

In 2019, Investors in People's efforts focus on calling for and growing a movement that puts people first. This will involve a number of activities aimed at creating a rallying cry for better workplaces.

Recent Developments

In 2018, Investors in People's first Managing Mental Health in the Workplace report sought

Brand History

1990 The employment department is asked to develop a national standard of good practice for training and development. The following year the first 28 Investors in People organisations are celebrated at a formal launch.

1993 Investors in People forms as a business-led, non-departmental public body. The first review of the Standard occurs, and an arm of the business opens in Australia.

2008 More than 7,000,000 people are now working in Investors in People organisations. An extended framework is introduced with different levels of recognition encouraging a route for progression and continuous improvement.

2010 The Health & Wellbeing award is launched to help organisations support their people more holistically.

2012 There are now Investors in People organisations across 80 countries.

2015 Investors in People evolves and launches the Standard. Based on the high-performance model, the Standard is designed to explore the full range of performance of an organisation. By providing insight into culture, support and the wider context and future of an organisation, employers can hear from their people and understand the best route for improvement.

2017 Investors in People is established as a Community Interest Company (CIC) with the mission to improve the working lives of people in all organisations and communities. The opportunity of self-determination empowers the team at Investors in People to look for more and better solutions.

2018 Investors in People develops four products and solutions in its first year as a CIC. Its free platform, Jumpstart, is launched to enable businesses of all sizes to start developing their people management and culture.

2018 The One Year accreditation is introduced to be more responsive and inclusive to the needs of smaller organisations. Working at their own pace, organisations become accredited for a year at a time.

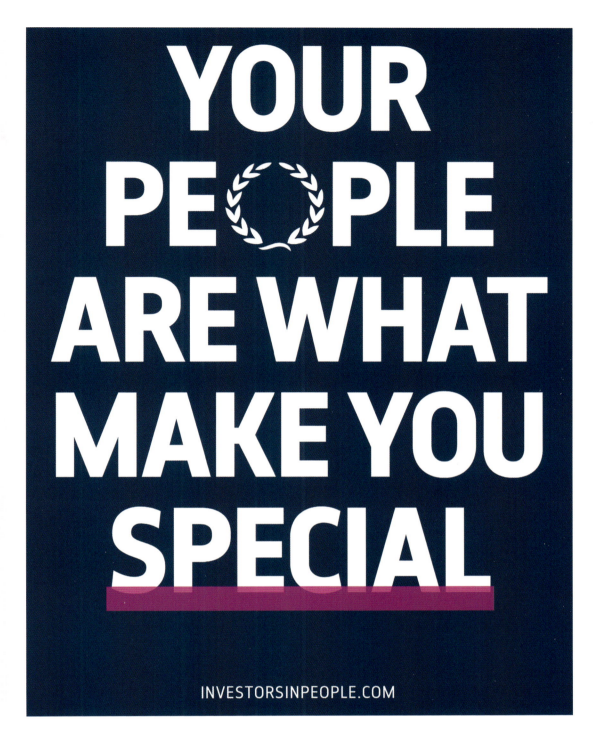

YOUR PEOPLE ARE WHAT MAKE YOU SPECIAL

INVESTORSINPEOPLE.COM

to unpick employee attitudes towards how their organisation cares for their mental wellbeing at work, and how this offer could be improved. The report highlighted that 80% of UK workers say they have experienced stress at work, as featured on BBC and ITV news, the report highlights the vital action needed from employers to support employee mental health.

Similarly, Investors in People's first Talent of Tomorrow report was developed with the intention of helping employers understand what the workforce of tomorrow wants from prospective employers today. Surveying 500 university graduates alongside 500 college leavers, the findings in this report gives clear insight into the ambition and motivations of the next generation of talent entering the workforce.

Exploring issues such as gender discrimination and wellbeing in the workplace, Investors in People's research will continue to provide more insightful trends in 2019 and beyond.

Promotion

In 2019 Investors in People will continue to address the importance of good people management practices across the world by speaking and exhibiting at events such as UNLEASH London, the Employee Engagement Conference, The Business Show, Engage Employee Engagement Conference, CIPD Festival of Work, HR360 Vienna and the Web Summit, to a combined delegate attendance of over 100,000 senior professionals.

Brand Values

As a community interest company, Investors in People's vision is to ensure every community prospers through investing in people.

Investors in People helps companies put people first by turning organisations into communities so that individuals can fulfil their potential. In turn, companies maximise their collective potential to make positive societal change.

Investors in People's brand values underpin the success of the organisation's purpose. Investors in People values are to be ambitious, driven, collaborative, empowered and always improving.

IM, irwinmitchell
solicitors

Nationally acclaimed, Irwin Mitchell is one of the few law firms that provide
a diverse range of legal and financial services to businesses and private individuals.
It has a strong customer-facing culture, and impressive client retention levels

Market

As one of the largest law firms in the UK, Irwin Mitchell provides a wide range of legal services to over 200,000 clients a year, with particular strengths in litigation. From its 14 UK offices, the firm provides a full range of consumer and business legal services, and is consistently recognised as a leader in its field.

It adopts a partnership approach with its clients, underpinned by the latest technology, innovative pricing and excellent service. It is the leading personal injury and medical negligence practice in the UK, covering all key injury types from road traffic accidents to international personal injury claims and workplace related illness and injury, including catastrophic brain injury and spinal cases. The firm also provides complimentary services from its national public law and leading Court of Protection practice.

Within the B2B market, Irwin Mitchell offers a wide range of commercial services and has strength in several sectors including real estate, manufacturing, technology, financial services, consumer businesses and education. Within these sectors the firm typically advises senior executives and management teams, general counsel and institutional investors.

Irwin Mitchell Private Wealth encompasses four main areas of law: residential property, tax, family and wills as well as trusts and estate disputes. Regarded as one of the top private client offerings in the UK, its prestigious client base includes high and ultra-high net worth individuals including business owners and entrepreneurs, high-level executives, investors and multi-generational families.

Irwin Mitchell's investment management business, IM Asset Management Ltd, provides specialist fund management services for private individuals. It acts for a wide range of clients including high net worth individuals – both personal injury claimants and those with business related or family wealth. IM Wealth

DID YOU KNOW?

The firm was the **Official Legal Services Provider** of the **2017 World Para Athletics Championships**

Management, which is owned by IM Asset Management, provides expert financial planning, helping clients of all ages prepare for their current and future financial needs.

Product

The company, which employs over 2,800 staff, has a group structure with Irwin Mitchell Holdings Limited sitting above Irwin Mitchell LLP and a number of subsidiaries with offices throughout England. Irwin Mitchell Scotland LLP is a separate Scottish legal practice, regulated by the Law Society of Scotland and has an office in Glasgow.

Achievements

Irwin Mitchell has the largest online market share in the personal injury and medical negligence markets, and the greatest share of voice in legal editorial coverage in the UK media. It has been recognised as one of The Times Best 200 Law Firms 2019 and the top three litigation firms in the UK (Source: The Lawyer). It has also recently received several other awards including Regulatory Law Firm of the Year at the Women in Compliance Awards as well as the Diversity and Inclusion Award from the Yorkshire Law Awards 2018.

Recent Developments

Irwin Mitchell has continued to see an increase in brand metrics, as a result of its integrated marketing strategy. Brand awareness, consideration, recommendation and leadership metrics have all strengthened year-on-year. Its footprint has also widened with greater consumer understanding of the wide range of services that the company offers.

Best known for its personal injury work, in recent years Irwin Mitchell has invested heavily in growing its private wealth and business divisions.

Promotion

In 2018 Irwin Mitchell continued to promote the brand through an integrated marketing strategy, bringing all component parts of its marketing capability together to drive brand awareness and presence.

Within this integrated marketing strategy, there are a number of key campaigns. In Personal Injury, the award winning 'Don't Quit, Do It' campaign showcases how sport can help people recover from serious injuries and other major traumas in their lives. The firm has partnered with well-known sports stars, such as Paralympic star Hannah Cockroft MBE and tennis star Alfie Hewitt, to demonstrate its commitment to rehabilitation. In 2018, the business also launched a disability sports grants programme and distributed £58,000 to 122 individuals and clubs. This aided the

continuation of sports being played or new sports being undertaken as well as the purchase of new equipment.

Irwin Mitchell Private Wealth partnered with The Times' 2018/19 coverage of the autumn rugby union internationals and the six nations championship and also sponsored the 'The Ruck' podcast. This provided a platform to launch a new creative strategy showcasing its core brand values and differentiating private wealth services to a relevant audience.

The business division has been promoted via thought leadership campaigns, such as the UK Powerhouse reports, which are published quarterly and examine economic growth in 48 towns and cities across the UK. The analysis, produced by the Centre for Economics & Business Research (Cebr), is unique. These reports generate significant media coverage and have resulted in Irwin Mitchell appearing in high profile media channels.

The latest creative for promoting the personal injury division shines a light on ability rather than disability and features real clients. It focuses on the progress that comes from the support that Irwin Mitchell is able to give its clients, allowing them to have the independence and confidence to take part in sport.

The business also has longstanding relationships with many charities and support groups, which offer vital help and advice to clients and their families. Irwin Mitchell has campaigned with these groups for many years to support their objectives, promote their awareness and key messages. In 2018 it supported Brake, the road safety charity, with its Bike Smart awareness campaign.

Brand Values

Irwin Mitchell places innovative client service and the delivery of client value at the centre of everything it does. Its unique approach of providing services with an expert hand and a human touch is embraced by its people, built into its processes and supported by technology. Everything the firm does is underpinned by its five values: pioneering, approachability, tenacity, efficiency and integrity.

Irwin Mitchell's social responsibility programme is a fundamental part of the essence of the firm. Its dedicated charity, the Irwin Mitchell Charities Foundation (IMCF), has raised more than £2m for charitable organisations since its inception in 1997.

All staff are encouraged to participate in the firm's award-winning CSR programme which is pulled together under four strands: people, environment, community and pro bono.

The Kingspan ethos can be summed up quite simply: **customer focused; solutions-driven; and innovation-led.** Through its diverse portfolio and global reach, it provides clients with a comprehensive range of building products and systems that **deliver value without compromising on quality or performance,** backed up by the very best technical support

Market

In a market that is increasingly subject to economic, environmental and regulatory influences, Kingspan has worked hard to ensure that its building envelope solutions are proven, compliant, energy efficient and durable. Its advanced systems can speed up construction processes, reduce carbon emissions, and help to create healthy buildings, all around the world. It is also responding to the growing need for water management systems, improvements in air quality, and renewable energy generation, as well as ways of reducing energy demand and meeting fire performance requirements.

Product

The Kingspan Group has five operational divisions: Insulated Panels, Insulation, Light + Air, Water & Energy, and Access Floors. Each division offers a comprehensive portfolio of construction products, backed by high levels of customer support, including design, technical services, Building Information Modelling (BIM), Building Energy Modelling (BEM), U-value

calculations, field services, compliance advice, waste take-back schemes, after sales care and comprehensive product guarantees.

Kingspan Light + Air is helping buildings to achieve excellent daylighting levels for a greater number of hours in the day with the launch of Kingspan Day-Lite Kapture – a precision engineered polycarbonate rooflight featuring an advanced, nano-prismatic layer, which uses microscopic structures to efficiently scatter light.

Kingspan Insulation has introduced Kingspan Thermataper TT44-K and Thermataper TT47-K, its first tapered roofing systems to incorporate its premium performance Kooltherm insulation, delivering excellent drainage and thermal efficiency with even slimmer, lightweight constructions.

DID YOU KNOW?

Polycarbonate is tough – it's used for riot shields as well as Kingspan rooflights

A new range of architectural floor finishes was launched at London Build 2018 as part of Kingspan Access Floors' product range. The new range of integrated, bonded and overlay finishes include a wide variety of Terrazzo, Porcelain and genuine timber.

Achievements

Kingspan Group has been placed on the CDP Climate Change 'A' list for a third year running.

In 2017, 69% of the total energy used by Kingspan's operations came from renewable sources, and the Group is on target to achieve its goal of Net Zero Energy (NZE) status by 2020.

The new Light + Air division performed ahead of expectations and expanded the range of product solutions the business offers. After a strong year in 2017 and the development of a unique US and European footprint, sales were up 57% in the first half of 2018.

Kingspan Insulation was a Regional winner for Best Use of Technology in the 2018 Chamber of Commerce Business Awards and was also shortlisted for the Made in the Midlands Awards, Manufacturer of the Year.

Kingspan Insulated Panels won Manufacturer of the Year at the BusinessGreen Leaders Awards 2018, was shortlisted for the Offsite Awards, Best Use of Steel and the Solar Power Portal Awards, C & I Storage Project of the Year.

Recent Developments

Kingspan Group joined some of the world's leading global companies in a commitment to the Science Based Targets Initiative (SBTi) to reduce greenhouse gas emissions by 10%.

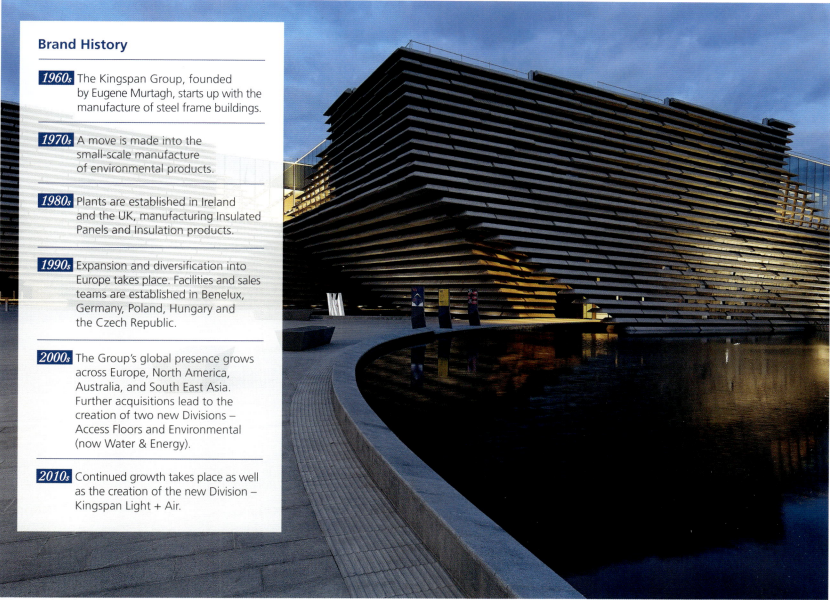

Brand History

1960s The Kingspan Group, founded by Eugene Murtagh, starts up with the manufacture of steel frame buildings.

1970s A move is made into the small-scale manufacture of environmental products.

1980s Plants are established in Ireland and the UK, manufacturing Insulated Panels and Insulation products.

1990s Expansion and diversification into Europe takes place. Facilities and sales teams are established in Benelux, Germany, Poland, Hungary and the Czech Republic.

2000s The Group's global presence grows across Europe, North America, Australia, and South East Asia. Further acquisitions lead to the creation of two new Divisions – Access Floors and Environmental (now Water & Energy).

2010s Continued growth takes place as well as the creation of the new Division – Kingspan Light + Air.

© Photography by Hufton + Crow

In September 2018 Kingspan Facades was launched – a new business incorporating Kingspan Group's portfolio of facade products under a single supply point, to provide the most appropriate solution for any type of facade requirement.

In response to the call for higher standards of installation and oversight on construction projects, Kingspan Facades will be underpinned by an industry-leading Compliance Assured scheme to support customers through design, installation training and on-site inspection during construction and handover of a BS 8414 tested, BR 135 certified Kingspan Facade system.

Kingspan Environmental Division was renamed Kingspan Water & Energy to better reflect its ambition to become a global leader in the design and supply of sustainable water management solutions, as well as environmentally responsible energy storage solutions, powered by smart monitoring.

A new whitepaper from Kingspan Insulation examined how insulation specification can have a significant impact on daylight levels within a building.

Kingspan Insulation invested €17m in two state-of-the-art, low waste production lines at its facilities in Derbyshire and North Yorkshire: a prototype Continuous Process Line 3 (CPL3), which is the latest evolution in the firm's Queen's Award-winning CPL technology, and a 2,400 m² manufacturing line for XPS insulation.

Kingspan Steel Building Solutions invested £1.4m in a state-of-the-art production line at its Walsall manufacturing facility, enhancing its capacity and capability to meet the growing market demand within the storage, handling and distribution sector.

Acquisitions included the Spanish polyurethanes business, Synthesia International, Poliuretanos and Huurre in the first quarter of 2018, Poland-based manufacturer of insulated panels and insulation boards, Balex Metal sp. z.o.o., Norwegian water-treatment company Vestfold Plastindustri, and the Brakel Group, a Dutch based leader in the daylight, natural ventilation and smoke management sectors. The Group also established Kingspan Jindal in India, and announced a US$10m investment in Invicara, a provider of transformative software solutions.

Promotion
The different divisions within the Kingspan Group have a healthy and active relationship with the relevant trade press, regularly contributing technical articles looking at industry issues and solutions. Other activities include presenting on testing, policy and legislation at trade events.

Regular Continuing Professional Development (CPD) training is run for construction professionals on a range of different topics, including facades and fire performance, building regulations and the real value of space.

Investment in Kingspan's digital offering has continued, with both Kingspan Insulation and Kingspan Insulated Panels launching free online learning hubs, offering customers online learning and comprehensive technical support.

Brand Values
Whether it is tackling climate change or fuel poverty, providing healthy buildings or social value, the Kingspan ethos is about investing in the future. It does this through high performing products, innovation, technical expertise, education and support. As a brand it represents quality, service, and corporate responsibility, and it always strives for excellence.

Established in 1896, **Knight Frank is the world's leading independent property consultancy** with a **mission to 'connect people and property, perfectly'**. Its residential and commercial teams form enduring relationships with clients to assist with all property requirements, from first homes to new office headquarters and world-famous landmarks

Market

Knight Frank's independent partnership sets it apart from its competitors. Its unique structure enables a vision committed to long-term growth and delivering industry-leading services and market-leading advice to clients.

Product

With more than 18,000 people in 523 offices across 60 territories, Knight Frank's four core global service lines – residential, valuations, global capital markets as well as occupier services and commercial agency – assist with clients' property requirements around the world.

On the residential side, Knight Frank is involved with some of the world's most prestigious homes. It offers a wide range of services including sales, lettings, residential development and consultancy, and counts more than 70 offices within its UK network.

Its UK commercial network, comprising two central London offices and 10 regional offices, provides investment, agency and professional consultancy services across core sectors including offices, retail, logistics and industrial, hotels, student property and healthcare.

Achievements

In 2018, awards won by Knight Frank included UK Residential Agency of the Year and Lettings Agency of the Year at the RESI Awards, and Professional Agency of the Year at the Property Week Awards.

Recent key transactions include: bringing the Northern Hemisphere's tallest building, 111 West 57th Street in New York, to market; letting homes to more than 2,000 overseas students in the UK; leasing London's landmark Adelphi building to tenants including Condé Nast, Spotify and The Economist; acting on one of London's largest ever townhouse sales for a reported £95m; and negotiating the largest ever single letting in Irish State history to Salesforce.

Little Pipe Cay, Bahamas

The firm's global corporate responsibility programme, Building Foundations, continues to grow. It is guided by five key areas: workplace, governance and ethics, environment, charity and community as well as marketplace. In 2017, Knight Frank's biennial Day of Giving raised a record £400,000 for charity and saw employees around the world support their local communities.

In addition, Knight Frank's Respect, Diversity & Inclusion steering group strives to ensure that employees are respected for being themselves in the workplace. The initiative hosts a series of regular events and communications to engage with employees and covers six key categories: age, disability, ethnicity and religion, gender, LGBT+ as well as working parents.

Recent Developments

2018 saw the expansion of the market-leading Private Office based in London. Dedicated to transacting the world's finest properties, the specialist group of global property experts delivers a bespoke and personal service to private clients, family offices and wealth advisers around the world.

Knight Frank's global presence is strengthened by part-owned and associate offices around the world as well as a number of strategic alliances. The latter includes: a joint venture with ZIEGERT in Germany; Santos Knight Frank in the Philippines; Bayleys in association with Knight Frank in New Zealand; and Newmark Grubb Knight Frank and Douglas Elliman Knight Frank in the USA.

Promotion

Every year, Knight Frank's research teams produce numerous market-leading reports.

Harptree Court, Somerset, England

Brand History

1896 Knight Frank & Rutley is founded and completes its first sale in Conduit Street, London.

1922 Chartwell in Kent is bought for Sir Winston Churchill.

1980 The company is involved with the £93m sale of Britannic House to BP, the UK's biggest property deal.

1981 Douglas Elliman Knight Frank sells Pan-American World Airways Intercontinental Hotels Corporation to Grand Metropolitan for US $500m.

1996 'Rutley' is dropped to become Knight Frank.

2008 The company moves its Global HQ to 55 Baker Street, London.

2010 Knight Frank is appointed on The Shard.

2011 The Knight Frank website launches in 21 languages as well as a new property app, which is listed in The Daily Telegraph Top 10 property apps.

2015 Knight Frank is instructed to sell 231 super-prime residences in the Royal Atlantis on the Palm Jumeirah, Dubai.

2018 Knight Frank is instructed to sell Australia's largest privately owned cattle enterprise, spanning 5.5 million hectares.

One Barangaroo, Sydney, Australia

LITTLE PIPE CAY, A US $85M PRIVATE ISLAND IN THE BAHAMAS, IS CURRENTLY FOR SALE THROUGH KNIGHT FRANK

Its flagship publication, The Wealth Report, launches via 30 events around the world with press coverage in top-tier media and an extensive social media reach. Other key reports include: Urban Futures, exploring global affordability; Private View, showcasing exquisite homes and luxury lifestyle interests; and (Y)our Space, presenting the future trends shaping global occupational markets.

Furthermore, Knight Frank regularly features in both local and national media around the world. In 2018, it was quoted in almost 40,000 pieces of press globally by the likes of the FT, The Times and The Wall Street Journal, as well as on broadcast channels BBC and Sky.

In recognition of the ongoing challenges faced by the residential sector, Knight Frank recently rolled out training accredited by The Institute of Customer Service, committed to building upon the firm's legacy and strengthening the exceptional service its customers receive, every time.

Brand Values

At the heart of Knight Frank are its people, clients and communities. It forms long-term relationships with clients to provide considered advice and personalised solutions on all areas of property across key residential and commercial markets. Supported by market-leading research and innovative technology, Knight Frank aims to ensure the quality of its service differentiates it from the competition.

knightfrank.com

Founded by Ole Kirk Kristiansen, the **LEGO**® **Group is one of the world's leading manufacturers of play materials.** The LEGO brand name is based on the Danish term, Leg Godt, meaning 'play well' and reflects **the brand's deep commitment to inspire and develop the builders of tomorrow**

Market

The LEGO Group is represented in many parts of the world and is a privately held, family-owned company with headquarters in Billund (Denmark) and main offices in Enfield (USA), London (UK), Shanghai (China) and Singapore.

Sixty years on from when the LEGO brick was patented, and 40 years after the creation of the first LEGO Minifigure, the LEGO brand belief in every child's right to play well is as strong as ever. It is the LEGO philosophy that 'good quality play' enriches a child's life – and lays the foundation for later adult life.

Product

LEGO play experiences enable learning through play by encouraging children to reason systematically and think creatively. They offer endless hours of engagement, as all LEGO bricks are based on the LEGO System in Play, which allows children to build anything they can imagine – over and over again.

The classic LEGO brick design has stayed the same over the past six decades. First patented in 1958, a LEGO brick purchased at that time would be compatible with a brand new 2019 brick.

From curious small hands to exciting roleplay and advanced building challenges over to engaging digital and educational exploration, LEGO products seek to provide an assortment broad enough to appeal to every child, no matter building ability or age.

Achievements

The LEGO Group has grown from being a small local company into being one of the world's leading suppliers of creative play and learning materials.

In 2000, the LEGO brick was awarded double honours being named Toy of the Century by both US FORTUNE magazine and the British Association of Toy Retailers in recognition of its longstanding success. Since this, the brand has

gone from strength to strength thanks to its dedication to innovation and being able to rebuild and reinvent. It is heralded for its ability to continue to inspire creative thinking and imagination in children.

There are now more than 60 different brick colours in production and the number of different types of LEGO elements – including all types of LEGO bricks and other elements – has reached in excess of 3,700.

THERE ARE 915,103,765 DIFFERENT WAYS OF COMBINING SIX EIGHT-STUD BRICKS OF THE SAME COLOUR

The first LEGO Movie™ was released in 2014, bringing the brand's iconic Minifigures to life. The much-anticipated sequel launched in 2019, once again delighting and amusing fans, young and old.

The new LEGO Harry Potter™ Hogwarts™ Great Hall set became one of the 23 LEGO sets to appear in the top 100 selling items in the UK toy market

(Source: NPD 2018) and topped Christmas lists across the UK after it was included in the prestigious 2018 DreamToys toys of the year.

January 2019 marked 50 years since the LEGO Group unveiled its inaugural large brick for small hands in 1969. LEGO DUPLO® derives from the Latin word 'duplex' meaning 'double' and are twice the size of classic LEGO bricks on all dimensions so all bricks fit into the LEGO System in Play.

Recent Developments

Today's children are seamlessly merging what is real and what is virtual, reinventing play – there are now endless opportunities for children's imaginations to run wild in both the real and virtual worlds.

Inspired by the blurred lines between the digital and physical worlds, this move into 'fluid' play, with physical and digital experiences inspired the launch of LEGO Hidden Side, the only play experience available today that fully and seamlessly integrates augmented reality (AR) and physical construction to reveal a hidden world of interactive play.

The LEGO Group is committed to innovating to bring new play experiences to all build levels and ages as it knows play is fundamental: not only is it great fun, it is vital to a child's ability to develop core life skills such as confidence, communication, creativity and critical thinking.

Promotion

The 'Plants from Plants' campaign in 2018 saw LEGO botanical elements such as leaves, bushes and trees being made from plant-based plastic sourced from sugarcane. This move is part of the LEGO Group's ambition to use sustainable materials in core products by 2030 and packaging by 2025.

The new sustainable LEGO elements are made from polyethylene, which is a soft, durable and flexible plastic, and while they are based on sugarcane material, they are technically identical to those produced using conventional

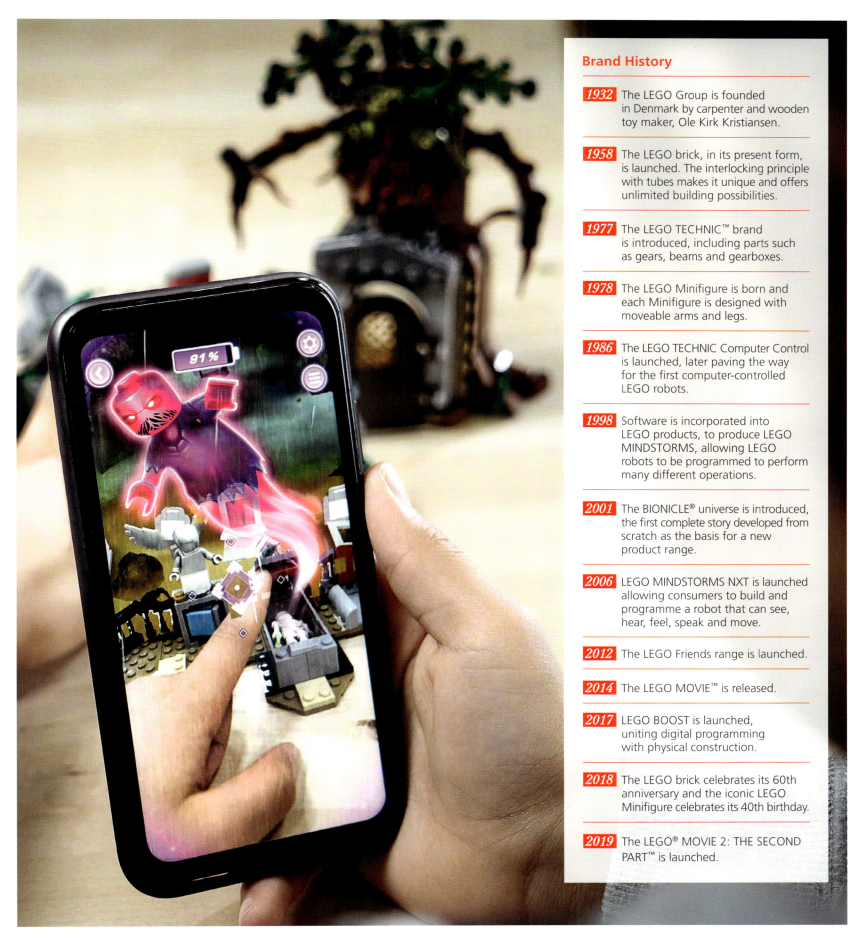

Brand History

1932 The LEGO Group is founded in Denmark by carpenter and wooden toy maker, Ole Kirk Kristiansen.

1958 The LEGO brick, in its present form, is launched. The interlocking principle with tubes makes it unique and offers unlimited building possibilities.

1977 The LEGO TECHNIC™ brand is introduced, including parts such as gears, beams and gearboxes.

1978 The LEGO Minifigure is born and each Minifigure is designed with moveable arms and legs.

1986 The LEGO TECHNIC Computer Control is launched, later paving the way for the first computer-controlled LEGO robots.

1998 Software is incorporated into LEGO products, to produce LEGO MINDSTORMS, allowing LEGO robots to be programmed to perform many different operations.

2001 The BIONICLE® universe is introduced, the first complete story developed from scratch as the basis for a new product range.

2006 LEGO MINDSTORMS NXT is launched allowing consumers to build and programme a robot that can see, hear, feel, speak and move.

2012 The LEGO Friends range is launched.

2014 The LEGO MOVIE™ is released.

2017 LEGO BOOST is launched, uniting digital programming with physical construction.

2018 The LEGO brick celebrates its 60th anniversary and the iconic LEGO Minifigure celebrates its 40th birthday.

2019 The LEGO® MOVIE 2: THE SECOND PART™ is launched.

---

plastic. The elements have been tested to ensure the plant-based plastic meets the high standards for quality and safety that the LEGO Group has, and that consumers expect from LEGO products.

The unique LEGO brick design, and the LEGO Group's uncompromised focus on quality and safety during the past 87 years, ensures that two LEGO bricks produced decades apart can still fit together. As the LEGO Group is working towards using sustainable materials in its core products and packaging, it will remain strongly rooted and driven by the uncompromised focus on high product quality and safety.

Brand Values

Guided by the company spirit, 'Only the best is good enough', the company is committed to the development of play experiences to inspire and develop the builders of tomorrow.

The brand's core values of Imagination, Creativity, Fun, Learning, Caring, and Quality are important not only because they define who the LEGO Group is as a company and what it stands for, but also because they guide its ambition of enabling future generations to build a better world.

With a global product strategy and commitment to improving air quality, LEVC continues to work towards pioneering zero-emission capable technology **across a range of electric commercial vehicles and providing flexible EV solutions** that meet the requirements of city regulators, vehicle operators and urban city dwellers

Market

As our cities expand and become more congested, concerns over air pollution continue to grow as the health impacts are better understood. With an urgent need for clean air in cities across the world, global demand for greener commercial vehicles is set to grow significantly.

Delivery of the LEVC vision is underpinned by the creation of a new global strategy focused entirely on electric commercial vehicles.

Product

While some manufacturers measure how long it takes to build a vehicle in hours, LEVC prefers generations. Perhaps that's why its vehicles are considered both timeless and part of the urban landscape.

The TX eCity marks a revolutionary start to a new chapter in black cab history. Engineered from the ground up yet unmistakably a black cab, the new vehicle embodies the collective experience and expertise LEVC has gained over the last century building commercial vehicles.

Achievements

With a commitment to leading the EV transition, last year LEVC helped taxi drivers secure more than £9m of Government grant funding to support the upfront cost of purchasing an electric taxi, enabling more drivers to make the switch to a greener vehicle.

DID YOU KNOW?

By switching to **an electric TX eCity,** black cab drivers can reduce their carbon footprint by seven million tonnes a year

There are now more than 1,500 TX eCity electric taxis on UK roads and the product has experienced export success in Germany and the Netherlands. Having secured a high level of positive exposure for TX in 2018 – gaining quality coverage in the top tier of international print and broadcast media – LEVC sales are set to double in 2019.

With the successful introduction of the TX eCity, LEVC has proved the vehicle concept and technology in the toughest commercial vehicle market in the world. With the company looking towards the next step on the electric revolution, LEVC and Geely New Energy Commercial Vehicles (GCV), LEVC's parent company, announced a move to create a seamless portfolio of electric commercial vehicles for markets across the world. This new product strategy will create a line-up of electric commercial vehicles, with potential for more electric van derivatives for cities, as well as ensuring that the company's electric commercial vans can be developed, manufactured and marketed globally.

This new approach, better strategic fit and opportunity to create a wider range of new products will allow LEVC, in partnership with GCV, to better meet customer requirements over the long term and to achieve its vision of becoming the urban commercial vehicle provider of choice. It also represents a huge vote of confidence in LEVC by Geely and will help to increase choice, while lowering development and production costs.

Recent Developments

Fully recognising that new on-street charging infrastructure remains critical if more drivers are to make the switch to an electric vehicle, LEVC throughout 2018 actively engaged in innovative technologies which would provide added value and operational benefit to its customers.

PowermyStreet, a new resource set up by LEVC in partnership with the London Evening Standard and CleanAir in London among others, helped Londoners improve the on-street EV charging landscape by nominating locations where they felt a charge point would be useful. Information provided then supports proposals and has a direct influence on London's on-street public EV charging infrastructure planning.

The brand's commitment to tackling air pollution by facilitating EV adoption also saw LEVC work with Ubitricity and Siemens, to launch an innovative new lamp post charging trial.

Brand History

1908 Mann and Overton's, a successful dealer group and coachworks company, introduces the 12/16 cab based on the Austin Model 15. It quickly becomes the most successful taxi in London.

1914 The Austin Model 15 is the only cab available and serves dual roles by also providing the chassis for a successful van series.

1948 What goes on to become know as the FX series, and the traditional black cab, comes into being and sets the standard.

1959 The FX4 brings diesel power, even more passenger space, and wheelchair access as standard and goes on to become a symbol of London as familiar and iconic as any landmark.

1997 The TX series is launched and sets a new standard for robust engineering, passenger comfort and safety.

2007 With the TXII and TX4, further innovations help to continually evolve what is still the only purpose-built professional taxi. From guaranteeing Euro 6 compliancy, to improving fuel efficiency and power, the TX series is the benchmark in the trade.

2009 The FX4 is recognised by the Design Museum, listing it in its '50 cars that changed the world'.

2017 LEVC's electric TX taxi becomes fully certified to carry fare-paying passengers.

2018 TX successfully launches in London, Manchester, Coventry, Birmingham, Edinburgh, as well as Germany and the Netherlands. More than 1,500 electric taxis arrive on UK roads.

2019 LEVC announces plans for a portfolio of electric commercial vehicles for markets around the world in response to growing demand for electric mobility. In addition, HRH The Prince of Wales visits LEVC and tours the EV manufacturing facility.

The trial, which involved the installation of EV charge points in existing street light lamp posts, helped drivers who do not have access to off street parking, enabling them to charge their vehicle outside their home.

Promotion

A taxi has one purpose – to carry passengers. LEVC engineered the TX eCity to be the pinnacle of hassle-free travel in the city. The interior style of the vehicle is elegant and contemporary. Along with the space, comfort and accessibility it provides, the aesthetic appeal and quiet refinement of the cabin make it a relaxed and pleasant place in which to be driven. Together, this makes TX the perfect vehicle to pioneer new inner-city mobility initiatives.

In 2018 the brand explored opportunities that responded to the changing urban mobility landscape. On-demand mobility apps CleverShuttle

and Ioki – currently operating in Hamburg and Munich, Germany – used the TX eCity to combine a personalised, eco-friendly chauffeur service with efficient ride sharing to offer a greener, more affordable transport service which gives drivers and passengers a notably superior ride, with greater comfort and connectivity.

Meanwhile in London, LEVC collaborated with British Airways to introduce a new and environmentally friendly electric taxi service at its Heathrow home.

The new service transports passengers at risk of missing connecting flights between planes; meaning even those with the shortest of stays in London can experience the world's most advanced electric taxi. The new zero-emission capable taxis have replaced conventional internal combustion engine vehicles at the airport, and successfully help British Airways to reduce emissions that impact air quality.

Brand Values

Whether urban dweller, city regulator, vehicle operator, or employee, 'People Driven' are two words which define LEVC. The human factor is integral to everything it does, and everything the business does is underpinned by four key values that aim to deliver a better quality of urban living for people all over the world: Dependability, Connectivity, Progression and Reliability.

LinkedIn is the **world's largest professional network with more than 610 million members** in more than 200 countries and territories worldwide. It aims to create economic opportunity by **connecting professionals and making them more productive and successful.** It is transforming the way companies hire, market, sell and learn

Market

LinkedIn serves the global workforce and their employers through its online professional networking and recruitment platform. It has a diversified business model with revenue coming from Talent Solutions, Marketing Solutions, Sales Solutions, LinkedIn Learning and Premium Subscriptions products. In December 2016, Microsoft completed its acquisition of LinkedIn, bringing together the world's leading professional cloud and the world's leading professional network. Headquartered in Silicon Valley, LinkedIn has offices across the globe.

LinkedIn has a wealth of workforce data and has developed The Economic Graph. This is a digital representation of the global economy, based on its 610 million members, 50,000 skills, 30 million companies, 20 million open jobs and 84,000 schools. In short, it's all the data on LinkedIn.

Through mapping every member, company, job and school, LinkedIn is able to spot trends like talent migration, hiring rates and in-demand skills by region. These insights help LinkedIn to connect people to economic opportunity in new ways. In addition, by partnering with governments and organisations around the world, it also helps others connect people to opportunities more effectively.

Product

LinkedIn believes that 'You are happiest when who you are lines up with what you do' and aims

to humanise the world of work. LinkedIn members create their own profiles and connections to build and maintain a unique professional network, helping them throughout their professional journey. The platform can be used to search and apply for jobs, interact with their professional community, and to learn and upskill. By joining public or private Groups or following hashtags, members can also be kept up-to-date with news, debate and developments in their areas of interest and tap into the knowledge of their networks. Members can also build their own profiles through sharing content and publishing posts and articles. LinkedIn also provides businesses and recruiters with a platform where they can find, connect with and tap into diverse talent pools. With more than 20 million active job listings and 20.5 million members who have indicated being open to new opportunities, LinkedIn helps recruiters find the right person by matching the open role with qualified candidates, so they can prioritise the ones most open to hearing from them.

The platform is available to anyone globally at no cost, with paid-for options for recruiters, talent and L&D leaders, and Premium members.

Advertisers can also use the platform for targeted display ads and InMail campaigns.

Achievements

LinkedIn has built a strong culture, fuelled by a diverse workforce. Its vision is to 'create

economic opportunity for every member of the global workforce' and its mission is to 'connect the world's professionals to make them more productive and successful'.

DID YOU KNOW?

LinkedIn started 'Bring In Your Parents Day' six years ago after finding that **one-third of parents don't know what their children do for a living**

In order to maintain a strong company culture, initiatives such as global company all-hands meetings take place every two weeks, led by CEO Jeff Weiner. For employees, this is an opportunity to hear how the company is doing, directly from executives in a non-filtered way. For executives, it's a chance to keep employees apprised on high-level decisions at the company, provide an update on the direction of the company, and hear constructive, honest and open feedback from employees. No question is off-limits.

Each month, LinkedIn also gives employees a day to focus on themselves, the company or the world. While this is an internal programme, LinkedIn

#InItTogether

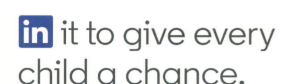

it to give every child a chance.

Ryan Evans
Education Specialist, Aspire 2Be

Brand History

employees often spend the day volunteering in their communities and inviting local non-profits into the office to work with employees.

LinkedIn also partners with OUTstanding/ Involve in the UK and Ireland. Employees attend Future Leader workshops and participate in its mentoring programme for LGBT and ethnic minority employees.

Recent Developments

Producing reports using its extensive data has become an important part of what LinkedIn does. LinkedIn's Workforce Report is produced monthly and reviews hiring and professional migration trends in the UK. It is timed in order to support the Office for National Statistics labour reporting cycle and covers the same time period.

LinkedIn has also carried out research analysing the attractiveness of the British labour market, which shows a clear decline in Britain's appeal to overseas job hunters searching in the UK, and a loss in market share of skilled immigration.

Meanwhile, its annual Top Companies and Top Start-Ups lists rank the most sought-after companies to work for, whilst its Top Voices list ranks members whose posts, articles, videos and comments are driving engaging conversations in their industries and countries.

LinkedIn also continues to develop its product portfolio having recently launched Talent Insights – a self-serve talent analytics product that taps into LinkedIn global data to provide real-time actionable insights to help businesses source talent more effectively.

LinkedIn also continues to develop its content. For example, it recently announced plans to move its core hiring tools – LinkedIn Recruiter, LinkedIn Jobs and Pipeline Builder – onto one single platform called the new intelligent hiring experience. For recruiters, the new interface will give them access to all their talent needs in one place, helping them be more efficient, aligned and collaborative.

Promotion

LinkedIn produced its first ever TV ad in 2016, which ran in the US and launched during the Academy Awards – widely considered to be the US advertising industry's second biggest TV slot, after the Super Bowl. The campaign also ran across print, digital and social. The creative concept was based on LinkedIn data, which found that three million of its members were qualified for NASA's latest astronaut job posting at the time. The ad used NASA footage with a voiceover from LinkedIn's CEO, Jeff Weiner.

LinkedIn's latest brand campaign 'In It Together' ran in the US, UK, Germany and France in 2018. The campaign has real LinkedIn member stories at the heart of its creative. The second wave of the campaign launched this year and hones in on people who have leaned on the LinkedIn community to help them secure their ideal jobs.

The campaign highlights the power of community and how members come together every day to help each other connect to opportunities.

The two phases of the campaign used a combination of out-of-home, digital, broadcast and on-demand media channels. Clever use of a campaign microsite also drove both content consumption and sign-ups. The campaign was further enhanced with influencer-led social activation and LinkedIn employee engagement.

Brand Values

LinkedIn aims to create economic opportunity by connecting professionals and making them more productive and successful.

linkedin.com

LLOYD'S

*As the **world's specialist insurance and reinsurance market**, Lloyd's provides the complex and critical insurance needed to underwrite human progress*

Market

Lloyd's is a unique insurance market with an unrivalled concentration of specialist underwriting expertise. The market comprises more than 50 leading insurance companies, more than 200 Lloyd's-registered brokers and a global network of almost 4,000 insurance agents (coverholders) licensed to write insurance on Lloyd's behalf.

Through this network, Lloyd's does business in more than 200 countries and territories around the world.

Lloyd's has been able to retain its pre-eminent position in global insurance due to a combination of its internationally recognised and respected brand, its underwriting expertise, its global network, a unique working culture and a continual commitment to innovation.

As risks evolve and emerge, the breadth, depth and responsiveness of the Lloyd's market gives customers the confidence to move forward in the face of uncertainty. Lloyd's aim is to remain the global centre for specialist insurance and reinsurance for many years to come.

Product

At Lloyd's, customers have access to the combined scale, expertise and capacity of the

DID YOU KNOW?

*In 2018 the Lloyd's market **insured Will Smith's** bungee jump over the Grand Canyon **for US $200m***

entire insurance market – which contains large international organisations to smaller specialists. Much of the business is carried out on a subscription basis, meaning risks are shared between multiple insurers. These insurers cover some of the world's most complex risks – everything from shipping, aviation and pandemics to nuclear, political risk and cyber.

The Lloyd's market has always been at the forefront of its industry, pioneering new forms of protection for a rapidly changing world. Its market's underwriters and brokers are among the very best in the world, anticipating and responding to new and emerging risks and using state-of-the-art modelling to create specialist products and solutions. For example, Lloyd's is now the world's largest cyber insurer, it insures businesses who are part of the sharing economy, space travel and more, giving companies the confidence to drive social progress and economic development.

Lloyd's is proud of its reputation for paying valid claims. In 2017, Lloyd's paid around £18.5bn in claims including for the Californian wildfires and the hurricanes that hit the US and Caribbean. Between 2012 and 2017 Lloyd's paid £75bn in claims, enabling millions of customers to recover from disasters, and get their lives and businesses back on track.

Achievements

Originally created to insure shipping ventures more than 330 years ago, Lloyd's has provided insurance for a huge variety of customers –

from Arctic explorers, international aid organisations and space missions to multinational companies and celebrities.

Today, as the world becomes more interdependent and society becomes more vulnerable to systemic shocks, Lloyd's remains well placed to meet the insurance needs of the global economy with significant operations in the US and Europe. It also has operations in Singapore, Shanghai, Beijing, Tokyo, Dubai and Latin America, and recently opened its first office in India.

Recent Developments

In 2018, Lloyd's launched a new technology accelerator – the Lloyd's Lab. This is a physical space in the Lloyd's building in London, where specially selected technology partners develop new concepts and products that could benefit Lloyd's market stakeholders, including ways to improve the customer experience, build digital relationships, make use of artificial intelligence and improve data analytics to enhance underwriting, and create 'smart' insurance products.

In November 2018, Lloyd's also launched its new subsidiary in Brussels. Lloyd's Brussels ensures that customers continue to have access to Lloyd's expertise, products and services after Brexit.

Promotion

With expertise earned over three centuries, Lloyd's is a name that resonates with customers beyond its headquarters in London into the US, Europe, Asia, Latin America and the Middle East and Africa.

Its reputation for risk expertise is supported by highly respected thought leadership and risk analysis, helping customers to quantify the costs of the threats they face and to understand the insurance solutions available to them.

Brand History

1688 Lloyd's coffee house is recognised as the place for obtaining marine insurance.

1774 The modern Lloyd's is born as it moves to the Royal Exchange and leaves the coffee business for good.

1904 Lloyd's writes its first motor policy, cementing its reputation for innovation.

1906 Faced with the devastation of the San Francisco earthquake, Lloyd's underwriter Cuthbert Heath instructs prompt payment: "in full, irrespective of the terms of their policies."

1911 Lloyd's writes its first policy for aviation.

1965 The first space satellite insurance is placed at Lloyd's and in 1984, Lloyd's launches a successful salvage mission to reclaim two rogue satellites, sending a shuttle and five astronauts into orbit in order to retrieve them.

1999 Lloyd's Asia opens in Singapore as part of its commitment to develop the insurance industry in new and emerging markets.

2001 The events of 9/11 change the world's perception of risk forever. It was also Lloyd's largest-ever single loss, impacting many different classes of business.

2015 Lloyd's launches its global City Risk Index which found that nearly half the economic risks faced by 301 cities around the world were linked to human made threats.

2016 Lloyd's expands its award-winning diversity festival across its global network of offices.

2018 Lloyd's Lab is opened.

Recent studies include Lloyd's City Risk Index, a partnership with the Cambridge Centre for Risk Studies, which quantifies the amount of annual GDP at risk in 279 cities from 22 threats.

In addition, the 2018 Lloyd's report, A World at Risk, calculates how much of the world is underinsured and is therefore exposed financially to natural catastrophes. Lloyd's also publishes reports on emerging risks for all its stakeholders including customers. Recent topics cover cyber attacks, the sharing economy, the internet of things and virtual reality.

By scanning the horizon, Lloyd's keeps its customers informed of emerging threats and trends, ensuring they can focus on the future with confidence, safe in the knowledge that Lloyd's is protecting them every step of the way.

Brand Values

Lloyd's key brand values are Trust, Modernity, Innovation, Expertise and Global. Lloyd's is clear about its aim to be the global centre of specialist insurance and reinsurance; meeting the challenges of a changing world and accessing the major overseas territories and emerging markets.

London
Stock Exchange Group

London Stock Exchange Group (LSEG) is a global markets infrastructure business. It provides valuable services for a wide range of customers, focusing on Intellectual Property, Risk and Balance Sheet Management and Capital Formation. The Group plays a vital economic and social role in enabling companies to access funds for growth and development

Market

LSEG plays a vital economic and social role within the global economy through its interconnected businesses, enabling companies to access funding for growth and development, make informed investment decisions and manage financial risks. In turn, on a broader macro-economic basis, this provides greater efficiency in accessing and managing capital, helping to fund innovation, generate wealth and create jobs.

With structural economic shifts and widespread regulatory change impacting the markets and communities served by the Group, the systemic importance of safe, transparent and trusted market infrastructure has never been more apparent.

Against this background, LSEG is acutely aware of its wider responsibilities as an acknowledged global leader in the field.

Product

LSEG delivers the infrastructure, products and services across the financial markets infrastructure value chain to provide a platform for serving customers at each and every point and meeting a wide range of their needs.

Its Information Services division provides customers with an extensive range of valuable information and data products that inform investment decisions and capital allocation, including indexes, data on pricing, trading and valuations. Through FTSE Russell, the Group is a global leader in financial indexing, benchmarking and analytic services with approximately US $16tn benchmarked to its indexes.

LSEG offers a full range of central counterparty (CCP) clearing services and collateral management solutions which provide strong risk management and capital efficiency benefits. Through leading global clearing house LCH, the Group provides proven risk management capabilities across a range of asset classes. During 2018, LCH's interest rate derivatives clearing service, SwapClear, processed over US $1 quadrillion in notional.

LSEG's primary markets provide choice and connections between a wide range of issuers and investors, enabling domestic and international companies to raise capital effectively. Through its secondary markets, it provides liquid and deep access to financial securities to enable improved price formation, transparency and trading efficiency.

Among the international equity, bond and derivatives markets operated by the Group are: London Stock Exchange; Borsa Italiana; MTS, Europe's leading fixed income market; and Turquoise, the pan-European trading platform. Nearly 2,700 companies from over 100 countries

DID YOU KNOW?

Since 1995, companies have raised more than £112bn on LSEG's AIM

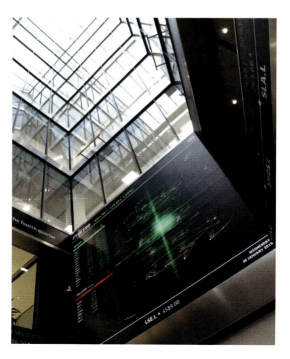

are currently listed on these markets, which offer businesses efficient access to capital while giving investors the opportunity to trade one of the world's most diverse ranges of securities.

The Group understands that ambitious small and medium-sized enterprises (SMEs) are key to growth and job creation in the real economy. AIM, launched in 1995, has raised more than £112bn in financing for these companies; and LSEG has also created ELITE, a business support and capital raising initiative for dynamic high growth private businesses across some 40 countries.

The Group's acclaimed annual celebration of UK SMEs, '1000 Companies to Inspire Britain' and sister publications, '1000 Companies to Inspire Europe' and 'Companies to Inspire Africa' continue to celebrate and support SME communities across the globe.

Through LSEG Technology, the Group develops and operates high performance technology solutions, including trading, market surveillance and post trade systems for over 40 organisations and exchanges, including LSEG's own markets.

Achievements

Having grown from a domestically focused national exchange, today's LSEG is a multi-asset, multi-platform business with an increasingly global presence. The purchase of a majority stake in LCH in 2013 greatly enhanced its post-trade capabilities, while the 2014 acquisition of the US-based Frank Russell Company led to the creation of FTSE Russell.

The Group offers some of the most deep and liquid markets, innovative products and services in global financial markets infrastructure – all offered, crucially, on an open access basis.

Recent Developments

Sustainable and green finance are becoming important issues for LSEG's clients, both issuers and investors, and are rising up the agenda

Brand History

1698 At Jonathan's Coffee House, John Castaing begins issuing a list of stock and commodity prices called 'The Course of the Exchange and other things'.

1801 The first regulated exchange comes into existence in London and the modern Stock Exchange is born.

1973 The 11 British and Irish regional exchanges amalgamate with the London exchange, which also admits its first female members.

1986 The UK market is deregulated in the 'Big Bang'.

2007 London Stock Exchange merges with Borsa Italiana, creating London Stock Exchange Group.

2009 LSEG acquires a majority stake in Turquoise, the pan-European trading platform.

2011 LSEG acquires the outstanding 50% of FTSE International, giving the Group full strategic control.

2013 LSEG completes the purchase of a majority stake in LCH Group, a leading global clearing house.

2014 LSEG completes the acquisition of Frank Russell Company and begins the integration of FTSE and Russell Indexes into FTSE Russell.

2016 CurveGlobal, LSEG's new interest rate derivatives venture launched in partnership with major dealer banks, goes live.

---

of governments and policymakers around the world. The Group is committed to supporting a financial ecosystem that fosters long-term investment horizons, that helps businesses across the world, specifically small and medium-sized companies, drive sustainable economic growth.

In 2018 LSEG further enhanced its credentials as a global centre for green finance, expanding and diversifying the portfolio of green bonds, green ETFs, renewable investment funds and environmentally focused corporates hosted on its markets. FTSE Russell continues to release new tools, including sustainable versions of its most popular indexes that further increase investors' ability to integrate environmental, social and governance (ESG) factors in their portfolios.

The combination of client relationships and product capabilities also drives innovation, often in partnership with LSEG's customers, in areas such as ESG. For example, FTSE Russell announced that the world's largest pension fund, the Government Pension Investment Fund of Japan (GPIF), had selected the new FTSE Blossom Japan Index as a core ESG benchmark.

In 2018, LCH compressed more than US $773tn in notional on behalf of its members and clients, estimated to have saved its customers US $39.5bn in capital.

Many other recent examples can be cited of fresh thinking driving innovative change across the breadth of LSEG's activities. One such example is Turquoise Plato, an unprecedented tie-in between Turquoise and boundary-pushing industry body Plato Partnership. Another is CurveGlobal, a groundbreaking venture that is supporting the transition from LIBOR to new SONIA futures. CurveGlobal offers increased efficiencies and lower costs in interest rate futures trading.

Promotion
Targeting a diverse range of audiences, the Group concentrates its activity on its four complementary business divisions: Information Services, Post Trade Services, Capital Markets and Technology Services.

Recent marketing activity has included campaigns focused on AIM, LSEG's support for the financial technology (fintech) sector, and the Group's distinctive open access philosophy.

Open access is the principle that lies at the heart of free and fair markets. The Group believes customers should have the choice of where they place their business. It provides access to all of its markets and products for a wide range of users, including those that offer competing services to parts of the Group.

Access to LSEG services is not conditional on taking a suite or bundle of different services.

A growing number of partnership agreements, such as the one underpinning the CurveGlobal venture, are already demonstrating the huge value of open access.

Brand Values
The Group is built on the core values of partnership, integrity, innovation and excellence. Convinced that collaboration is the key to long-term growth, LSEG prides itself on working with its customers as a partner, not merely a supplier. It cherishes a pioneering spirit, and a passion for delivering quality in everything it does. Finally, its motto – 'Dictum meum pactum' (My word is my bond) – expresses an unwavering commitment to building markets based on transparency and trust.

Marshalls

Creating Better Spaces

Marshalls is the UK's leading manufacturer of hard landscaping products, and has been supplying **superior natural stone and innovative concrete products to the construction, home improvement and landscape markets since the 1890s.** Marshalls strives to create products that improve landscapes and create better environments to **develop happier and healthier communities**

Market

A global leader in creating better spaces, Marshalls strives to improve environments for everyone, from creating integrated landscapes that promote well-being and using fairly traded stone, to providing products that alleviate flood risks and creating innovative protective landscape furniture. Working in both the public sector as well as domestic and commercial markets, Marshalls provides a complete external landscaping, interior design, paving and flooring products service – from planning and engineering, to guidance and delivery. Marshalls is committed to producing new products that better any existing market offering, and to make them from the best materials it can source. Over the years, Marshalls has continued to develop and expand its products and services – whether working alongside architects, local authorities and contractors or providing homeowners, driveway installers and garden designers with innovative domestic products.

Product

Marshalls' domestic customers range from garden designers and professional landscapers to DIY enthusiasts and driveway installers, and specialises in helping to create beautiful and practical outdoor spaces that families can enjoy for years to come. Designed to inspire, Marshalls' extensive product ranges combine quality, elegance and durability in both traditional and cutting-edge designs, with products to suit every taste and style. In the public sector and commercial market, Marshalls

works with a diverse commercial customer base, including local authorities, commercial architects, specifiers, contractors and house builders, by offering them unrivalled technical expertise, manufacturing capability and an enviable product range, including superior natural stone, innovative concrete hard landscaping products, water management solutions, rail products, landscape furniture and protection products, and natural stone cladding as well as facades.

OVER 14.5 MILLION
MINUTES OF MARSHALLS' YOUTUBE VIDEOS HAVE BEEN VIEWED

Achievements

Having been the first organisation to achieve verification against BRE Global's newly launched Ethical Labour Sourcing Standard (BES 6002) in 2017, Marshalls achieved verification for the second year running. It continues to focus on being a successful and profitable business whilst minimising its impact on the environment, looking after people and communities, striving to be innovative and to respond to market challenges and opportunities as well as taking the lead in its sector. Having remained a signatory of the United Nations Global Compact since its acceptance in 2009, Marshalls is committed to aligning operations and strategies with the

10 universally accepted principles in the areas of human rights, labour, the environment and anti-corruption. In 2018, Marshalls was again awarded The Fair Tax Mark in recognition of the business' commitment to transparent tax processes along with being recognised as a Living Wage Employer. The Carbon Trust has reaccredited Marshalls three times. Since 2009, Marshalls has reduced its relative carbon footprint by almost 16% and has made a commitment to reduce its carbon emissions by 3.1% per year until 2020.

Recent Developments

Marshalls is spearheading Future Spaces, a project set up to foresee how commercial, public and domestic spaces might adapt and evolve over the next 10 years. The result of intensive research, Future Spaces aims to predict how changing lifestyles, technology and economic conditions might dictate the look, feel, colour, shape, textures and materials used to create those spaces. Sustainability remains at the heart of everything Marshalls does, and the company continues to be at the forefront of sustainable business. As the first company in its sector to belong to the Ethical Trading Initiative (ETI), Marshalls has unveiled its ETI Strategic Plan 2018 - 2020. Objectives have been developed to further embed and integrate ethical trade into business activities and decision-making as well as seeking to improve conditions for workers, their families and communities. Marshalls published its second Modern Slavery

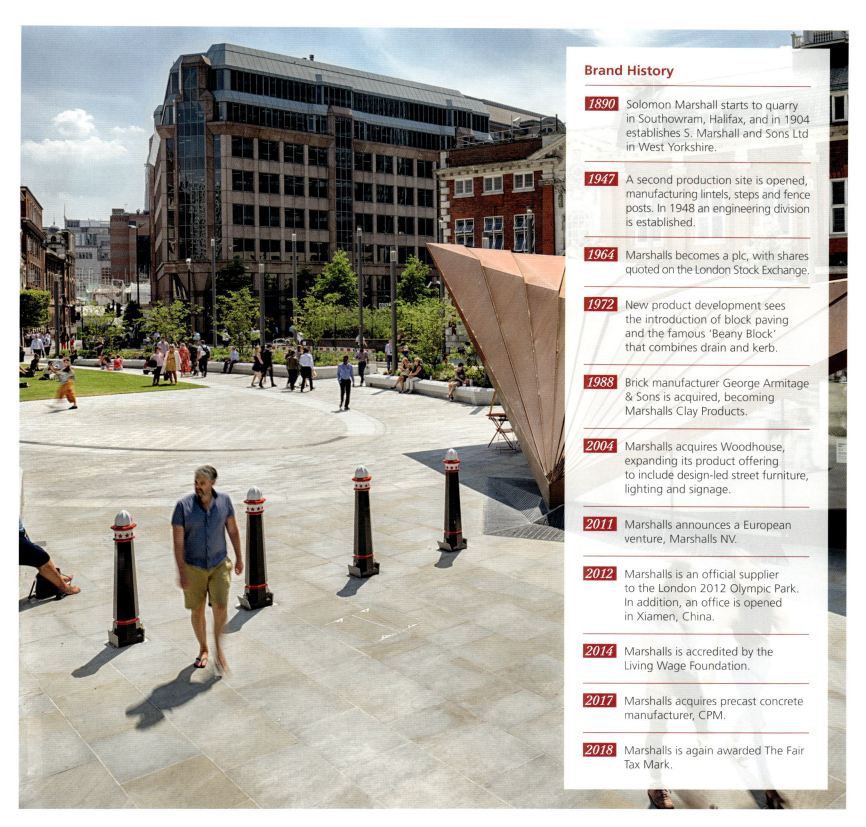

Brand History

1890 Solomon Marshall starts to quarry in Southowram, Halifax, and in 1904 establishes S. Marshall and Sons Ltd in West Yorkshire.

1947 A second production site is opened, manufacturing lintels, steps and fence posts. In 1948 an engineering division is established.

1964 Marshalls becomes a plc, with shares quoted on the London Stock Exchange.

1972 New product development sees the introduction of block paving and the famous 'Beany Block' that combines drain and kerb.

1988 Brick manufacturer George Armitage & Sons is acquired, becoming Marshalls Clay Products.

2004 Marshalls acquires Woodhouse, expanding its product offering to include design-led street furniture, lighting and signage.

2011 Marshalls announces a European venture, Marshalls NV.

2012 Marshalls is an official supplier to the London 2012 Olympic Park. In addition, an office is opened in Xiamen, China.

2014 Marshalls is accredited by the Living Wage Foundation.

2017 Marshalls acquires precast concrete manufacturer, CPM.

2018 Marshalls is again awarded The Fair Tax Mark.

Disclosure Statement, as required following the introduction of the UK Government Modern Slavery Act 2015. Together with anti-slavery partner, Hope for Justice, Marshalls has made good progress in preventative education work with employees, suppliers and those in and around overseas supply chains, especially in Vietnam and India. In 2018, Marshalls became a Patron Partner of CRASH, sharing practical skills, building materials and donations to help homelessness charities and hospices with their vital construction projects. Marshalls also became the first in the construction sector to join the Co-op's Bright Future programme, offering the opportunity of a paid work placement and a job for those who have been rescued from modern slavery in the UK.

Promotion

Marshalls' digital strategy continues to increase in momentum across its operations. The strategy combines digital trading, digital marketing and digital business and is focused on the customer experience. The strategy places the interests of stakeholders and the requirements of customers as its key priorities. Customers are able to use web and mobile applications to model their requirements and allow for full digital access. A new commercial web platform was launched in 2018 and a new domestic platform will follow. Marshalls' strategic direction is 'digital by default', which seeks to define digital as a core part of the company's culture. Marshalls continues to lead the way in thought leadership, by highlighting the growing importance of Landscape Protection products. In response to the need for better

protection from terror attacks, Marshalls takes a multi-layered, holistic approach to landscape protection products, ensuring that they are attractively integrated into landscapes without compromising on a design's aesthetic or affecting pedestrian movement and interaction.

Brand Values

Marshalls' shared values of Leadership, Excellence, Trust and Sustainability underpin the company and are important to the continued success of the business. Marshalls aims to be the supplier of choice for every landscape architect, contractor, installer and consumer, and for the brand to remain synonymous with quality, innovation and superior customer service.

marshalls.co.uk

ODEON®

The most well-known cinema brand in the UK and Ireland, **ODEON is synonymous with the very best in immersive cinematic experiences.** Transporting imaginations since the 1930s, today ODEON operates more than **120 cinemas and 950 screens**

Market

ODEON is part of the ODEON Cinemas Group, Europe's largest cinema operator. Each year, more than 115 million people visit the Group's 360-plus cinemas – and 2,900 screens – across 13 European countries. The ODEON brand is among the cinema market leaders in the UK and Ireland, Spain, Italy, Sweden, Finland, Estonia, Latvia and Lithuania, and holds a strong position in Germany, Norway and Portugal. As an AMC Theatres company, the Group is part of the largest movie exhibition group in the world.

Product

When the first ODEON cinema opened in 1930, it established the brand as not simply somewhere to watch films, but somewhere to experience them too. Elegant Art Deco architecture and the latest technology were its hallmarks: you didn't just go to see a film, you went to the cinema.

Today, ODEON's passion for film sees it remain at the forefront of the modern cinematic experience – including operating the largest cinema screen in the UK, London's BFI IMAX. From box office movies to specialist genres and live events, screenings are brought to life through a distinctive ODEON presence and cutting-edge technologies.

iSense is ODEON's premier film experience, designed with cutting-edge technology that allows customers to see every detail and hear every sound exactly as it was intended. Dolby Atmos 3D sound complements a vast wall-to-wall screen that's the canvas for state-of-the-art 4K digital projectors: four times the resolution of standard projectors, they deliver an even brighter, more detailed picture for a breathtakingly real spectacle.

For dedicated film fanatics, the Limitless monthly subscription service launched in 2016 gives cinema-goers the chance to see as many films as they want, as often as they like, while ODEON Event Cinema brings the world's greatest live performances straight to the big screen, from theatre and opera to sporting events. Additional

DID YOU KNOW?

Almost **2,000 tonnes of popcorn are sold** at ODEON's UK cinemas every year

ODEON sub-brands offer a tailored experience for audiences of all ages, from ODEON Newbies (baby-friendly screenings of new releases) and ODEON Kids through to ODEON Silver Cinema (for over 55s).

The ODEON experience extends beyond the screening room, with an enhanced food and beverage offering that includes classic hot and chilled snacks, branded concessions such as Costa Coffee and Ben & Jerry's ice cream, and sophisticated new bars serving premium drinks. For a VIP experience at selected cinemas, The Gallery provides unlimited popcorn, nachos and soft drinks as well as extra-wide seats with added leg room.

ODEON Events is a natural progression of the brand's emphasis on creating the very best customer experience, combining the magic and excitement of cinema with seamless corporate hospitality. ODEON Events offers venues across the UK, with satellite link-ups connecting colleagues and guests globally, high-end AV equipment ensuring company messages make a real impression on the big screen, and a specialist events team providing support at every step.

Achievements

ODEON Cinemas Group operates 360 cinemas and 2,900 screens across Europe, entertaining

2.2 million guests per week. London's world-famous ODEON Luxe Leicester Square is the brand's flagship site, hosting more than 700 of Europe's biggest film premieres since it opened in 1937 and claiming the title of the first Dolby Cinema in the UK. This combination of brand reach, heritage and an ever-improving customer experience has generated strong loyalty.

The company is as committed to its employees as it is to its customer experience. In 2018, ODEON made it onto The Sunday Times Best Big Companies to Work For list for the second consecutive year, being placed at 25 once again. In the same year, ODEON achieved the 15th spot in Ireland's Great Places to Work (Best Large Workplaces) list, having been awarded 16th place in 2017.

Brand History

1930 Oscar Deutsch and associates open the first ODEON cinema in Perry Barr, Birmingham.

1937 An Art Deco icon, the ODEON Leicester Square cinema opens in London.

1942 The Rank Organisation acquires controlling shares in the business after the death of Oscar Deutsch.

2016 ODEON is acquired by AMC Theatres.

2017 The first ODEON Luxe cinema in Europe opens in East Kilbride, Scotland.

2018 The flagship ODEON Luxe Leicester Square reopens after an 11-month, multimillion-pound refurbishment. It is the UK's first Dolby Cinema.

2019 ODEON has more than 120 cinemas and 950 screens across the UK and Ireland.

Recent Developments

Innovation has played a key role in ODEON's success, and there's no better illustration of this than 2018's multimillion-pound refurbishment of the iconic ODEON Luxe Leicester Square, which now boasts a restored heritage interior alongside state-of-the-art technology. The first cinema in the UK to feature the full Dolby Cinema experience, its transformation cements the venue as a 21st-century entertainment icon in the heart of London's West End. Dolby Cinema enables richer and more action-packed storytelling through a unique combination of Dolby technologies and a tailored cinema design.

ODEON Cinemas Group plans to introduce seven Dolby Cinemas in the UK, while also continuing its roll-out of the new ODEON Luxe cinemas. The first ODEON Luxe opened its doors in October 2017 and there are now more than 16 across the UK. Each features cutting-edge sound and projection technology, luxurious recliner seats, an Oscar's Bar and innovative food and beverage counters, all setting out to recapture the charm of the golden age of cinema.

Promotion

ODEON is famed for being passionate about film with its distinctive logo remaining a long-standing beacon for cinema goers. The magic of cinema and its ability to transport guests to another world that is at the heart of brand promotions. Whether they are shining the spotlight on the brand, a film or practical information, all ODEON creative brings the wonder of film to life through the use of engaging imagery that reflects a sense of escapism and drama.

Brand Values

The essence of the ODEON brand is encapsulated in the phrase 'Transporting Imaginations'. Businesses under the ODEON Cinema Group are united by an aim to develop excellent cinemas, create unbeatable experiences for guests and offer fantastic careers for their employees. The Group's ambition is to use its expertise in hospitality and retail to deliver an inspiring entertainment experience at all of its sites, and to continuously strive to innovate and improve its services.

odeon.co.uk

OLYMPIA London

The home of inspirational events, Olympia London opened its doors in 1886.
Established as a London architectural, cultural and events landmark,
it is the capital's busiest venue, welcoming more than 1.6 million visitors attending
over 220 events and contributing £1.2bn to the economy each year

Market

The events sector is worth £42.3bn to the UK economy, with conferences and meetings accounting for £19.9bn and exhibitions and trade fairs generating £11bn (on direct spend).

Olympia London is one of the capital's preferred exhibitions and conferences venues, thanks to its world-class offerings and location – only 25 minutes from Heathrow airport and reachable by various public transport connections in Kensington.

Combining seven spaces to form 45,000 sq ft, this iconic venue hosts over 220 events welcoming 1.6 million guests each year, contributing £1.2bn to the UK economy annually.

Product

Showcasing unrivalled heritage and architecture, the Victorian Grade II listed building offers clients more than a venue space, but an extension of the award-winning expert team. From operations to marketing and an event industry blog to sustainability; the results are seen in increased footfall, which has risen from 700,000 to 1.6 million guests since 2011.

Achievements

The home of inspirational events, Olympia London opened its doors in 1886 and was established as an architectural, cultural and events London landmark. It is a prime choice for exhibitions, conferences and live events; making it one of the busiest venues in London. Holding a strong link to the capital's history, it has survived two world wars and seismic political changes whilst

DID YOU KNOW?

All monarchs from Queen Victoria to Queen Elizabeth II have attended an event at Olympia London

hosting centenary events such as The London International Horse Show and Ideal Home Show.

Its elegant Victorian arches have also seen inspirational personalities such as Vivienne Westwood hold her first catwalk show as well as performances by Jimi Hendrix and Pink Floyd; not to mention showcasing contemporary themes such as inclusivity with Drag World and the biggest fashion trade event in the county: Pure London.

Over the years, the venue has been recognised with an array of accolades and in 2018 achieved Superbrand status for the second consecutive year. It was also awarded the Silver Green Tourism Awards; acknowledged with the London Healthy Workplace Achievement Certificate; and recognised with British Safety Council's Five Star Health and Safety Accreditation.

Recent Developments

2018 marked the announcement of a £1bn investment plan, set to enhance Olympia London's world-class offering and to cement it as a destination for events, creativity and entrepreneurship, positioning the venue for the next 130 years.

The plans, approved by Hammersmith & Fulham Council, will turn the 14-acre site into a destination. The award-winning practices Heatherwick Studio and SPPARC are leading on the design and implementation of the project. The transformation, set to begin in 2020, is expected to create more than 3,000 new construction jobs over the next five years, in addition to approximately 5,400 new jobs locally once it is completed. It will also bring an extra £9m per year in consumer spending to Hammersmith & Fulham.

Working closely with English Heritage to preserve its original architecture, the project will also bring new features to London, such as a 1,500-seat theatre; a 1,000-seat performing arts venue and 670,000 sq ft of creative office space. In addition, there will be 2.5 acres of new public spaces such as botanical gardens, restaurants and retail, accessible to everyone.

Brand History

1886 Architect Henry Edward Coe reveals Olympia London's elevation, showing the iconic 170 ft clear span of the roof. On Boxing Day, Olympia London opens its doors to the public with the Paris Hippodrome Circus.

1888 The First Great Horse Show takes place, and remains one of Olympia London's calendar highlights as The London International Horse Show.

1908 Olympia London hosts the first Ideal Home Show, which is still held at the venue today.

1919 The Cycle and Motor Cycle Show is held at Olympia London.

1955 Olympia London hosts the first Boat Show.

1958 Olympia London hosts the first computer exhibition, the British Electronic Computer Exhibition, in Olympia National.

1967 Jimi Hendrix, The Animals and a young Pink Floyd play Olympia London.

1992 The Smash Hits Awards are hosted at the venue.

2012 Olympia London celebrates 125 years with specially commissioned works of art, including pieces by artist Peter Blake.

2013 Following a multimillion-pound revamp and disassociation from Earls Court, the business is rebranded as Olympia London.

2019 A £1bn project to transform Olympia London into a destination for events, culture and business is approved by Hammersmith & Fulham Council. Conceptualised by British designer Thomas Heatherwick, it is the biggest investment in the venue to date.

Promotion

Despite its 133-year history, Olympia London as a brand is fairly young, being established six years ago following disassociation from its bigger sister, Earls Court.

It has since grown exponentially, reaching Superbrand status in 2017, and owns the fastest growing social media audience in its sector with a 28% growth rate in 2018 (compared to an average of 5% among direct competitors).

Recent news covering the venue's redevelopment has been seen or heard an estimated 215 million times over print, online and broadcast.

Brand Values

Reflecting a strong set of values encompassing care, commitment, passion, trust and respect,

Olympia London holds one of the highest employee retention rates in the sector. In 2019, 45% of permanent staff had been with the venue for 10 years or more. Carrying unrivalled industry expertise, the venue's teams are one of the top indicators to drive customer satisfaction.

Sustainability is at the core of a world-class offering, which includes grassroots initiatives championing environment, community and education.

For more than a decade, Olympia London has sent 0% waste to landfill with 98% recycled and the remaining 2% converted into renewable energy. More recently, single-use plastic has been one of the focuses of sustainability at the venue, with plastic straws and cutlery abolished and disposable coffee cups recycled via a 'closed loop' system.

Engaging with the local community is another integral part of its values, with initiatives that include electing a local charity to support each year and backing local causes whenever necessary, such as fundraising for the local Grenfell Tower residents.

Over the course of its 133 years, the 'home of inspirational events' has created lifelong memories for millions of people. Keeping true to its brand values and showcasing a solid vision for the next 130 years, Olympia London continues to 'wow' with its rich heritage and bright future.

P&O Ferries is a leading pan-European operator with in excess of 20 ships.
Every year with 27,500 sailings, it carries more than 10 million passengers and 2.2 million freight units. With P&O Ferries people get **unconstrained, flexible, more adventurous holidays.** The brand also has a sister logistics company P&O Ferrymasters

Market

P&O Ferries operates eight main routes between Britain, France, Northern Ireland, Republic of Ireland, the Netherlands and Belgium. Its core audience are car passengers, though it also services freight, coach and foot passengers. The ferry market is complex, with varying passenger and competitor profiles. Across the English Channel, P&O Ferries runs up to 46 sailings a day between Dover and Calais. On the Irish Sea, P&O Ferries operates the fastest and shortest crossing, running between Cairnryan and Larne. Here it helps those travelling to see friends and family, students, or business people. On the North Sea, it operates a daily overnight sailing from Hull to either Zeebrugge or Rotterdam as well as minicruises. Outbound, it takes many British passengers to Europe for their holidays.

DID YOU KNOW?

The perfect flag indicates **history, meaning and symbolism.** In this respect the P&O flag is one of **the most perfect I know**

Boyd Cable, 1937

Inbound, it brings many EU passengers to Britain for holidays, especially from France, Germany and the Netherlands. Across all its routes, P&O Ferries competes with other ferry companies, train operators and airlines. However, it has the highest brand awareness scores in the UK ferry market. The English Channel is its busiest route and on it P&O Ferries has a 60% share of all ferry passengers.

Product

P&O has been around for over 180 years, but the ferry side of the business began in the 1960s, when it pioneered this mode of travel. In 2006, P&O Ferries was acquired by Dubai based DP World.

With new leadership the innovative spirit has continued, driven by the brand's customer-centric ethos – striving to bring freedom, flexibility and choice to each passenger.

P&O Ferries offers a full range of tickets, including a Standard Flexi, which allows customers to sail on any crossing up to four hours earlier or later than originally booked, at no extra cost. A new two day ticket on the Dover to Calais route was launched in 2018 to offer more choice for customers. Across the P&O Ferries routes, customers can enjoy a range of services from complimentary champagne in the Club Lounge to delicious meals in The Brasserie Restaurant, Starbucks coffee on the sundeck or cocktails in the live jazz Sunset Bar.

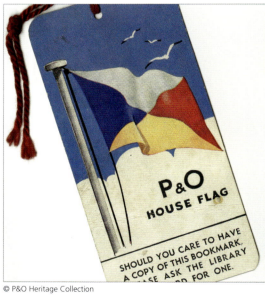

© P&O Heritage Collection

P&O Ferries has an award-winning website that helps customers book tickets, add accommodation and research destinations.

Achievements

Along with being nominated as a Consumer Superbrand for the last six years, P&O Ferries is very proud to have held Best Ferry Operator for the last 11 years running, from the respected and prestigious British Travel Awards. P&O Ferries

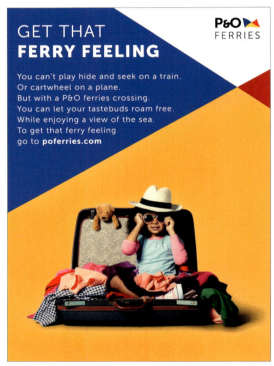

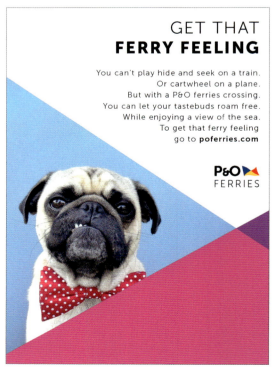

THEY CAN'T PLAY HIDE AND SEEK ON A PLANE

poferries.com

Brand History

1837 The 'Peninsular Steam Navigation Company' is founded on a mail contract to Spain and Portugal.

1840s 'Peninsular & Oriental' (P&O) is incorporated by Royal Charter and begins a regular mail service to India.

1850s P&O launches the largest steamship in the world, the Himalaya.

1887 P&O celebrates the Jubilee by launching its largest and grandest steamers at 6,000 tons each.

1904 P&O offers its first pleasure cruise.

1924 P&O becomes the largest shipping company in the world.

1964 P&O Ferrymasters is born, entering the ferry business via the P&O subsidiaries GSNCo.

1971 P&O short sea shipping division is established and by 1975 it has been restyled as P&O Ferries, using the P&O House Flag on the funnels.

1987 P&O celebrates its 150th anniversary with HM The Queen as guest of honour.

2000 P&O Cruises becomes an independent company.

2012 P&O Ferries launches its latest ship, Spirit of France, sister to the Spirit of Britain, creating the biggest and most luxurious service on the Channel.

2014 The new brand identity launches.

2017 P&O Ferries has the highest number of cross-channel passengers in August for 12 years.

2018 P&O Ferries announces plans to increase capacity on the Zeebrugge-Teesport route by almost 25% in order to create a gateway to Scotland via the north-eastern port.

---

also currently holds Best Ferry Booking Website and Best Ferry Mini Cruise Operator, both of which the brand has won year-on-year since the awards introduced these categories. In 2019, P&O Ferries was also delighted to again secure the public vote for Favourite Ferry Company and was also awarded Best Ferry Company, at the 2019 Globe Travel Awards.

Recent Developments
Over the past five years, P&O Ferries has promoted the benefit of adventurously-minded flexible travel via a colourful visual identity that has injected vibrancy and modernity across all touchpoints.

At the end of 2018, the brand design evolved to increase visual differentiation and ownability further, taking inspiration from the brand's heritage and the single biggest, most recognisable P&O Ferries brand asset: its four-coloured quadrant flag.

This provides an infinitely flexible branded design system and set of components to embed across the multitude of creative media and physical brand environments, including partnership activity, such as Visit Britain.

THE COLOURS OF THE P&O HOUSE FLAG HAVE REMAINED UNCHANGED SINCE 1837

Promotion
To achieve the brand focus of attracting new audiences, P&O Ferries has tapped into the insight that in a world where borders are closing in and competitive modes of transport such as planes, Eurotunnel and Eurostar leave passengers feeling confined, there is a yearning for travel experiences which give freedom and the feeling of being a 'traveller', not just a holidaymaker.

The brand uses this insight to showcase the authentic spirit of freedom P&O Ferries enables onboard and through taking a car on holiday, with the story of a couple enjoying moments of surprise and inspiration in its ads and through the endline 'Get that ferry feeling'.

Brand Values
Travelling on P&O Ferries gives the freedom of an independent, car-based holiday, enabling customers to broaden their horizons in the true spirit of travel.

The result? P&O Ferries is bold, uplifting, optimistic and charming in tone, and its brand values are Inspirational, Insightful, Trustworthy, Reliable and Simple.

19 **65**

Since 1965, when Peter Boizot opened the first PizzaExpress restaurant in London's Soho, the same values of **'great food, evocative music, and distinctive design'** have remained central to the brand's DNA. The **one recipe that has never been changed**, this powerful vision has created an iconic brand, which now **has over 600 restaurants globally**

Market

PizzaExpress remains resilient in a challenging market and continues to pioneer new restaurant formats and further develop its brand – 2019 sees the sociable pizzeria undertake a significant brand refresh, reflecting the values and vision of founder, Peter Boizot.

With people at the heart of the business, PizzaExpress works closely with industry bodies such as UK Hospitality, with the aim of professionalising the industry and instilling the belief that hospitality is, and will remain, a viable career option.

Product

PizzaExpress continues to adapt its menu in line with consumers' ever-evolving tastes and dietary demands, and leads the industry with its innovative menus. The restaurant's award-winning Vegan Giardiniera is now one of the best-selling pizzas across restaurant, retail and delivery.

The team at PizzaExpress works tirelessly to bring the finest ingredients to favourite recipes that customers know and love. This year, for the first time, a dedicated vegan menu was launched in more than 470 restaurants, further demonstrating PizzaExpress' leading position in the marketplace and its aim to bring people together over great food. The health and wellbeing of customers is also incredibly important, and the brand provides clear information that enables people to make informed decisions about their food and drink choices.

DID YOU KNOW?

PizzaExpress sells over 32 million pizzas per year in supermarkets

The growth of the Leggera Lighter range has provided further choice for customers seeking a lighter option, whilst the understated Margherita pizza still ranks as the best-selling dish. The iconic Dough Balls also continue to be a crowd-pleaser, with the limited edition Snowball Dough Balls making their way onto the Christmas menu. Signalling the arrival of the festive season, the brand hosted 'Snowball Dough Ball Day' when the dish was available for a reduced price of £1, with all proceeds going to Macmillan Cancer Support.

Achievements

Industry awards have recognised the innovative menus that PizzaExpress provides. This has included the 2018 FreeFrom Eating Out Awards and the PETA Vegan Food Award for the Vegan Giardiniera pizza in 2017. Furthermore, the Leggera Lighter range has been welcomed by the media and customers alike.

PizzaExpress has also been recognised by the Good Housekeeping Institute as the UK's 'favourite high street restaurant' and by Which? magazine

for being the 'healthiest and tastiest pizza on the high street'. In November, a YouGov survey found the brand to be the UK's favourite high street restaurant, illustrating the brand's popularity and ability to weather difficult market conditions.

The brand regularly wins 'gold' awards from Mumsnet for its 'family friendly' offering, with its extensive children's menu and welcoming approach to families.

PizzaExpress has also won marketing awards for its use of technology and launched its new app in 2018, which offers exclusive rewards for customers, and achieved the number two slot in the iTunes free app charts, behind WhatsApp. Continuing with its endeavour to put people at the heart of the business, the brand has also been closely associated with charitable causes, building upon Peter Boizot's original aim to raise funds for the Venice In Peril charity. PizzaExpress also works with Macmillan Cancer Support, with one simple goal: to bring people together, so that no one faces cancer alone. Funds raised by teams and customers during the company's 'Go Green Week' and from PizzaExpress products sold in restaurants and supermarkets, have topped £1.5m raised for the charity over the past two years.

Recent Developments

PizzaExpress has continued to invest in innovation to ensure that it remains relevant for the future.

2018 saw the opening of the brand's inaugural 'Global Innovation Centre' in Central London, providing a kitchen and event space designed to deliver a dedicated area for menu and brand development. 2019 sees the rollout of a significant brand refresh, demonstrating the brand's pioneering approach.

With the aim of bringing people together through shared passions, the brand's test and learn strategy will see successful initiatives rolled out at pace. This will impact all areas of the business including the service experience, restaurant design, food and drink and music, as well as marketing.

The planning of this project has been 18 months in the making, and has included in-depth consumer research, with much of the new direction taking inspiration from founder, Peter Boizot's original vision. The recent logo refresh illustrates the brand's heritage, as it highlights '1965', the opening date of the inaugural PizzaExpress in Wardour Street, London.

Importantly, people remain at the heart of the business, with much planned to improve the customer experience. Over the last year, there has been significant investment in a leadership programme which continues into 2019 with more than 470 restaurant managers taking part. The PizzaExpress Live brand will continue to evolve and all refurbishments and future openings will feature new design formats, the first of which will open in London's Oxford Circus in spring 2019.

2019 will also see the launch of ZA; a new, all-day fast casual dining offering. The brand builds on the early inspiration for PizzaExpress – Peter Boizot started out selling fresh, hot slices of PizzaExpress pizza. The company is responding to consumer demand and bringing back Peter's pioneering attitude, entering the fast-casual market with an offering that is new and fresh.

Promotion

PizzaExpress has worked hard to remain at the forefront of technological advances, whilst connecting with customers on a more emotional level. Over the past two years, the brand has tapped into real customer stories and created emotive content distributed through its owned-media channels. It has also created bespoke offers to encourage customer loyalty.

PizzaExpress' 2018 'Gather Round Good Food' Christmas film saw distant family and friends across the globe reuniting during a virtual dining experience with a twist – an experience that placed the brand's core values of bringing people together at the fore. The project resulted in an emotive video that achieved more than 1.5 million views, and extensive media coverage.

On National Pizza Day, the brand found superfans and confirmed the nation's favourite pizza to be Pollo ad Astra, which grabbed column inches. More recently, the brand has supported these initiatives with online and print advertising.

Brand History

1948 Peter Boizot works as a reporter for the Associated Press in Rome whilst also selling postcards from a barrow in St. Peter's Square.

1965 Peter discovers that, unlike in Italy, pizzerias don't exist in the UK. This inspires him to open the first pizzeria in London's Soho.

1967 Renowned Italian designer, Enzo Apicella, joins forces with Peter to open a second restaurant in London. He then goes on to design a further 85 PizzaExpress restaurants.

1969 PizzaExpress Jazz Club in Dean Street, Soho opens. The venue goes on to host a wealth of talent including Ed Sheeran, Jessie Ware and Newton Faulkner.

1970 PizzaExpress brings Peroni to the UK.

1971 PizzaExpress launches the 'Pizza Veneziana' initiative, providing a donation to the Venice In Peril fund from every pizza sold.

1986 Peter Boizot is awarded an MBE.

2003 Gluten-free pizzas and beer are launched onto the menu.

2006 PizzaExpress introduces the Piccolo menu for children.

2014 PizzaExpress wins 'Best Restaurant Chain' in the FreeFrom Eating Out awards.

2017 PizzaExpress launches its first vegan pizza – the award-winning Vegan Giardiniera.

2018 The brand has over 600 restaurants in 13 countries around the world and launches a dedicated vegan menu.

2019 PizzaExpress launches a brand refresh and extends into the 'on-the-go' sector with the launch of ZA.

Brand Values

PizzaExpress still works in adherence with its founding principles of bringing people together over great food. Pride is taken in offering a high standard of hospitality in all the brand's restaurants: from London's Soho to the heart of Mumbai, the cultural district of Beijing or the glitz and glamour of Dubai.

It appeals to customers who appreciate 'great pizza and good times'. Whether it be a family pit-stop, a leisurely lunch, a first date or a celebration, PizzaExpress continues its mission to be the world's most sociable pizzeria and remains the nation's favourite pizza in the UK to this day.

Polypipe helps professionals **create sustainable, engineered water management and climate management solutions** for the built environment, and is one of **Europe's largest and most innovative manufacturers** of piping, underfloor heating and energy-efficient ventilation

Market

Having built its business around the residential, commercial, civils and infrastructure markets, Polypipe has a detailed understanding of the applications in which its systems are used – including the activities of the New Build and Repair, Maintenance and Improvement (RMI) sub-sectors.

Product

With over 25,000 product lines, a fleet of over 400 vehicles and more than 2,600 employees, Polypipe has the capability to design, manufacture and deliver a wide range of innovative systems, including above and below ground drainage, plumbing and rainwater systems, cable protection and water management and climate solutions, including energy-efficient ventilation and underfloor heating systems.

Examples of new product development are InfraGreen tree boxes, allowing trees to be located in otherwise restricted areas, whilst ArborRaft units, installed below the road surface, provide the roots with room to spread without damaging the surface above. Furthermore, to help vegetation self-manage water efficiently and effectively, Polypipe's Permavoid units can include unique capillary cones, providing plants with essential water – creating drainage solutions through planting.

To comply with new BS55534 Standards, Polypipe's Manthorpe dry roofing products deliver a high-performance, easy-to-fix, maintenance free ridge and hip tile solution, negating the need for wet trades at height and reducing risk and time on site. In addition, SwiftBrick helps provide swifts with a readymade nesting space in an effort to increase the dwindling numbers and attract biodiversity into new-build environments.

As the industry adapts to the opportunities and challenges of digitisation and Smart technologies, Polypipe continually invests in providing its customers with industry-specific technical support,

BIM Modelling and product and process information to help the industry make informed product and system selections.

Achievements

From Polypipe's people to its continued investment recognition through award schemes and nominations for innovative excellence, it helps the industry adapt to the challenges of progress. Working with the material Polypipe has become synonymous with; plastic, Polypipe has placed sustainability at the heart of its offering, helping customers to safely manage water and air. It has invested heavily in the right technology and people to develop its own polymer recycling and processing plant, producing good quality recycled polyethylene which can then be reformulated and compounded for pipe production. Control of raw material on this level means Polypipe can convert recycled bottles, such as standard plastic milk bottles, into high quality HDPE Twinwall Pipe in just 55 minutes (see image on the right).

Recent Developments

Polypipe has always been a company of innovators, problem solvers and solution providers, which is why it continues to invest in new manufacturing technology and expansion strategies, to deliver products, systems and processes that help the construction industry achieve cost-effective results. Within its ventilation division, Nuaire has developed the IAQ-VALVE for example, which reduces contaminated air from inbound traffic emissions and provides filtered fresh air indoors. It's the first time a carbon filter has been added to a standard MVHR supply air valve.

Polypipe's commitment to making space for water is clear with the acquisition of the Permavoid business worldwide, while the recent acquisition of Manthorpe Building Products takes its product offering even further – providing solutions to site-specific challenges and Health and Safety risks through the use of innovative roofing systems.

High quality HDPE Twinwall Pipe made from recycled milk bottles

DID YOU KNOW?

Polypipe has launched **two large-scale MVHR systems** through its Domus brand

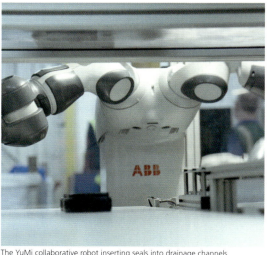

The YuMi collaborative robot inserting seals into drainage channels

The Permavoid system, making space for water

Polypipe has expanded its offering, acquiring the Permavoid, InfraGreen and Manthorpe businesses

The business's ongoing innovation includes the introduction of YuMi robotics to help increase manufacturing output through automation. The picture, at the bottom of the previous page, shows a YuMi collaborative robot being used for a repetitive task that requires a high degree of dexterity, here inserting seals into drainage channels. Meanwhile, the company's Enhance® programme has seen significant investment to deliver products which feature BioCote® antimicrobial technology, single-piece moulding construction and fixed Ring Lock Seal technology.

Promotion
By working with its customers and understanding the key market sectors, Polypipe is able to deliver campaigns that highlight its innovation and technical advances. To support its underfloor heating systems, Polypipe launched a campaign which would boost recruitment for its Registered Heating Engineers Network (RHEN), engaging with the audience through a programme of training, the promotion of membership benefits, and new product developments.

Polypipe has also developed a series of print and digital collateral, CPD resources and presentations, covering the effects of urbanisation and climate change on our cities, and how this can be diminished through the adoption of Green Infrastructure within its projects. It's an initiative which was launched at a conference featuring key industry experts and attendees across the construction, landscaping and local authority sectors.

Brand Values
Polypipe understands the specific needs of the construction industry and provides solutions to satisfy key market drivers. Trust. Support. Experience. Innovation. Polypipe stands by these words as a philosophy, constantly exploring new ways to help the industry succeed – demonstrated by the acquisition of the Permavoid and Manthorpe businesses in 2018, providing sustainable, cost-effective solutions to meet industry standards and help make space for water. Thinking throughout each and every project it undertakes, Polypipe is able to maintain the market-leading position for creating surface water drainage technology and sustainable products that are intelligently engineered for a more resilient future for all.

The illustration to the right shows the Permavoid system as it is used in-situ, making space for water whilst creating important Green Infrastructure.

Brand History
1980 Polypipe is formed in Doncaster.

1988 A full range of plastic drainage products for the residential construction market launches.

1996 Polypipe moves into mainland European construction market manufacturing.

1997 Entry into the civils and infrastructure market takes place.

1998 Plastic hot-and-cold-water plumbing and heating systems are launched.

2000 Polypipe's underfloor heating range is launched and Polypipe enters the Italian market.

2004 A new range of SuDS products and solutions are launched.

2007 Polypipe Water Management Solutions team is launched and entry into Commercial market takes place. Polypipe Gulf is also formed.

2012 Carbon-Efficient Solutions is launched.

2014 Polypipe is admitted to the London Stock Exchange.

2015 Polypipe Underfloor Heating makes its TV debut and the acquisition of Nuaire Ventilation and SureStop businesses takes place.

2018 Acquisition of the Permavoid, InfraGreen and Manthorpe businesses takes place.

Rolls-Royce is recognised around the world for **pioneering cutting-edge technology that meets the planet's vital power needs.** Its systems deliver safe, reliable power solutions that are predominantly used in the Civil Aerospace, Defence, and Power Systems markets. **A key focus is now being placed on electrification and digitalisation**

Market

Rolls-Royce operates across markets that have highly complex power needs and require very long development cycles – usually measured in decades. Growth in these markets is linked with growth in the overall global economy, or in the case of the defence markets, growth in global security and defence budgets. Rolls-Royce has customers in more than 150 countries, with over 400 airlines and leasing customers, 160 armed forces, 4,000 marine customers including 70 navies, and more than 5,000 power and nuclear customers. The company's annual revenues in 2017 were more than £15bn, half of which came from services.

Product

As the second largest manufacturer of widebody aircraft engines in the world, Rolls-Royce is best known for its jet engines. In Civil Aerospace, with a fleet of over 13,600 engines in service, it is the leading supplier for large passenger aircraft and high-end corporate jets. Its Trent engines are in service on the Airbus A330, A340, A350 and A380, alongside the Boeing 777 and 787 Dreamliner.

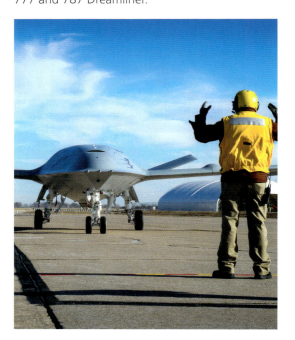

In Defence, Rolls-Royce is a market leader in aero engines for military transport and patrol aircraft with strong positions in combat and helicopter applications. In total there are more than 16,000 Rolls-Royce aero engines in service with more than 160 military customers. It has significant scale in naval markets across the world and provides the nuclear power plant for the Royal Navy's submarine fleet. It has been the industry leader in Short Take-Off and Vertical Landing (STOVL) technology for more than 60 years, with its latest technology on the F-35B Lightning II fighter.

DID YOU KNOW?

Rolls-Royce is building the world's fastest all-electric aeroplane. The zero-emissions aircraft, named 'Spirit of Adventure', will be able to travel over 3oomph

Since 2016, Rolls-Royce has also had full ownership of German high-speed diesel engine manufacturing brand MTU, whose engines are used across a wide range of applications from trains, super-yachts and ferries to mining trucks, tractors and for power generation.

Rolls-Royce also has vast experience in developing nuclear energy power solutions. As one of the largest employers of nuclear designers, engineers and scientists in the UK, it has been the sole provider and technical authority for nuclear power to the Royal Navy for more than 50 years. Using this experience, it is now bringing its technical expertise to the civil nuclear market, through the development of small modular reactors. In addition, it provides nuclear Instrumentation and Controls safety systems to around half of the world's operational reactors.

Achievements

Rolls-Royce has been recognised with Industry Leader, Industry Mover and Gold Class awards for the Aerospace and Defence sector in the Dow Jones Sustainability Index. It is also listed in both the DJSI World and DJSI Europe indices.

Recent Developments

To support the growing demand for cleaner, safer and more efficient power, Rolls-Royce is continuously developing new technologies for its core markets. In Civil Aerospace, the UltraFan® design will deliver more thrust, more efficiency and more reliability than ever before, providing further refinements of the highly successful Trent XWB engine. With industrial technology markets striving for cleaner, more sustainable power, Rolls-Royce is continuing its pioneering tradition with a focus on 'championing electrification'. The company is already developing micro-grids and hybrid electric power technologies. It has challenged itself to build the world's fastest all-electric small aircraft and last year unveiled an electric vertical take-off and landing (EVTOL) concept.

Digitalisation is another major element of Rolls-Royce's strategy, with the company already deploying the latest digital technologies to enable its own transformation and

Brand History

1904 Henry Royce meets Charles Rolls, whose company sells high-quality cars in London.

1914 At the start of World War I, Royce designs his first aero engine, the Eagle, which goes on to provide half of the total horsepower used in the air by the Allies.

1940 Royce's Merlin powers the Hawker Hurricane and Supermarine Spitfire in the Battle of Britain.

1953 Rolls-Royce enters the civil aviation market with the Dart.

1976 Concorde, powered by the Rolls-Royce Snecma Olympus 593, becomes the first and only supersonic airliner to enter service.

1987 Rolls-Royce returns to the private sector, becoming the only company in Britain capable of delivering power to use in the air, at sea and on land.

1999 Rolls-Royce acquires Vickers for £576m, transforming Rolls-Royce into the global leader in marine power systems.

2003 BMW takes over responsibility for Rolls-Royce cars.

2011 Trent 1000 engines power the new Boeing 787 Dreamliner into service.

2012 Rolls-Royce opens a new 154,000m^2 aero engine build facility in Singapore.

2015 The two Rolls-Royce marine gas turbine engines that power the Royal Navy's new aircraft carrier, HMS Queen Elizabeth, go into operation for the first time.

2017 Rolls-Royce launches R^2 Data Labs, a development hub for new data-led services.

2018 Rolls-Royce launches the IntelligentEngine.

2019 Rolls-Royce collaborates with Sunseeker International to build its first production yacht with hybrid power.

deliver improved performance for customers. Rolls-Royce has been at the forefront of performance data analytics for nearly 30 years, providing equipment for health monitoring as part of its TotalCare® aircraft engine maintenance programme. Now, using the latest digital technologies, Rolls-Royce is developing new opportunities to improve its capability and services. Most recently, Rolls-Royce launched IntelligentEngine, its vision for the future of aircraft power. In addition to designing, testing and maintaining engines in the digital realm, this vision sets out a future where an engine will be increasingly connected, contextually aware and comprehending, helping to deliver even greater reliability and efficiency.

Promotion

The company vision is to 'pioneer the power that matters'. In 2017, Rolls-Royce invested £1.4bn into research and development, and had more than 700 technology patents approved for filing. Through a global network of 31 University Technology Centres, Rolls-Royce is at the forefront of scientific research, delivering leading-edge technologies that reduce fuel burn, emissions and noise across all its platforms.

Rolls-Royce is going through an exciting time of change. Technology is driving core products to ever-higher levels of performance, while electrification and digitalisation are continuing its long-held tradition of creating new, market-shifting opportunities – for both its customers and itself.

Brand Values

Rolls-Royce exists to be the 'Pioneers of Power'. The company vision is to pioneer cutting-edge technologies that deliver clean, safe and competitive solutions to meet the planet's vital power needs.

Beginning as a small business, Sage has grown to serve three million customers in 23 markets. It is a technology leader that helps organisations of all types manage everything from money to people with Sage Business Cloud, the business management platform that works intelligently to fit businesses' changing needs

Market

Building on a legacy of trusted business technology and close relationships with customers, partners and accountants, Sage has set out its vision of becoming a great SaaS (Software as a Service) company for customers and colleagues alike. Significant progress has been made, with £434m of annualised recurring revenue in FY18, growing at 51%. Operating globally across small and mid-market businesses gives Sage access to a significant total addressable market, set to be worth US $33bn in 2019, comprising 92 million businesses. In many of its markets, Sage is the leader, with particular strength in cloud adoptive countries like the US, Canada, the UK, France and Australia. Sage is particularly successful in serving mid-market businesses, which represent 90% of the addressable market by value.

For more than 35 years, Sage has been helping organisations of all sizes keep pace with change – whether they are growing, exporting, merging, downsizing, acquiring, or responding to market conditions. It has supported these customers through its experience in navigating changes in the business environment, a dedication to personalised service and investment in technology that works intelligently.

For small businesses, simple time-saving tools help customers take control of their finances and reduce time spent on admin so that they can focus on running their business.

For mid-market businesses, there are solutions that let business leaders take control of their entire business, from supply chain to sales to people, to gain greater efficiency, flexibility and insight.

For accountants and bookkeepers, there are solutions for accounting, payroll, payments, client and practice management, as well as compliance, so that they can provide the best service to their clients.

£3·2tn IS ANNUALLY MOVED THROUGH SAGE SOFTWARE

Product

Sage prides itself on providing the only business management solution that companies will ever need. Unlike other vendors, who only have point solutions that require customers to evaluate new products and vendors every time they add complexity to their business, Sage Business Cloud offers a one-stop shop for all its customers' business management needs, with purpose-built solutions and an ecosystem of applications.

Sage's cloud connected solutions, Sage 50cloud and Sage 200cloud, provide the power and productivity of the desktop, with the freedom

and security of the cloud. Cloud native solutions – Sage Business Cloud Accounting, Sage Intacct and Sage People – are fully functional and flexible, with open APIs, giving customers access to a busy ecosystem. Sage Business Cloud Enterprise Management, for larger businesses, can be deployed on-premise or in both private and public clouds – providing a sophisticated and deeply functional solution for end-to-end business processes.

Achievements

Sage has been recognised at Britain's Most Admired Company awards for IT services, software and equipment. Sage Business Cloud has also been named Accountancy Software of the Year at the British Small Business Awards and Cloud Innovation of the Year by Channelnomics.

In 2018, Sage 50cloud was awarded the 2018 Expert's Choice award from Finances Online; Sage Intacct was heralded as 'Visionary' in the 2018 Gartner Magic Quadrant; and Sage Enterprise Management was named in the Gartner Mid-Market ERP Magic Quadrant as the cloud solution to watch in 2019.

Sage prides itself on being a responsible corporate citizen. The Sage Foundation invests time, money and technology into helping the communities in which it operates. This has become a core part of the organisation's internal culture and external brand. It is fully integrated into working life at Sage, across all colleagues in all markets. Sage colleagues are encouraged to take five 'Sage days' a year, which in 2018 totalled 24,000 working days, to volunteer for a grassroots charity that is close to their heart. Furthermore, last year Sage awarded 162 grants to not-for-profit organisations. In 2016, Sage CEO Steve Hare pledged to lead Sage in raising US $1m through active colleague, partner or customer led challenges. The company is expected to hit the target this year.

Brand History

1981 Sage is founded in Newcastle upon Tyne.

1989 The company is listed on the London Stock Exchange.

2016 Pegg, the world's first accounting chatbot, is launched.

2017 Sage acquires Intacct and Fairsail; in addition, Sage Business Cloud is launched.

2018 Sage Accountant Cloud is launched.

2019 Sage's Making Tax Digital programme launches.

Sage customer, The Split Screen Coffee Company

Recent Developments

Today, Sage innovates through improvements for customers on its 'product roadmap' and in the longer term, through the incremental adoption of emerging technology as well as more experimental innovation.

In 2016 Sage introduced Pegg, a smart assistant to help businesses manage everything from money to people by texting requirements through a familiar-style messaging platform on their phone, tablet or laptop. In 2017, the Pegg framework – a smart artificial intelligence (AI) platform – was launched to help customers manage a diverse range of business functions.

As an industry leader in AI, customers trust Sage to innovate in an ethical way, which is why in 2018 it launched the Roadmap for Ethical Business, which was built with customers as well as government. The framework highlights four areas for creating a competitive but ethical AI economy, namely: create a governance framework; make your AI accountable; build trust through transparency; and empower your workforce.

Driven by its core belief that 'AI will replace, but must also create', Sage has started to build a wealth of talent through Sage FutureMakers Lab. The programme was designed to showcase the exciting opportunities a career in AI may provide. Free to attend, the sessions educated over 150 young people on the diverse range of skills required for a future career in AI, including ethical design as part of the course curriculum. After these initial courses, 30 young people were offered a more in-depth one-day course, with around 15 attendees finally being offered a relevant work placement.

Promotion

Sage's SaaS transition has shaped its brand and marketing – seeing increased use of owned content, mass personalisation, tighter relationships through Account Based Marketing and deeper vertical insights, particularly for larger organisations. At a brand level, Sage continues to highlight its deep experience of navigating change for customers, expert service and intelligent technology.

In 2018, entrepreneur Peter Jones became Sage's brand ambassador, fronting TV, digital and display campaigns to highlight his long-term relationship with Sage and raise awareness of the upcoming Making Tax Digital programme. At the Drum B2B Awards, Sage received Best Social Campaign, Best Brand Campaign as well as Best Product Launch Campaign for its Peter Jones campaign, whilst payment campaign 'Sage Pay: changing the conversation on payment gateways' received an International B2B Award.

A significant legislative change in 2018 was the introduction of the General Data Protection Regulation (GDPR) in Europe, which came into force in May 2018. Sage was active in arming its customers with the information they needed to prepare their business for this, running integrated marketing campaigns and acting as a media thought leader in many of its key geographies.

Around the world, Sage has placed importance on continuing to help small and mid-market businesses navigate change, providing them with support and advice, and lobbying for them on policy issues, when required.

Brand Values

Sage believes that today's organisations are built by 'business builders' – professional visionaries who see opportunities rather than obstacles and are driven by their passion and values. These professionals and the organisations they work for fuel the worldwide economy; and because of this, they are the heart of the Sage brand.

The mantra, 'Be Sage. Build On.' evokes the essence of the Sage brand and the company's purpose. To 'Be Sage' is to be profoundly wise, famed for good judgment and experience. In that spirit, Sage encourages all people in business to 'Build On' – to transform the way they think and work so their organisations can thrive.

Sainsbury's
live well for less

Sainsbury's **commitment to helping customers live well for less** has been at the heart of what it has done **since 1869.** Today this means **enabling its customers to live better every day by offering great quality and service at fair prices** – across food, clothing, general merchandise and financial services – **whenever and wherever they want to shop**

Market

J Sainsbury plc operates over 600 Sainsbury's supermarkets, more than 800 Sainsbury's Local convenience stores and over 800 Argos locations and 16 Habitat stores – almost 2,300 locations in total. In addition, it has online channels for food, clothing, general merchandise and financial services. Sainsbury's sells over 90,000 products and employs over 185,000 colleagues across the UK and Ireland. Sainsbury's Bank offers accessible financial services products such as credit cards, insurance, travel money, mortgages and personal loans that reward customers.

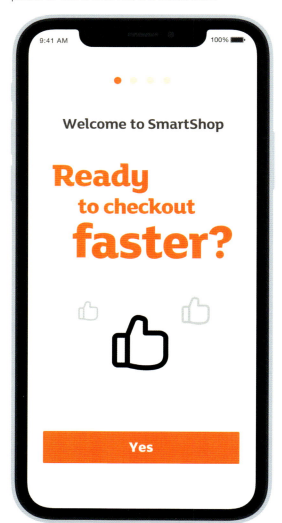

DID YOU KNOW?

In 2012, Sainsbury's was the **first ever Paralympic-only sponsor**

Product

Sainsbury's aims to offer customers quality and convenience as well as great value, such as Taste the Difference, Deliciously FreeFrom and Food to Go. The strong trend towards gourmet-quality ready meals led it to launch the Supper Club range and its restaurant-quality Slow Cook range has become the market leader since its launch two years ago. The growth of these new food innovations shows customers trust both Sainsbury's high quality standards and its commitment to using the best ingredients while offering low prices. Sainsbury's has also developed a range of distinctive products including Love Your Veg, which is in response to changes in consumer habits such as flexitarian diets, and is outperforming the growing meat-free market. Another success story has been the launch of an internally developed new craft beer, Hyde & Wilde, which has already become Sainsbury's second largest craft beer brand, a great feat in a short period of time.

Achievements

Sainsbury's colleagues continue to deliver excellent customer service and the brand has won The Grocer Gold Awards for Service and Availability for the past six years. There is a strong focus on making it a great

DID YOU KNOW?

In 2016, Sainsbury's became the **first major UK retailer** to axe food multi-buys

place to work, and this is reflected in the fact that over 20,000 colleagues have worked in the business for more than 20 years. It is important to Sainsbury's that its colleagues reflect the diversity of the communities it serves, especially at management level. The inclusive recruitment policy means it is committed to training and developing all colleagues, treating everyone fairly and equally when they come and work for Sainsbury's. Since 2008, 26,000 colleagues have been employed through YouCan – Sainsbury's scheme that provides jobs for people who might otherwise struggle

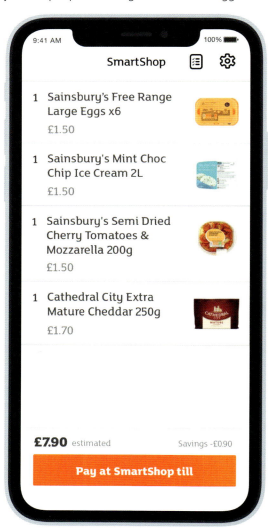

Brand History

1869 John James Sainsbury and his wife Mary Ann open the first Sainsbury's store on London's Drury Lane.

1903 Sainsbury's opens the 100th branch in London and the south-east and Sainsbury's Red Label tea is introduced, becoming an instant favourite.

1931 The pioneering pilot Amy Johnson becomes the first public figure to feature in Sainsbury's adverts.

1946 The first issue of 'The Journal', the company's internal magazine, is published and is still running today.

1955 Sainsbury's opens the largest self-service food store in Europe.

1958 Sainsbury's first TV advert airs.

1959 The first appearance of 'Good food costs less at Sainsbury's' is described by BBC News as 'probably the best-known advertising slogan in retailing'.

1973 Own brand clothing is launched.

1986 Sainsbury's become the first supermarket to offer organic food.

1997 Sainsbury's Bank is launched.

1998 The first Sainsbury's Local store opens.

1999 Sainsbury's launches a partnership with Comic Relief.

2005 The Active Kids programme is launched.

2011 The 'Live Well for Less' campaign is launched.

2016 The purchase of the Home Retail Group s completed.

2018 Nectar, the UK's largest loyalty programme with 20 million collectors, is acquired.

2019 Sainsbury's celebrates its 150th year, a milestone that a minority of businesses have reached.

to find employment. In addition, more than 2,000 female colleagues have been paired with a mentor through the female mentoring programme.

150 Sainsbury's
Est. 1869

Due to Sainsbury's close connections with many communities, it is in a strong position to bring business and the charity sector closer together. Sainsbury's is passionate about giving back to its neighbours as well as supporting national charities, such as Comic Relief and The Royal British Legion. Sainsbury's encourages every store to get involved in food donation, volunteering and its local Charity of the Year programme. Sainsbury's has pledged to support its local communities in relevant and impactful ways and generate over £400m for charitable causes by 2020.

Recent Developments
After the acquisition of the Home Retail Group, there are now more than 250 Argos stores in Sainsbury's stores, giving customers more choice. In addition to this, Sainsbury's is achieving growth in clothing sales online thanks to its Tu brand now being available at Argos. In line with making it easier for customers to shop, Sainsbury's is continuing to roll out the SmartShop app, which allows customers to 'scan, bag and go' as they shop, eliminating the need to queue at the till. Growing customer

choice is an ongoing theme as Sainsbury's looks to serve new grocery missions, with the trial of seven beauty areas, with specially trained colleagues and over 1,400 new beauty products, as well as the launch of the Boutique range, which is 100% cruelty-free. Efforts on sustainable packaging have also been stepped up, with a 35% reduction in packaging, specifically own brand, since 2005, and an aim for 50% by 2020. Overall, 83% of the packaging on Sainsbury's own brand products is classed as widely recycled and 38% is made from recycled content.

Promotion
The Sainsbury's brand underwent a large scale review and update in 2017, completely reinventing its visual identity and tone of voice, in order to build a set of distinctive assets. This strategy has proved to be successful, with advertising campaigns often over-indexing on benchmarks for recognition and brand attribution. The recent Christmas campaign, which enlisted The Greatest Showman director Michael Gracey, was positively received among the public and media.

This year the brand is celebrating its 150th year, with a range of exciting communications and initiatives planned for colleagues and customers in the communities Sainsbury's serves.

Brand Values
Sainsbury's vision is to be the UK's most trusted retailer, where people love to work and shop. Its core values are integral to how it does business and enable the company to drive lasting, positive change in communities across the UK and overseas. These are based on five

core values: health, sourcing, environment, community and colleagues. Sainsbury's supports the UN Sustainable Development Goals and wants to play its part in ending poverty and tackling climate change, injustice and inequality. These 17 goals also offer great economic opportunity and in a highly competitive industry like grocery, they make strong commercial sense.

the Luxury Included® holiday

By offering **luxury, innovation and choice,** Sandals and Beaches Resorts have been at the forefront of the Caribbean all-inclusive travel sector for 37 years. In an industry brimming with new contenders, the combined knowledge and experience of Sandals' management team and resort staff has maintained its **market-leading position**

Market

Over 35 years ago, along the white-sand shores of Jamaica, a visionary with a passion to share his beautiful home with the world introduced the Luxury Included® holiday. Today, Sandals Resorts sets itself apart by steering away from off-the-shelf five-star package holidays, to placing an emphasis on personal choice, always aiming to offer more for the price of the holiday. Sandals Resorts' prices include 5-Star Global Gourmet™ speciality restaurants, premium brand drinks, tips and taxes, in addition to land and water sports such as golf and complimentary scuba diving for certified divers. There are 16 Sandals Resorts created exclusively for 'two people in love' located in Jamaica, Saint Lucia, Antigua, the Bahamas, Grenada and Barbados. Its sister brand, Beaches Resorts, currently comprises three resorts in Jamaica and Turks & Caicos and caters for families, groups, couples and singles.

Product

In 2018, Sandals Resorts announced new additions to the company's flagship resort, Sandals Montego Bay, including an Over the Water bar, Latitudes° and an Over the Water wedding chapel with a glass-bottomed aisle. Sandals Resorts launched the Caribbean's first Over the Water Maldivian-style suites in Jamaica at Sandals Royal Caribbean Resort & Private Island in 2016, with more Over the Water additions at resorts in Jamaica and St Lucia thereafter.

Sandals Montego Bay also benefited from new dining options including Butch's Steak and Seafood, Jerk Shack and Soy, giving couples a wide choice of global gourmet cuisine.

Nine new room categories were launched at Beaches Negril Resort and Spa in summer 2018 including the Tropical Beachfront Two-Bedroom Grand Butler Family Suite.

The company's newest resort, Sandals Royal Barbados opened in December 2017 featuring 222 butler and concierge level suites, a rooftop

THERE ARE AS MANY AS **21 DIFFERENT CUISINES** FROM AROUND THE WORLD AT EACH SANDALS RESORT

infinity pool, bowling alley and barber shop. Plans were also recently announced to develop another family-friendly Beaches Resort in Barbados.

In addition, the tenth Wedding Inspiration service, Band of Gold, has been launched, giving brides and grooms inspiration when designing their weddings – assisting couples looking to be on trend, with a sense of metallic flair and modern elegance.

Achievements

In 2018, Sandals Resorts received an array of travel trade awards including the coveted Travel Company of the Year Award and Hotel & Resort

Operator of the Year, for the tenth consecutive year, at the TTG Awards. Sandals Resorts also took home the award for Best All Inclusive Resort Operator at the Travel Weekly Globe Awards, amongst others. The company was also awarded 10 gongs at the prestigious World Travel Awards including Caribbean's Leading Hotel Brand 2018, Caribbean's Leading All-Inclusive Family Resort 2018 for Beaches Turks & Caicos Resort Villages & Spa and the Caribbean's Leading Resort 2018 for Sandals Barbados, amongst others.

Sandals Resorts' philanthropic arm, The Sandals Foundation, is celebrating its tenth anniversary in 2019. The organisation aims to unite the region with one common goal: to elevate its people and protect its delicate ecosystem under the pillars of community, education, and the environment. Sandals Foundation has implemented projects and programmes valued at over US \$46m.

Sandals Resorts is the only hotel chain in the world to have six resorts holding Master Certification from EarthCheck, the world's leading scientific benchmarking, certification and advisory group for sustainability in travel and tourism. Six resorts hold Platinum, three hold Gold and three hold Silver EarthCheck Certifications.

Recent Developments

Sandals Resorts is currently developing plans for the company's fourth resort in Saint Lucia. The new property will include the island's first rooftop infinity-edge sky pool with 360° views of the island's beautiful north coast. It is also the first Sandals property to have continuous winding river pools surrounding every room block, all with unobstructed access to the main pool.

Over the Water additions have opened at Sandals South Coast with 12 new Over the Water bungalows at the end of 2017 as well as an Over the Water wedding chapel and Over

Brand History

1981 Sandals Montego Bay, the flagship resort, opens with Sandals Inn in Montego Bay launching four years later.

1986 Sandals Royal Caribbean opens becoming the only resort in Jamaica with a private island. Three years later, Sandals Ochi makes its debut in 'Butch' Stewart's hometown.

1991 Sandals Grande Antigua – the first destination outside of Jamaica to have a Sandals presence – opens.

1994 Sandals Halcyon in Castries, Saint Lucia opens with Sandals Royal Bahamian in Nassau, Bahamas launching two years later.

1997 Sandals introduces its first family resort in Jamaica, as Beaches Negril opens its doors. Beaches Turks & Caicos opens in Providenciales, becoming the second family resort.

2002 Both Sandals Grande St. Lucian, Saint Lucia and Beaches Ocho Rios, Jamaica open.

2005 Sandals South Coast, Jamaica opens with Grand Pineapple Beach Resort in Negril, Jamaica launching three years later.

2009 The Sandals Foundation is announced.

2010 Sandals Emerald Bay, Great Exuma, Bahamas opens.

2013 Sandals LaSource Grenada opens and Sandals Barbados is acquired. Two years later, Sandals Barbados opens following an extensive renovation project.

2016 Sandals opens its first ever, dedicated high street retail experience, Sandals Luxury Travel Store, in Chelsea, London.

2017 Sandals Royal Barbados opens.

2018 Sandals launches a tour operation in the UK.

the Water bar at Sandals Montego Bay, Jamaica. In September 2018, Sandals Resorts International announced that all 19 Sandals and Beaches Resorts would eliminate the 21,490,800 single-use plastic straws and stirrers used across the resorts each year by November 2018.

Sandals acquired the Cap Estate Golf Club in St Lucia in 2018, which is currently being redesigned with the help of pro golfer, Greg Norman. The 18-hole Championship golf course will be the second partnership between the two global brands – Sandals and Norman – following the development of the golf course in Emerald Bay, The Bahamas.

Promotion

Sandals' marketing activity is largely upweighted around the group's key selling periods and uses a broad mix of media with the primary objective of acquiring new customers. Repeat guests are rewarded through the Sandals Select Rewards Programme, giving the most valuable customers access to a wide selection of offers – from room upgrades to free nights. Events are regularly held at the Sandals Luxury Travel Store in Chelsea, allowing Sandals the opportunity to interact with potential and existing customers as well as showcase exciting new product launches and updates.

In 2018, a large customer profiling project was undertaken, which resulted in insightful customer persona profiles being created. 2018 also saw the launch of mobile responsive websites for Sandals and Beaches UK. As well as this, Sandals became the official sponsor of the West Indies cricket team.

Looking forward, Sandals will increase its focus on growth throughout Europe; particularly in France, Germany and Italy. To achieve this, its online offering is currently being optimised to create an improved user experience.

Brand Values

Sandals Resorts was created with the vision of sharing the beautiful Caribbean with the world through Luxury Included® holidays. Thirty-five years later, Sandals has achieved this by combining an authentic Caribbean holiday with all the luxury of a world-class, five-star resort – where the best of everything is always inclusive, all the time, anytime. Guests therefore have more time to relax and less time to worry about the finer details of their holiday.

Savills plc is a global real estate services provider with more than 600 offices and associates throughout the Americas, the UK, continental Europe, Asia Pacific, Africa and the Middle East. Its 35,000-strong workforce combines entrepreneurial spirit and a deep understanding of specialist property sectors with high standards of client care

Market

Savills has an international network of more than 600 offices and associates across the UK, continental Europe, Asia Pacific, Africa, the Middle East and the Americas. With 138 strategically located offices throughout the country, Savills has a substantial national footprint and is the largest multi-service property advisory business in the UK, providing more sector specialisms than any of its competitors across the commercial, residential, rural and energy sectors.

Product

During its 164-year history, Savills has grown from a family firm of chartered surveyors into an international property services group. Servicing all aspects of the residential, rural and commercial property markets, the firm continues to adapt its offer to cater for a diverse and evolving client base.

Achievements

In its continued dominance of market-leading deals, in 2018 Savills jointly advised Deka on the purchase of the 318,000 sq ft Verde office block in Victoria, London, for £455m. It also advised Hengli Investments Holding

---

MARK RIDLEY HAS BEEN WITH SAVILLS SINCE 1996 AND HAS OVER 30 YEARS OF PROPERTY EXPERIENCE

(Group) Limited on the acquisition of the headquarters of Lloyds Banking Group at 25 Gresham Street, London – the Hong Kong investor's first purchase in the UK.

Savills won Residential Adviser of the Year for a third consecutive year at the 2018 EG Awards, and beat shortlisters CBRE and Knight Frank to the coveted Global Real Estate Adviser of the Year prize. Property Investor Europe magazine also selected Savills as 2018's European Broker of the Year, while Property Week named Savills specialists the Industrial Agency Team of the Year in the UK.

In addition, Savills is The Times Graduate Employer of Choice for Property for the 12th consecutive year, a position that it has held since the category's inception in 2007. It also appears in The Times Top 100 Graduate Employers list 2018. The firm continues to be the only real estate agent to make the list, which rates UK businesses across all sectors and geographies.

As one of the founding members of 'Changing the Face of Property' in 2014, an initiative run by a number of major property firms, Savills remains committed to developing a culture of inclusivity and diversity within the property profession with five areas of focus: gender, disability, LGBT, socio-economic and ethnicity.

Charitable activity is strongly encouraged across the business. LandAid, the property industry charity, is Savills' corporate charity, while YoungMinds, the UK's leading charity championing the wellbeing and mental health of young people, continues to be Savills UK graduates' charity of choice in 2018/19.

Recent Developments

In the past 12 months Savills acquired Cluttons Middle East, an established leading consultancy business in the region with 190 employees across seven offices, which has been rebranded as Savills Middle East. It also expanded its Indian business into a full-service platform to operate from Delhi, Mumbai, Bangalore and Hyderabad.

In the UK, Savills acquired British Land's third-party portfolio within its property management business, Broadgate Estates, to enhance its

Photo, left to right: James Sparrow, Mark Ridley and Richard Rees

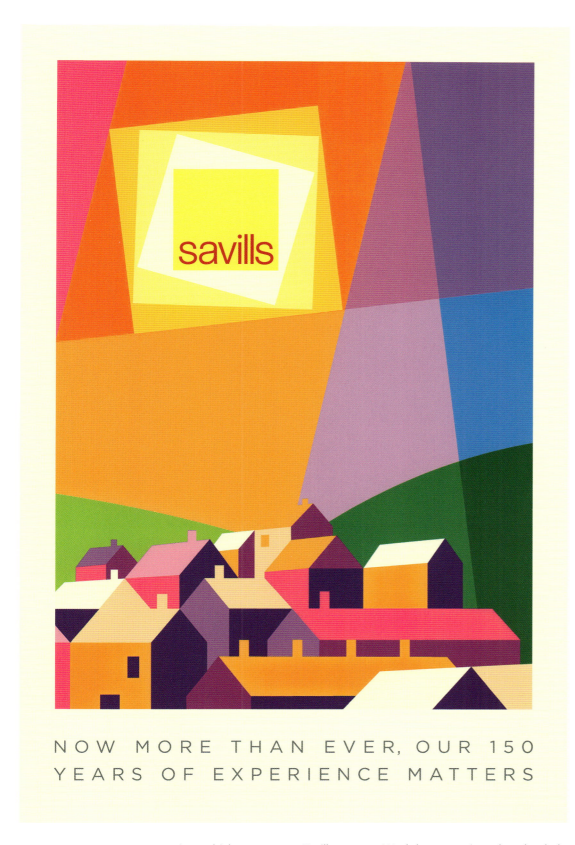

NOW MORE THAN EVER, OUR 150 YEARS OF EXPERIENCE MATTERS

Brand History

1855 Savill & Son is founded by Alfred Savill.

1972 The firm is rebranded as Savills and moves to Mayfair.

1988 Savills is listed on the London Stock Exchange and begins trading as a plc.

1997 A 20% share of Savills is sold to First Pacific Davies – one of Asia's foremost property companies – and the subsidiary is rebranded FPDSavills.

2000 Savills plc is listed in the FTSE 250 and acquires First Pacific Davies in April.

2004 To coincide with the company's 150th anniversary in 2005, the decision is made to drop 'FPD' from FPDSavills. The rebrand brings all the subsidiaries back under the Savills umbrella.

2013 Commercial Chairman Mark Ridley becomes CEO of Savills UK.

2014 Savills announces its biggest ever acquisition: US firm Studley at £154m.

2015 Savills completes its largest ever UK acquisition, the merger of Smiths Gore.

2016 Savills strengthens its position in the Midlands with the acquisition of GBR Phoenix Beard as well as acquiring specialist residential management business Chainbow Ltd.

2017 Savills confirms the completion of its acquisition of Aguirre Newman S.A., the leading independent Spanish and Portuguese real estate advisory firm.

2018 James Sparrow is appointed CEO UK & EMEA and Richard Rees is appointed UK MD. Savills acquires the third-party portfolio management business within British Land's Broadgate Estates. Savills also acquires Cluttons Middle East, an established leading consultancy business in the region with 190 employees across seven offices, rebranding the business as Savills Middle East from 1st January 2019.

2019 Mark Ridley, former Deputy Group CEO, succeeds Jeremy Helsby as Savills Group CEO. After 11 years in the role, Helsby becomes a consultant to the Plc Board in the USA.

---

property management operation, which covers 360 million sq ft of space; Porta Planning LLP, a planning and development consultancy business based in London; and Currell, a leading property services company in East London.

Promotion

In the residential sector, which is undergoing huge disruption, Savills, as a premium brand, needed to actively differentiate itself from the rest of the market. Through market research it uncovered a real insight about consumers: they have relationships with their homes that are akin to those they have in real life. Savills used this in its TV adverts and through a number of other channels in an engaging and humorous way to reach new people in new markets.

Savills venture, Workthere, was introduced to help growing businesses find flexible, co-working and serviced office space. It has expanded into Ireland, Germany, France and the Netherlands, as well as taking its first steps into Asia with an offer in Singapore, with further global launches planned.

Brand Values

Savills attracts the best individuals within its market, and through careful selection and the preservation of a unique culture, provides a global platform from which its talents and expertise can not only benefit clients but also the wider community.

The firm's vision is to be the real estate adviser of choice in all the markets it serves, focusing

not on being the biggest company, just the best in the eyes of its clients. Its values capture its commitment not only to ethical, professional and responsible conduct but also to the essence of real estate success; an entrepreneurial, value-embracing approach.

As a **trusted advisor, combining people, knowledge and technology** to deliver six protective services, Securitas brings value to its customers through the **design and delivery of effective security, fire and safety solutions**. This is how it contributes to a **safer society and shapes the global security of tomorrow**: protecting homes, workplaces and societies

Market

Securitas is the leading global security services provider, employing more than 335,000 people in 55 countries, throughout North America, Australia, Europe, Latin America, Africa, the Middle East and Asia.

Always looking ahead, Securitas observed that market conditions were changing and formed a strategy to develop protective services that were more effective and cost efficient.

Securitas has invested significantly and is leading the industry in delivering risk-based security solutions which continuously flex to meet the changing requirements of clients, across a wide range of industries and customer segments.

Securitas is transforming the security industry moving from traditional guarding to a broader spectrum of protective services combining on-site, mobile and remote guarding with electronic security solutions, fire and safety, and corporate risk management.

Product

At Securitas, intelligent security is the way forward. By capturing and analysing internal and external data sources, Securitas completes risk analysis to predict and prevent threats and future incidents.

Securitas also provide open source intelligence to help customers combat the growing risk of insider threat and social media screening for enhanced vetting of individuals.

The rise in mobile, electronic and remote security reflects changing customer needs towards an output-based specification. Given technology is an increasingly important part of Securitas' business, its unique, in-house City & Guilds accredited training programme teaches its Protective Services Officers to deliver an integrated service to the highest standards.

DID YOU KNOW?

Securitas is the **UK's first and only government-certified canine security** provider

Achievements

The state-of-the-art Securitas Operations Centre (SOC) monitors thousands of system signals every day and was the first UK SOC to receive European accreditation to BS EN 50518 and the industry leading NSI Gold Standard.

The Securitas Learning and Development Academy was awarded City & Guilds training centre status in 2015 for its multiple training and development solutions including e-learning, classroom based, on-site and blended learning.

In 2016, Securitas UK became the first Home Office approved training provider to deliver Project Griffin counter-terrorism awareness training to employees.

Securitas provides a wide range of Fire & Safety services including fire risk assessments, business continuity and emergency planning, specialist first response teams, and City & Guilds accredited Fire Marshall training. In 2017 Securitas UK successfully achieved British Approvals for Fire Equipment (BAFE) accreditation.

Securitas is the UK's first and only government certified canine security provider, achieving Free Running Explosive Detection Dogs (FREDDs) certification in 2017 – the EU standard for the use of dogs in aviation cargo security.

Securitas UK relaunched Security Trained Assistance and Reception Services (STARS) in 2018 – highly professional front of house receptionists with SIA security qualifications.

Recent Developments

Securitas UK has announced its accreditation as the 100th Recognised Service Provider, working closely with the Living Wage Foundation (LWF). The only global security company currently accredited by the LWF, Securitas UK has made a commitment to offer a Real Living Wage option alongside every tender opportunity.

Brand History

1934 Erik Philip-Sörensen founds Hälsingborgs Nattvakt in Helsingborg, Sweden. It quickly expands as Sörensen acquires a number of other security companies.

1935 Securitas Alarm is founded in Sweden to meet the demand for alarm technology as a complement to the guarding services.

1936 All companies owned by Erik Philip-Sörensen are gathered under the collective name Securitas. The logotype of three red dots – for Integrity, Vigilance and Helpfulness – quickly becomes a well-known symbol, first in Sweden, then internationally.

1985 Investment AB Latour becomes Securitas' new owner, with a renewed focus on security.

1991 Securitas AB is listed on the Stock Exchange.

2010-2011 Securitas purchases Reliance Security Services and Chubb Security Personnel.

2015 Securitas announces Vision 2020 combining people, knowledge and technology to deliver six protective services.

2017 Securitas UK is accredited as a Recognised Service Provider working with the Living Wage Foundation.

2018 Magnus Ahlqvist is appointed as President and CEO of Securitas AB. In addition, Securitas UK acquires MK Group Security and R & R Frontline Services.

In 2019, Securitas UK was recognised as a Top Employer by The Top Employers Institute.

Promotion

Recently Securitas relaunched its UK Experience Centre; an interactive, hands-on experience for new and existing clients. With live demonstrations, case studies, augmented and virtual reality applications, the Experience Centre showcases the latest in intelligent security technology.

With a focus on digitalisation, Securitas UK has replaced its printed marketing collateral using a digital e-zine format available to clients via the website and to Protective Services Branch Managers through an online app.

Securitas LEAD, the company's augmented reality app, brings each of the six Securitas Protective Services to life, engaging the reader in a unique hands-on experience.

Meanwhile, Stay Ahead, Securitas UK's digital e-zine, encourages readers to think about the security landscape in the face of a changing world and ever-increasing security threats.

Brand Values

Securitas' brand purpose is the promise it makes to its customers.

In Roman mythology Securitas was the goddess of security and stability. Today, the global Securitas brand reflects those values: Securitas knows security, understands risk and how it affects its customers and the industries in which they operate.

Together with its promise, the Securitas values – integrity, vigilance and helpfulness – are at the very heart of who the company is and what it does. The things that matter to Securitas are what matters most to its customers – keeping people, property and assets safe.

The brand promise and values differentiate Securitas. They unite its people towards common goals, and secure the trust and loyalty of its customers.

securitas.uk.com

Shred-it is one of the **UK's leading information security companies**. It provides advice on confidential information protection and secure destruction and recycling services to organisations of all sizes in the private, public and third sectors. With more than **5,000 team members** and **operating a fleet of over 2,000 trucks globally**, the Shred-it focus is to protect what matters

Market

Shred-it is one of the UK's leading information security companies operating in a worldwide market that is forecast to grow 8.7% to US$124bn in 2019 (Source: Gartner Inc.). Year-on-year spending on information security products and services has continued to rise as security compliance and risk management becomes an increasingly critical part of the business landscape. Key drivers for the growth in the market are numerous, but include an increased focus on detection and response capabilities as awareness of security risks and data breaches grows; privacy concerns and stricter regulation such as the EU's GDPR around data loss prevention; and business digital transformation initiatives that reinforce the need to view sensitive data and related systems as critical infrastructure.

Product

Since its founding in 1988, Shred-it has become one of the world's leading information destruction companies, with more than 5,000 team members and a fleet of over 2,000 trucks globally. Shred-it's fundamental

brand proposition is focused on protection. It does this through its team of information protection experts whose one goal is to help organisations comply with stringent privacy laws, legislation practices and procedures via certified state-of-the-art information security products and industry-compliant regulated services. This ensures people, customers, businesses, brands and the environment are Shred-it protected.

DID YOU KNOW?

Fewer than **1 in 5** business leaders **describe their business as paperless**[*]

*Source: Ipsos 2018

Shred-it's protection solutions and services, which include secure document destruction, media destruction, branded goods and uniforms destruction as well as recycling services, meet the

daily or ongoing needs of today's organisations in the private, public and third sectors. It safely disposes of unwanted or outdated confidential information across all major sectors from local and central government, healthcare, retail, legal, engineering, property, education, to police forces, banks and financial institutions. After paper has been securely shredded, the confetti-sized pieces are mixed with millions of pieces of other shredded documents, baled and recycled into paper products.

Achievements

Shred-it specialises in providing a tailored information destruction service that helps businesses to comply with legislation and ensures that customer, employee and confidential business information are protected at all times. Shred-it provides a consistent service based on its unique security measures, and has a standard Data Processing Agreement (DPA) which sets out the basis on which the company provides its services and, where relevant, processes data on behalf of a customer. The technical and organisational security measures that are applied when dealing with confidential information are explained in detail in its Security Information policy document. Shred-it's accolades include: ISO 9001, ISO 14001, EN 15713, NAID member, Waste Carrier's Licence (UK), British Security Industry Association Certificate, Fleet Operator Recognition Scheme and it is recognised by the ICO.

Brand History

1988 Greg Brophy founds Shred-it.

1993 Shred-it grows and expands overseas. It also launches a manufacturing division.

2002 Further expansion takes place, with state-of-the-art records management and storage facilities.

2014 Shred-it merges with Cintas Document Shredding, operating under the Shred-it brand.

2015 Shred-it is acquired by Stericycle and becomes a wholly owned subsidiary.

2018 Shred-it operates in 170 markets throughout 18 countries worldwide, servicing more than 500,000 global, national and local businesses.

Recent Developments

In 2014, Shred-it merged with Cintas Document Shredding to create a new company that operates under the Shred-it brand. In 2015, Shred-it was acquired by Stericycle and is now a wholly owned subsidiary of Stericycle, a global business-to-business services company, serving more than 500,000 customers around the world. As an integrated company operating for over 30 years, Shred-it's focus is to continue developing, delivering and improving solutions to meet the ongoing needs of a diverse customer base, while helping them manage their confidential information and aid compliance with stringent data privacy laws to protect what matters.

Promotion

In an increasingly commoditised market, Shred-it sought a clear point of differentiation in recent years to distinguish its offering from rivals. Following market research of its extensive worldwide customer base, Shred-it identified a number of key insights which led to the brand's positioning around the 'We protect what matters' strapline. Shred-it protects people, it protects customers, it protects brands and reputations and it protects the environment.

This has enabled the brand to better focus the message around the core idea of protection – the brand's red thread and its very reason for existence. This core message is transferable across markets, sectors and channels.

Brand Values

Shred-it has a one team, one goal motto with a customer first approach, to ensure the safeguarding, understanding and managing of confidential information. Shred-it's values around excellence in service provision, depth of experience and sector knowledge, accountability and integrity, together with sustainability and continuous improvement underpin its leading market position. The values deliver peace of mind and help organisations stay in control through being Shred-it protected. They are encapsulated in the brand's strapline 'We protect what matters'.

The secret to a great night's sleep

Silentnight is the **UK's largest and most trusted manufacturer of branded beds, mattresses and sleep accessories. With a wide consumer profile, Silentnight's mission is to use its passion, product knowledge, exceptional quality and sleep expertise to provide sleep solutions for all the family**

Market

The UK retail bed and mattress market is worth around £1.98bn (Sources: Mintel, Conlumino, NBF Sales Statistics). Furthermore, Silentnight is the UK's favourite bed and mattress manufacturer (Source: GfK data) and remains well known, with strong brand recall and consideration from consumers, in particular the brand's iconic Hippo and Duck characters.

Product

Founded in 1946 in Skipton, North Yorkshire, Silentnight's factory and offices have always remained in Lancashire and, in 2016, the brand celebrated 70 years of quality and innovation. Over the years it has developed a strong core product offering to cater for the mass market, with families being the key audience. Products include a wide selection of mattresses using its exclusive Miracoil® and Mirapocket® advanced spring system technologies, bases with different storage options and a comprehensive children's proposition. Silentnight is also available across bed frames, sleep accessories such as pillows and duvets, a range of heating and cooling products and even pet beds.

As the UK's leading bed and mattress manufacturer, Silentnight is committed to working to the highest quality standards for its customers. For example, all of its mattresses and upholstered beds are handmade in its UK factory. The products and raw materials are rigorously tested in Silentnight's in-house SATRA-approved testing lab, which was established in 1980. Experienced staff, proficient in materials testing, structural testing of finished products and flammability testing, ensure customers can sleep safe in the knowledge that their bed or mattress meets all safety, quality and flammability standards.

Achievements

Silentnight has been awarded a Which? Best Buy for its mattress-now® Memory 3 Zone rolled mattress for five consecutive years. The 1200 Eco Comfort Pocket mattress has also been

DID YOU KNOW?

One in five homes in the UK have a **Silentnight product**

recognised by Which? as being "one of the best value mattresses we've tested". Furthermore, in June 2017, the brand gained its third Which? Best Buy with its Studio medium mattress, which was the 'Top scoring bed-in-a-box mattress'.

Silentnight Beds is a member of the Furniture Industry Sustainability Programme, having shown commitment to social, economic and environmental sustainability across its business. In 2011, Silentnight achieved Forest Stewardship Council certification for all the timber used in the production of its divans and headboards.

In 2017, Silentnight was also recognised for its commitment to the environment, being awarded The Furniture Makers' Company Sustainability Award, which was also re-awarded for 2018.

Since the award, Silentnight's commitment to sustainability has gone to new levels and will continue to be a main focus with the introduction of the Eco Comfort range. Silentnight is seeing more and more demand for eco-friendly products and building on the success of the Eco Comfort Collection, it has developed an eco-mattress for everyone in the family. All mattresses use Silentnight's Eco Comfort Fibres™, a luxury comfort filling that is made from recyclable plastic bottles, which not only benefits the environment but also offers value for money.

In August 2018 Silentnight launched the Eco Comfort Breathe mattress collection, which has a fresh and distinctive look and feel. The exclusive patented Micro Climate System delivers the ultimate in breathability and moisture management – guaranteeing a refreshing night's sleep. In addition, there is an environmentally friendly product for children, Safe Nights nursery mattresses as well as the new Healthy Growth range. This provides a foam and chemical treatment free solution that is comfortable and supportive for children.

Recent Developments

Silentnight is committed to new product innovation in its drive to give consumers the best sleep experience possible and to remain at the forefront of the marketplace. Studio by Silentnight continues to appeal to consumers. One mattress that is available in three comforts, Studio by Silentnight is designed with the reassurance of the Silentnight brand with a fresh, contemporary experience, rolled and boxed for the consumer's convenience.

Another product innovation, only available in the UK to the Silentnight Group, is Geltex®. This high-performance gel-infused foam offers

Brand History

1946 In North Yorkshire, Tom and Joan Clarke form Clarke's Mattresses Limited.

1948 Tom and Joan register Clarke's Mattresses Limited and rent their first shop, moving operations to a bigger site a year later, due to huge demand.

1951 Clarke's Mattresses changes its name to Silentnight Limited.

1961 The business continues to expand and moves to its current premises in Barnoldswick.

1986 Silentnight launches its 'Ultimate Spring System'. To demonstrate its unique no-roll-together properties, Hippo and Duck are introduced.

1990s The unique spring system is improved and renamed Miracoil® Spring System.

2002 Hippo and Duck star in an animated TV commercial, set to a version of Hot Chocolate's 'You Sexy Thing'.

2003 Silentnight begins production of children's beds and mattresses.

2008 mattress-now® – the first Silentnight 'convenience' rolled mattress is launched.

2012 Safe Nights and Healthy Growth ranges are launched. A refreshed brand identity is rolled out, with Hippo and Duck still central to communications.

2013 The Geltex® inside collection is launched and Silentnight is awarded two Which? Best Buys, and the Safe Nights Memory Wool cot-bed mattress wins several parenting awards.

2016 Silentnight celebrates its 70th anniversary and launches Studio by Silentnight with the mini-pocket system, Ultraflex, following a year later.

2018 Sustainability becomes a prime focus with the launch of an eco-friendly product.

unparalleled breathability, ideal pressure relief and optimal body support for a truly restful night's sleep. Silentnight has placed emphasis on increasing the use of Geltex® across its range. The latest innovation to the brand is the minispring Ultraflex. Working in harmony with Silentnight's spring systems to provide enhanced comfort and increased breathability, it aims to take sleep to the next level.

Promotion

Silentnight's advertising activity has focused on 'A great night's sleep shouldn't cost the Earth' and celebrates its sustainable mattresses. The iconic bed on a beach has captured the attention of the trade and consumers, with a multi-media campaign that ran across press, outdoor and digital channels. PR and social media activity has also supported the campaign, seeing Silentnight announce a partnership with The Marine Conservation Society.

Brand Values

Silentnight's mission is 'to help everyone in the family find their perfect sleep solution'. To ensure Silentnight remains an authority in sleep expertise, it invests in continuous research into sleeping habits, building the latest scientific developments and technical innovations into its products.

THE BEST START IN LIFE

Silver Cross is a **leading international premium nursery brand,** **renowned globally** for designing beautiful and innovative baby products. For more than 140 years, it has been **dedicated to the highest standards of craftsmanship** to give babies the best start in life

Market

Silver Cross is a market leader in the nursery sector, with a broad portfolio of products including contemporary travel systems, lightweight strollers, luxury coach prams, car seats, nursery furniture and baby bedding.

The brand was founded in 1877 by William Wilson, who invented the first patented baby carriage. This revolutionary idea changed parents' lives forever, allowing them to transport their children in comfort and safety.

Silver Cross' dedication to quality and British craftsmanship has stood the test of time and it continues to meet the needs of modern parents by designing products which are stylish, practical and beautiful.

Today, Silver Cross is a global brand, loved and trusted by millions of parents worldwide. Its products are now sold in

DID YOU KNOW?

Silver Cross founder **William Wilson** is credited with **inventing the baby pram** concept

42 countries worldwide and, in addition to its UK headquarters, it has offices in Hong Kong, Shanghai, Melbourne, Dubai and Barcelona. It also has flagship stores in Hong Kong, Shanghai and Moscow.

Product

Founded on a love of high-quality craftsmanship and an obsessive attention to detail, Silver Cross has an unwavering commitment to design and innovation.

It has an award-winning team of in-house designers, engineers and product development specialists based at its Yorkshire head office.

Driven by a desire to create beautiful products that meet the demands of modern family life, Silver Cross has an outstanding range of innovative and contemporary travel systems and strollers. Each combines the latest advances in technology with stylish design and functionality.

In addition, Silver Cross has an expanding home and nursery division featuring beautifully crafted furniture sets and exquisite baby bedding.

It also continues to produce the iconic Balmoral and Kensington coach prams, a masterpiece of design and engineering and the only prams still hand-crafted exclusively in the UK.

Achievements

Silver Cross continues to impress industry experts and parents alike with its products, winning the most prestigious awards from parenting websites and magazines.

Among its latest key launches is Jet, a unique baby stroller that's so light and compact it can be taken on board an aircraft and stored in the overhead locker. Ideal for family travels, it's already proved a big success, winning several industry awards.

Coast is the newest travel system from Silver Cross, offering parents a super stylish single pram with the option to evolve it to a double for two babies or a baby and an older sibling. It incorporates the patented One plus One® connection system first seen on the award-winning Wave – the brand's first single to double travel system.

A luxury capsule collection, developed with childrenswear designer Princess Marie-Chantal of Greece, has proved another success. The Princess' passion for classic, elegant and timeless design is shared by Silver Cross and provides the inspiration for this exclusive range of luxury prams, nursery furniture and baby bedding.

Brand History

1877 Silver Cross is founded by William Wilson, who invented the first baby carriage.

1950-1970s Silver Cross is crowned the number one baby carriage for royalty.

1980s New manufacturing techniques for lightweight pushchairs are developed and The Wayfarer is launched. It becomes Britain's best-selling pushchair.

2002 Led by CEO Nick Paxton, Silver Cross develops a new approach to innovation and product development.

2006 Silver Cross goes global, forging partnerships with distributors around the world.

2017 Silver Cross celebrates its 140th birthday.

2019 Growth continues in the UK, Asia Pacific, Middle East, South Africa, Europe and North America and the company continues to invest in product, people and customer service.

In addition, Silver Cross enjoys an ongoing collaboration with Aston Martin, uniting two iconic and premium British brands. New additions to the collection include Silver Cross' most luxurious stroller yet, the Reflex Aston Martin, while the Aston Martin Cot and Fine Linen Collection offer the ultimate in exclusivity for the nursery.

Globally, Silver Cross continues to broaden its customer audiences with significant expansion in China and North America. The brand continues to be loved by new parents who demand the highest quality, fine detailing and innovation as well as intelligent design.

Silver Cross is proud to retain its enduring craftsmanship, embodied in the classic handmade Balmoral collection, whilst ensuring each new development is at the forefront of the latest design innovation.

Recent Developments

Silver Cross is continually driving forward its product range to meet the demands of today's families, with more key launches planned for 2019.

To accommodate its planned growth strategy, work is currently under way to double the size of its Yorkshire headquarters.

The company's newest acquisition, Micralite, enjoyed a successful launch in 2018, revealing a performance-driven, thoughtfully engineered collection of multi-terrain strollers, targeted at millennial parents.

In addition, Silver Cross continues to expand into more global markets, including Canada, France and New Zealand.

Promotion

Silver Cross' strong brand values of trust, quality and craftsmanship remain at the forefront of its appeal.

Thanks to its long heritage and a focus on British design, it continues to provide a beautiful start in life for babies everywhere.

Social media channels remain a key tool to communicate and engage with consumers around the world. However, the brand's strongest marketing tool has always been endorsement from those who have first-hand experience of Silver Cross products.

Brand Values

More than 140 years after it was founded, Silver Cross continues to develop the most innovative products, with a focus on design excellence and premium quality. A strong, evolving product range is key to its success, while an uncompromising approach to customer care has helped Silver Cross become a global brand, loved and trusted by millions of parents worldwide.

STAEDTLER®

Designing and manufacturing premium quality writing instruments since 1835,
STAEDTLER offers a comprehensive range of stationery and craft products for the school,
home and office, **including instantly recognisable classics such as the yellow and black Noris pencil.**
Innovation remains key to the company's success with **regular breakthroughs
in design, performance and manufacturing**

Market

In a competitive marketplace, STAEDTLER is the market leader for blacklead pencils, coloured pencils and fineliners. It is also number one in colouring felt pens, targeted at teenagers and adults, in the retail market (Source: GfK data, 2017).

STAEDTLER supplies retailers, the education sector and B2B markets as well as having other independent trade customers.

The brand has a presence in 150 countries worldwide and is the largest manufacturer of wood-cased pencils, non-permanent markers, erasers, mechanical pencil leads and modelling clays in Europe.

Ongoing innovative product development to explore new colours, techniques and trends drives the brand forward. For example, the popular adult colouring sector was pioneered by STAEDTLER.

Product

The STAEDTLER product range has evolved over centuries to encompass a vast selection

DID YOU KNOW?

Almost **three-quarters**
of total **production**
is in Germany

of premium quality writing and drawing instruments for the school, home and office. Its stationery range caters for every age group, starting with learner pencils for very young children. Alongside this, STAEDTLER also offers an extensive craft range including the popular FIMO polymer modelling clay.

STAEDTLER is renowned for producing high quality products and its iconic, market-leading yellow and black Noris pencil has a market share of more than 53%. Amongst its other internationally recognised classics are the Mars plastic eraser and the Lumocolor marker.

Achievements

Quality, reliability and design innovation, together with a clear environmental pledge, are at the heart of everything STAEDTLER does. This standpoint has helped to maintain the brand's position as one of the top three brands in the UK writing instruments market.

DID YOU KNOW?

STAEDTLER
sells over 96 million
wood-cased pencils
in the UK

Over the years, STAEDTLER has won numerous accolades for marketing excellence, product innovation as well as customer supplier awards.

In 2018, STAEDTLER's FIMO Kids Form and Play sets gained recognition at the 2018 Mums Choice Awards, winning a Highly Commendable award in the 'Best Toy for ages 8-11 years' category.

Recent Developments

Consistent commitment to new product development has led to regular breakthroughs in product design, performance and manufacturing. Innovations include the award-winning triplus range of triangular writing instruments; Anti-Break-System (ABS), the revolutionary break-resistant protective coating for coloured pencils; WOPEX, a ground-breaking production process that maximises the usage of raw materials; as well as Noris colour, an eco-friendly, premium quality coloured pencil.

MADE IN GERMANY · **STAEDTLER** · Noris · HB 2

Brand History

1662 Ancestor of the STAEDTLER founder, Friedrich Staedtler, works as a pencil maker in the German city of Nuremberg.

1835 Johann Sebastian STAEDTLER sets up his pencil manufacturing plant in Nuremberg.

1866 STAEDTLER employs 54 people, producing more than two million pencils annually.

1966 In the UK, STAEDTLER acquires the Royal Sovereign Pencil Company.

1968 Approximately 275 people are now employed at the UK factory.

1973 The STAEDTLER (UK) Ltd company name is introduced.

1977 Royal Sovereign-STAEDTLER Ltd becomes a wholly owned subsidiary of STAEDTLER Noris GmbH.

2016 STAEDTLER (UK) Ltd celebrates its 50th anniversary in the UK with a year-long programme of activities.

2017 STAEDTLER has 21 manufacturing and distribution subsidiaries globally, employing more than 2,100 people and announces plans for its own plantation, to maintain the highest ecological standards of production.

2018 World Kids Colouring Day, STAEDTLER's international charity initiative, raises over £19,000 for its Malawi school project.

In 2019, STAEDTLER will launch its biggest new product range to date. Exciting new products include a complete collection of premium products for the hobby artist under the new 'Design Journey' banner, trend ranges which include pastel highlighters and comic art-style stationery, as well as an exciting and extremely versatile new modelling material for the craft world.

draw your future, earn your stripes.

for back to school, choose STAEDTLER.

Promotion

The promotional activity of STAEDTLER is tailored to meet the requirements of the various channels that it sells into. In addition, it is also strongly promoted to consumers through carefully targeted, high profile campaigns including TV and cinema advertising. One such TV campaign won a CANMOL award at the Wales Marketing Awards, which was hosted by the Chartered Institute of Marketing.

2018 saw the launch of the Noris campaign, designed to promote STAEDTLER's hero product, the Noris school pencil. The 'Draw your future, earn your stripes' campaign focused on the role of the iconic pencil in helping children

to shape their future and the eye-catching campaign visuals demonstrated real schoolchildren and their career aspirations, everything from barristers and scientists to referees and astronauts.

Not only did the campaign reach almost two million people through digital advertising, it also incorporated striking outdoor advertising, stretching across the UK, which reached over 25 million people.

In support of 2019's major product launch, STAEDTLER will implement an integrated programme of creative marketing campaigns to further increase brand awareness and reach new audiences.

Brand Values

With its impressive heritage and international reputation, STAEDTLER remains committed to pioneering new product development and attaining the highest possible standards of quality and reliability. At the same time, the company ensures that the premium quality product range is produced in the most efficient, environmentally friendly way with consideration for both natural resources and everyone involved in the process.

The company is also committed to a CSR programme within the local community, working in particular with schoolchildren.

Stobart Group is a **well-respected and highly visible brand with operations across the UK**. Whether you're travelling abroad, passing a Stobart Energy transportation vehicle on the roads, spotting teams working on a rail project, or walking past one of its civil engineering work sites, you're likely to see Stobart employees hard at work

Market

Stobart Group is involved in the aviation, energy and civil engineering markets.

In the aviation sector, Stobart Group operates London Southend Airport. The market for London airports is dominated by a significant and growing demand for available slots for aircraft in an otherwise capacity-constrained

DID YOU KNOW?

London Southend Airport is the **capital's fastest growing** airport

Stobart Energy has contracts to supply biomass fuel to generate clean energy equivalent to the annual electricity needs of 2% of the UK population.

Stobart Rail & Civils is one of the UK's leading providers of innovative and efficient rail and non-rail civil engineering projects. It provides specialist rail, civil and infrastructure

capital. This creates a considerable opportunity for London Southend, which is the only remaining London airport that has invested in free capacity to allow growing airlines to launch new routes to and from London.

Stobart Energy operates in the renewable energy market and is the number one supplier of biomass in the UK. It has obtained this market-leading position in part due to its investment in employee training and high-quality infrastructure.

Stobart also provides expert services in the rail and civil engineering sectors. It has built a strong

reputation over 20 years thanks to its innovative approach to solving engineering challenges.

Product

Stobart Aviation includes London Southend Airport and Stobart Jet Centre, which launched at the airport in 2018 offering executive jet services. The division also includes Carlisle Lake District Airport, which is due to open in 2019 to commercial flights for the first time in over two decades, and Stobart Aviation Services, which provides ground handling and check-in services for airlines including easyJet and Loganair.

engineering and management services to third-party customers including Network Rail.

Achievements

London Southend Airport has been rated London's favourite by Which? readers five years in a row and is the capital's fastest growing airport.

Stobart Energy saw a 72% growth in terms of the tonnes of biomass fuel it sold in the first half of 2018. Furthermore, Stobart Rail & Civils is designing and constructing the new

Brand History

1960s The business is founded by Eddie Stobart as an agricultural contractor in the Lake District.

1970s Edward Stobart, Eddie's son, takes over the business.

2004 The business is acquired by rail and civil engineering group, WA Developments and grows steadily.

2005 The first Tesco contract is secured.

2007 The enlarged business is listed on the London Stock Exchange and the Group acquires London Southend Airport.

2010 Stobart Energy is formed.

2014 Stobart Group sells a controlling interest in Eddie Stobart Logistics.

2017 Stobart Group reduces its ownership of Eddie Stobart Logistics to 12.5% and Eddie Stobart is floated on the AIM market of the London Stock Exchange.

2019 Stobart Group is focused on three core operating businesses, Stobart Aviation, Stobart Energy and Stobart Rail & Civils.

maintenance facility at Newton Heath which will accommodate Arriva Rail North's new fleet of trains.

Recent Developments

Stobart Group was in the news at the beginning of 2019 as part of a consortium with Virgin Atlantic and Cyrus Capital, aiming to acquire regional airline Flybe and consolidate it with its own aviation assets.

In 2018, Stobart Group also announced a landmark agreement with Ryanair to base three of its planes at London Southend Airport from the summer of 2019, with the aim of welcoming over one million passengers a year. These aircraft will now sit alongside four easyJet planes, with easyJet welcoming over one million passengers through London Southend Airport in 2018.

Promotion

In 2019 Stobart Group intends to review new ways to promote its brand and its values, such as greater community engagement close to the areas in which it operates. For example, at the beginning of 2019, it announced a sponsorship agreement between its London airport and Southend United Community and Education Trust, with a focus on participating in future community engagement activities.

Brand Values

Stobart Group has strong brand recognition thanks to its highly visible operations across the UK that are supported by fantastic employees who are committed to ensuring quality customer service, improving efficiencies and introducing innovative approaches to solving customer challenges.

tommee tippee® is the number one baby feeding accessories brand in the UK (Source: IRI November 2018) and one of the top brands of infant products and accessories in the global market providing innovative, intuitive and stylish products loved by babies and recommended by generations of parents

Market

The UK baby accessories market is estimated to be worth approximately £170m (Source: IRI 2018 & Company Data) and encompasses everything from bibs and bottles to monitors and harnesses. It does not include nappies, wipes, toiletries, formula milk, baby food or nursery furniture. tommee tippee® is number one in six of the top 10 categories in the baby accessories market (Source: IRI November 2018).

tommee tippee® has more than one-third of the total market share by value (Source: IRI November & Company Data 2018). Internationally, it is sold in over 70 countries.

Product

Every tommee tippee® product has been designed around one key principle – to make the life of parents easier. Since the introduction of the original spill-proof cup, tommee tippee® has earned a reputation for its clever ideas and the quality of its intuitive products that support children on their journey from their first feed to independent feeding.

In recent years, significant additions to the product portfolio have included Closer to Nature®, Perfect Prep™ and Sangenic® Tec. Closer to Nature® feeding bottles are the cornerstone of the tommee tippee® portfolio. Designed to mimic the natural flex, feel and movement of a nipple, the original breast-like teat can be found on all Closer to Nature® Bottles, for a natural latch and smooth transition from breast to bottle.

2018 saw the launch of two key products in the tommee tippee® portfolio including Perfect Prep Day & Night, the latest edition to the Perfect Prep range and the new Advanced Anti-Colic bottle.

DID YOU KNOW?

Seven **Perfect Prep Machines** are sold every hour in the UK*

*Source: IRI & Company Data, Nov 2018

The bottle combines tommee tippee's award winning breast-like teat with the latest in anti-colic innovation to create Advanced Anti-Colic. The unique anti-colic venting system draws air away from the milk and the star valve keeps milk from travelling up the tube meaning 80% less wind, reflux and fussing. Plus, a built-in heat sensing straw gives extra reassurance that milk is just the right temperature, so baby can feed comfortably.

Achievements

Now in its fifth decade, tommee tippee® continues to impress industry professionals and parents alike with its products winning an array of awards. Once again, tommee tippee® swept the board at the Loved By Parents awards with 11 awards in total, including Platinum for Best New Product to Market with Perfect Prep Day & Night and Platinum in Best Product for Bottle Feeding with the New Advanced Anti-Colic bottle.

In 2018 tommee tippee® was also awarded a coveted Mother & Baby Award, winning Best Weaning Product with its Steamer Blender which steams fruit, vegetables and meat, then blends, with no transfer between cycles. The aim being less mess and stress at meal times.

Recent Developments

tommee tippee® is committed to helping parents throughout the roller-coaster ride of parenting,

developing stylish and practical products to meet the needs of babies around the world.

In 2018 tommee tippee® acquired the Gro Company, marking a new period of growth for the group. Known as the 'official' baby sleep bag brand, having sold over three million Grobags worldwide, Gro has an impressive range of well-loved and respected products, which help parents get babies to sleep safely.

Over the past year, tommee tippee® has extended its full global footprint to 13 offices in eight countries – UK, France, Australia, Hong Kong,

Brand History

1965 Manufacturing rights are acquired for Tommee Tippee baby products in the UK and Europe.

1986 Tommee Tippee introduces Pur™, the first silicone teat to the market with Sip 'n' Seal, the first non-spill baby cup, launching two years later.

1997 Tommee Tippee buys Sangenic – a patented nappy disposal system.

2001 Easiflow becomes the first baby cup to be accredited by the British Dental Health Foundation.

2006 The launch of Closer to Nature® changes the face of newborn feeding.

2009 Tommee Tippee's new 'star' brand identity is introduced and the following year the brand launches in the US and Canada.

2011 The Explora toddler range is relaunched followed by The Closer to Nature® Digital Video Monitor in 2012 and the Closer to Nature® Perfect Prep™ Machine in 2013.

2015 The Express and Go system and tommee tippee® #ParentOn are launched.

2017 tommee tippee® launches in China.

2018 The company acquires The Gro Company and launches Perfect Prep™ Day & Night in the UK as well as Advanced Anti-Colic, worldwide.

China, Italy, Morocco and, following investment in new offices, the US. The year also saw the global headquarters in the UK move to a new £2m office, giving its employees a fantastic environment to work in and helping attract further talent to fuel its international growth plans.

The group continues to show strong, above industry average growth across its core markets powered by new product development and a very active digital strategy.

Promotion
tommee tippee® is committed to a digital first approach across all aspects of its business and has invested heavily in a dynamic digital programme including social media, email marketing, SEO, PPC and online retailer activity. In addition to this, it also receives a substantial amount of PR and

editorial endorsement from the parenting press and online sources as well as having a strong relationship with the parenting blog community.

In 2018, tommee tippee® launched its biggest ever campaign to coincide with the launch of Perfect Prep Day & Night. Using social media, email marketing, advertising and PR, tommee tippee® has had a strong start to the year, reaching thousands of parents with its 'Dream Machine', for night time feeds.

The brand's strongest marketing tool however, comes from word of mouth, with parents providing first hand recommendation of products and the love that they have for the brand.

tommee tippee® is also a key exhibitor at UK baby shows, which attract more than 75,000

parents and pregnant women every year. The one-on-one interaction ensures that the brand is closer to parents, engaging them with product demonstrations and answering feeding questions.

Brand Values
This award-winning brand was launched in the UK over 50 years ago and was founded with one simple goal – to make everyday life just a little easier for parents around the world.

The brand is as fully committed to that original goal today as it was in 1965, working tirelessly to create innovative and stylish products that are designed to look and feel as impressive as they are functional.

tommeetippee.com

TONI&GUY™

OFFICIAL SPONSOR | LONDON FASHION WEEK

TONI&GUY has long been **renowned as an innovator within the hairdressing industry,** **bridging the gap between high fashion and hairdressing.** Toni Mascolo OBE's franchise model has maintained the company's **high education and creative standards,** protected the brand and made **successes of thousands of TONI&GUY hairdressing entrepreneurs worldwide**

Market

In the years since the birth of TONI&GUY, hairdressing has become a sophisticated industry worth billions, spawning some of the most influential and creative artists in the beauty and fashion sector. From individual salons to global chains, competition is fierce with consumers demanding the highest quality and service.

Having helped to change the face of the industry, the multi-awarded Superbrand has 592 salons globally, 201 in the UK plus a further 391 in 45 countries, whilst sister brand essensuals has 144 salons worldwide.

Product

TONI&GUY salons aim to offer a consistent level of service, guaranteed quality, exceptional cutting and innovative colour, including a recently introduced client-friendly Colour Menu, in contemporary but well-designed salons at an affordable price. All techniques practised by the stylists are taught by highly trained and experienced educators in 20 academies around the world.

The multi-award-winning label.m Professional Haircare range was created by Toni and his daughter, Sacha Mascolo-Tarbuck, in 2005. The brand has a presence in 44 countries globally, boasts more than 80 products and is the Official Haircare Product of London Fashion Week. In 2018, label.m launched its most successful and profitable range to date, called Anti-Frizz – a range of seven tailored solutions developed to replenish moisture, repair and eliminate frizz with smoothing, longer-lasting results for all hair textures.

Achievements

TONI&GUY has a worldwide brand presence and is recognised for its strong education network. "Education, education, education," was often quoted by Toni Mascolo as it is considered the cornerstone of the hairdressing powerhouse. An average of 100,000 hairdressers are trained each year, with more than 5,500 employees in the UK and a further 3,500 worldwide.

DID YOU KNOW?

Co-Founder and **CEO Toni Mascolo OBE still cut hair** one day a week, **alternating between London's Sloane Square and Marylebone stores,** until shortly before he passed away in 2017

This philosophy of motivation, inspiration and education is key to the brand's success.

Co-Founder and CEO, Toni Mascolo OBE, sadly passed away in 2017. During his illustrious career, he guided the direction of TONI&GUY and received much recognition for his work. Toni won London Entrepreneur of the Year and received an OBE for his services to the British hairdressing industry in 2008. He was also honoured with an International Achievement Award from the Fellowship for British Hairdressers and an International Legend Award at the Association Internationale Presse Professionnelle Coiffure Awards. Toni was also an Honorary Professor of Durham University and recognised as one of the 10 most successful Italians in the UK.

Undoubtedly one of the most celebrated entrepreneurs in hairdressing, Toni also received the Primi Dieci Award at BAFTA.

Toni's daughter, Global Creative Director Sacha Mascolo-Tarbuck, was the youngest ever winner of Newcomer of the Year at 19 years old. Additional awards include London Hairdresser of the Year, Hair Magazine's Hairdresser of the Year, Creative Head's Most Wanted Look of the Year, and its Most Wanted Hair Icon in 2009, and Fashion Focused Image of the Year from the Fellowship for British Hairdressing, as well as Hairdresser of the Year.

Recent Developments

The legendary Artistic Team, under the direction of Sacha Mascolo-Tarbuck, has received numerous awards over the years. Most recently this has included three British Hairdressing Awards in 2018, which brings its impressive tally to 71.

Although established more than 50 years ago, the globally recognised brand prides itself on 'moving with the times' and investing in the careers of young hairdressers. 2018 saw Gianluca Caruso win Newcomer of the Year at the British Hairdressing Awards – a category which the company has been recognised in no less than nine times: 1991, Sacha Mascolo; 1997, Andre Pante; 1999, Cos Sakkas; 2001, Nicole Liddon; 2002, Nina Beckert; 2004, Jose Boix; 2005, Efi Davies; 2015, Sophie Springett; and 2018, Gianluca Caruso.

Promotion

TONI&GUY juggles the need for consistency, the desire to be fashionable and the reassurance of solid service values, with the excitement of avant-garde styling, supported by its philosophy of continual education. TONI&GUY.TV launched in 2003 to enhance the in-salon experience. Containing up-to-the-minute content, today it still receives more than 83,000 views per week in the UK.

TONI&GUY Magazine was also launched in 2003 to communicate the brand's heritage

Brand History

1963 TONI&GUY is launched from a single unit in Clapham, South London by Toni Mascolo and his brother Guy.

1982 The TONI&GUY Academy launches.

1985 TONI&GUY's first international salon opens in Tokyo, Japan.

1987 TONI&GUY's first franchise salon opens in Brighton.

2001 The TONI&GUY signature haircare range is launched. The following year, Toni and Pauline Mascolo launch the TONI&GUY Charitable Foundation.

2003 TONI&GUY Magazine and TONI&GUY.TV are launched in the UK.

2004 TONI&GUY becomes the Official Sponsor of London Fashion Week.

2005 label.m Professional Haircare by TONI&GUY launches.

2008 Toni Mascolo receives an OBE for his services to the British hairdressing industry.

2010 Sacha Mascolo-Tarbuck and James Tarbuck join the British Fashion Council / Vogue Designer Fashion Fund.

2011 TONI&GUY becomes Official Sponsor of the British Fashion Awards.

2013 TONI&GUY celebrates 50 years of hairdressing success.

2015 TONI&GUY launches its first dedicated barber shop in Shoreditch, London and label.m celebrates 10 years of success.

2016 TONI&GUY enters a partnership with Samsung to bring the latest window screen technology to 150 salons.

2018 TONI&GUY wins three accolades at the prestigious British Hairdressing Awards: London Hairdresser of the Year, Avant-Garde Hairdresser of the Year and Newcomer of the Year.

and philosophy, focusing on key trends in fashion, the arts, beauty and travel. Distributed in salons across the globe, the magazine promotes the inspirational, accessible face of the company. Furthermore, it won Best Consumer Publication in 2011 at the APA Awards.

Fashion has always been a major pillar of the brand. In 2004, the link grew even stronger when it first began sponsoring London Fashion Week.

More than 30 seasons later, the partnership continues to grow through the endorsement of its professional haircare range, label.m, which is the first product line London Fashion Week lent its name to. In addition, for the 14th season, TONI&GUY and label.m offered support backstage to key designers showing at the 2018 London Fashion Week Men's shows.

The TONI&GUY Session Team works on more than 80 shows per year in London, New York, Paris, Milan, Tokyo and Shanghai, offering support to key designers including Mary Katranzou, Pam Hogg, Paul Costelloe and House of Holland, among many others. TONI&GUY has also been awarded Consumer Superbrand status for 12 years and is proud to support the industry as a leading sponsor of the British Fashion Awards.

Brand Values

TONI&GUY's reputation has been built on an impeccable pedigree and foundation of education, fashion focus and friendly, professional service. TONI&GUY aims to encompass the importance of local and individually tailored, customer-led service, promoting an authoritative, cohesive and – most importantly – inspiring voice.

TATA
CONSULTANCY
SERVICES

The fastest-growing – and third largest – IT services brand in the world,
TCS is a growing and influential force in the UK digital economy. With 17,000 UK employees
and more than 200 customers, including 42 of the FTSE 100, its influence
is felt across UK regions and business sectors

Market

TCS has had a presence in the UK for more than 40 years and is its second largest market. TCS is integrated across the UK's regions and industries, from retail and manufacturing to energy and the public sector, and employs more than 17,000 people in 60 locations. TCS in the UK is proud of how it reflects the diversity of the country as a whole, with more than 50 nationalities represented among its UK-based associates.

UK businesses are continuing to explore, understand and apply technologies such as artificial intelligence and big data analytics. These emerging technologies have led to a rapid and ongoing transformation into a new economic era, one in which the old rules and ways of working no longer apply. Analytics now rules over instinct, customer experience defines your brand, and the winners are determined not by size or scale, but by their innovation, insight and agility.

Product

Many iconic UK brands work in partnership with TCS to transform their business models for the digital era, creating new revenue streams and enhancing the customer experience to drive growth.

In 2018, TCS announced that it is helping Marks & Spencer transform into a digital retailer in a project that will involve new apps, increased use of APIs, automation and blockchain. TCS has also helped Virgin Atlantic transform its culture towards agile ways of working. In the engineering sector, TCS' partnership with Rolls-Royce has seen the latter launch new analytics and agile capabilities, as well as a new UK customer delivery centre.

Achievements

TCS was recognised as the number one IT services organisation for customer satisfaction in the UK by Whitelane, a leading European research agency. The Whitelane study surveyed more than 240 business leaders (CIOs, CEOs, CFOs and their direct reports) and TCS received a customer satisfaction score of 81%, leaving it in first place in a field of 31 providers. TCS also ranked number one in application development, maintenance, testing and SaaS, data centre, managed infrastructure and hosting.

Furthermore, Brand Finance named TCS the Fastest Growing Brand of the Decade in IT Services,

while the CRF institute recognised TCS as the UK's top employer. TCS is also the largest software consultancy in the UK to have been certified gold for the UK's 'Investors in People' marque. Overall, TCS UK won, or was nominated for, more than 50 awards across departments and disciplines.

Recent Developments

TCS' role as Official Technology Partner of the London Marathon was elevated to another level in 2018. It built on the success of the 2017 event, where the TCS-developed official event app launched for the first time, being downloaded on nearly 300,000 devices. The 2018 edition improved on this total, setting a world record for marathon apps being downloaded to over 360,000 devices. The partnership also allowed TCS to promote digital wellbeing, mindfulness and physical fitness via social media activations.

Elsewhere, TCS cemented its position at the heart of the UK's digital economy by hosting an Innovation Forum in London, focused on the topic of driving the Business 4.0 agenda. TCS provided a forum for C-suite executives, customers and technology innovation speakers to come together and discuss how businesses need a mindset shift from 'optimising scarce resources' to 'harnessing abundance'. TCS looks to help its customers focus technology platforms on using resources which are in abundance – such as capital, talent and capabilities – in real-time to move away from limited thinking.

Promotion

In 2018, TCS proved the value of integrated thought leadership campaigns. These campaigns go beyond announcements and really reflect the growing presence and importance of digital technologies in the world, and the effect they are having on businesses, societies and communities. In a climate that is full of scare stories about technology, it is vital to show how innovation can help to build a positive future.

TCS' #DigitalEmpowers site highlights inspiring examples of how technology is being used as a force for good and improving lives around the world. Whether it's drones helping protect forests in Europe or technology empowering women in rural India to set up as global sole traders, #DigitalEmpowers puts TCS at the head of the 'tech for good' movement. TCS won eight prizes at the Corporate Content Awards which took place in London, including a gold award for best branded content site for #DigitalEmpowers.

Brand Values

TCS understands that the UK's skills challenges can be addressed by raising the profile of digital skills and exposing young people to the opportunities of digital career paths at an early age. In 2018, TCS hosted the Digital Explorers – Experience Work programme. The scheme gives young people aged 14 to 19 the chance to experience work in digital industries and come away with a greater chance of succeeding in the sector.

The 2018 programme included a workshop week in the summer, where TCS invited groups of students to present their ideas for possible new digital applications to a panel of experts who took on the role of judges. Combined, TCS' award-winning UK STEM outreach programmes have inspired more than 300,000 young people to explore a digital future.

In 1810 the Reverend Henry Duncan did something revolutionary.
He built the Trustees Savings Bank, whose sole purpose was to help hard-working
local people thrive. Six years ago, TSB, Britain's challenger bank, was re-born based
on his values, to make banking better for all UK consumers

Market

In 2013 the big five banks controlled more than 85% of all UK bank accounts. Following the banking crisis, TSB was created to bring more competition to UK banking and actively make banking better for all consumers.

TSB delivers a different kind of retail banking that it calls 'Local Banking'. The bank only champions local people and local businesses, helping them and the communities they live in to thrive. It refuses to engage in any risky practises like overseas speculation and investment banking. In short it's High Street, not Wall Street.

Product

Fundamentally, TSB believes that when people help people we all thrive together. It's this belief which means it actively helps people make the most of their hard-earned money, stopping them missing out on things that could make them better off.

That is why TSB designs its products and services the way it does. Its Classic Plus account pays interest whilst not charging a fee. Likewise, its Fix and Flex personal loans and mortgages enable people to borrow well by allowing them to take repayment holidays should life change.

DID YOU KNOW?

The **Classic Plus** current account appeared in independently produced **Best Buy** tables every week during 2018

This is also why the TSB Business current account offers free business banking for over a year and comes with a suite of services which can help its customers start, run or grow their businesses better.

Achievements

TSB believes purpose-driven brands build strong businesses. Therefore it has continued to celebrate people who help other people in their communities through its #TSBLocalPride programme. At its heart is a long-term partnership with Pride of Britain and Pride of Sport. Pride of Britain is the nation's biggest annual awards ceremony of its kind, celebrating ordinary people across the UK who have gone to extraordinary lengths to help others.

But celebrating isn't enough. Through the TSB Local Charity Partnership programme, every branch and site supports a local, independently registered community group with fundraising and volunteering. TSB Partners and customers raise more than £500,000 for 450 causes every year. Furthermore, on Local Charities Day 2018 TSB celebrated the great work of these organisations and announced the first Local Community Fund winners – most of whom operate in a sector that often struggles to raise funds.

This commitment to its purpose has helped TSB build a strong brand. Those aware of the partnership with Local Pride were not only more likely to consider TSB as a brand, but also more likely to consider TSB products, such as its current account, too.

At the same time, TSB prides itself on creating a culture that encourages and builds diversity and inclusion. For example, TSB was one of the first companies to proactively publish and explain its gender pay gap and had a strong presence at LGBT Pride events across the country.

Recent Developments

TSB has helped personal banking customers be better off since launch. In 2018 it also turned its attention to the backbone of the economy – small businesses. This group often feels undervalued, underserved and overcharged.

TSB Business Banking launched to change this. It only focuses on the smaller, independent businesses of Britain. As well as developing products to help them be better off, TSB has also partnered with expert service providers to ensure these smaller businesses receive the support they need to start, run and grow their business.

Unlike many of the tech start-ups and the big banks, TSB is right where people most need it, at the heart of local communities right across Britain.

We're here to help the smaller, independent businesses of Britain start, run and grow.

tap | click | call | visit

Local banking for businesses

CURRENT ACCOUNT SWITCH GUARANTEE

Are you missing out on 5%_{AER} interest?

Come in and talk to a TSB Partner about the Plus account.

tap | click | call | visit

Local banking for Britain TSB

Brand History

1810 The Trustee Savings Bank is established by Reverend Henry Duncan of Ruthwell.

1986 TSB Group plc is founded.

1995 TSB is bought by Lloyds Bank. TSB disappears as a separate brand, living only as part of the name LloydsTSB.

2013 TSB separates from Lloyds Banking Group and becomes an independent entity, tasked by the EU with increasing competition in the British banking sector after the banking crisis.

2014 TSB Bank plc goes public with successful IPO.

2015 TSB is bought by Sabadell, Spain's fifth largest banking group.

2016 TSB is recognised as Britain's most recommended high street bank.

It's notoriously difficult to get customers to switch current accounts – fewer than 2% did in 2018. But by not switching, millions of people across Britain are missing out on having a banking relationship, which could make them better off. In this case, millions of people are missing out by having a current account that doesn't pay them any interest; whereas TSB's Plus account pays interest to all its customers with no monthly fee.

To jolt people out of this costly inertia and help them make the most of their hard-earned money, the campaign built on creating FOMO, the fear of missing out. This culturally familiar behavioural economics tactic has been proven time and time again to get even the most reluctant people to spring into action.

Brand Values

The bank is driven by a set of values – pioneering, straightforward, transparent, collaborative and responsible – that are very different from those which banking has come to be associated with. They continue to inform everything TSB does, just as they have done from the very start.

But, even though the brand has achieved a great deal, TSB's work is far from done. Millions of people across Britain are still missing out on banking which can truly make them better off. That is why TSB is going to continue to champion customers to fulfil its mission of making banking better for everybody.

TSB doesn't think customers ought to choose between digital services and branches. It therefore offers business banking customers the kind of service they would expect whether it is on mobile or in person; from a TSB Partner in branch who actively helps, rather than just selling things; or an expert Relationship Manager who will get to know customsers and their businesses over the long term.

Furthermore, TSB has used some of its marketing budget to actively encourage people to support their local businesses during their key trading periods, such as Christmas.

Promotion

As a purpose-driven business, TSB seeks to use its promotions to make banking better for everyone and its latest campaign focuses on the core banking product, the current account.

worldpay

Worldpay is a **global leader in payments processing technology** and solutions for its customers, **simplifying payments by breaking through borders and obstacles to help businesses grow**. It is a partner for connected commerce **for businesses around the world**

Market

Appetite for simplicity, immediacy and ubiquity is driving major changes in how people transact and make payments: from purchasing a coffee without needing to take cash out, to pre-booking an airline ticket on a mobile phone, to buying an upgrade seamlessly whilst playing a video game. Worldpay has embraced innovation in technology solutions for in-store, online and mobile payments throughout its history.

Worldpay processes over 40 billion transactions annually, through more than 300 payment types across 146 countries and 126 currencies.

It operates in the global payment processing technology market, which enables one of the essential needs of the world economy – making a payment for goods or services – and continues to be characterised by rapid growth and innovation.

Product

Worldpay serves some of the world's newest, smallest entrepreneurs and its biggest, most recognisable brands. Ultimately, the company helps make payments easier for businesses and consumers around the world.

Worldpay has a unique capability to power global integrated omni-commerce, through its

DID YOU KNOW?

Worldpay processes over US $1.5 tn payment volume globally each year and is the UK's number one acquirer*

*Source: The Nilson Report: The World's Top Card Issuers and Merchant Acquirers 2018

industry-leading scale and an unmatched integrated technology platform, which offers customers a comprehensive suite of products and services – delivered through a single global provider with expert local knowledge.

Achievements

Worldpay was named number one UK acquirer by The Nilson Report: The World's Top Card Issuers and Merchant Acquirers 2018, and it processed over US $1.5tn in global payment volume in 2017. Testament to its ability to scale, Worldpay continues to invest in specialist technology and local expertise to grow its global reach.

At the UK Card and Payments Awards 2018, Worldpay won 'Best Initiative in Mobile Payments' for its 'My Business Mobile' innovation, which turns a smartphone into a payment device.

The Sunday Times Best Big Companies List 2018 ranked Worldpay 14th, naming it first when it comes to work-life balance, with 72% of employees considering their jobs to be good for their personal development.

Recent Developments

Worldpay's continued investment in people has seen the launch of a successful graduate scheme,

Consumer Behaviour and Payments Report

Brand History

1989 The company is founded as Streamline, a subsidiary of National Westminster Bank.

1994 One of the world's first internet payments is processed.

2002 NatWest is acquired by RBS and renamed as RBS Worldpay.

2010 Advent International and Bain Capital acquire 80% of Worldpay.

2011 Worldpay acquires leading eCommerce solution, Envoy Services Ltd.

2013 Worldpay Zinc is launched, a mobile card processing terminal that links to mobile. RBS sells its remaining 20% stake in Worldpay.

2015 Worldpay is listed on the London Stock Exchange through an initial IPO.

2017 Worldpay invests in Cambridge-based Featurespace, a leading machine learning company for fraud prevention. In addition, Vantiv announces its intention to acquire Worldpay.

2018 Vantiv acquires Worldpay for US $10.4bn.

now in its second year. As a key part of their learning programme, graduates partner with The Prince's Trust to run 'Million Makers' entrepreneurial projects that contribute both to the charity and their professional development.

Recently, Worldpay invested in UK-based fraud prevention and machine learning firm, Featurespace. This has allowed it to provide even more intelligent, automated protection for its customers, harnessing the scale of its data resources.

Worldpay's Simplicity pricing plan was introduced in 2018 to give its small business customers a single, blended rate making it easier to understand the cost of payment services and simpler to plan against. Further assisting the UK's smaller businesses, Worldpay's Business Finance scheme, delivered in partnership with Liberis Limited, continues to grow, having already provided over £80m as an alternative source of funding.

Promotion
To amplify and elevate the 'new Worldpay' following its merger, a rebrand has taken place to reflect its increased ability to provide ever

simpler, always progressive payments to the world's consumers. Worldpay's tagline 'Advancing the ways the world pays' clearly encompasses what it does and who it is.

Worldpay's highly respected annual Global Payments Report demonstrates its commitment to helping global businesses to understand and tailor their strategy based on the payments landscape of 36 key countries. It highlights payment trends around the world, such as frictionless payments, the dominance of Chinese eCommerce and the rise of the eWallet. In 2018, a series of 10 videos for use at events, on social media and for internal communications quickly provided a snapshot of each payment trend and key market, encouraging viewers to read the full report.

Similarly, the Mobile Payment Journey is a useful and interactive ongoing content piece which deep-dives into the app and mobile user experience, and helps Worldpay customers to reduce lost sales by helping them to think 'mobile-first' for their audiences. The global retail team enlisted the support of eight partner organisations for a microsite developed to complement the expert advice of Worldpay's own team.

Global events under the Worldpay Rethink name are a chance for the company to take its consultative approach to new heights, enabling it to build relationships that go beyond simply sales. For customers, prospects and partners, and with selected publicly-available online sessions, Rethink takes the form of a payments conference. It brings the topics businesses want to discuss to the forefront – so that the company can learn, share and connect with its customers directly.

Brand Values
Worldpay is advancing the ways the world pays – one happy customer at a time. As the brand name suggests, the aim is to help customers make, simplify and optimise payments around the world, helping businesses of all sizes to prosper.

Worldpay believes its corporate responsibility strategy will guide the relationships it has with customers, colleagues and the world. It's part of how it makes sure it is doing the right thing in the right way, in accordance with the company's values.

Learning from Unicorns

How brand responsiveness is evolving

NICK MORRIS
Founding Partner, Canvas8

The 1950s were a good time for business. Big brands became icons. Coca-Cola launched its contoured bottle, The Marlboro Man redefined tobacco, and one million car sales were Cadillac's testament to the American dream.

In the 1950s, the average lifespan of an S&P 500 business was 60 years. Fast forward to 2019, and it's less than 20.

What has triggered this change? 2018 saw 112 new 'unicorns' join the market – companies valued at over a billion dollars. These brands are disruptive, challenging established businesses and creating new human norms. They are geographically and technologically diverse, ranging from India to Sweden, and reinventing everything from food delivery to webhosting.

What unites them, though, from Allbirds to Lime Scooters, from Lyft to Sweetgreen, is human-centricity. The new breed of challenger brands is born out of a deep frustration with the status quo – one led by brands people perceive as static and no longer fit for purpose. Combined, they are redefining brand responsiveness with clear-headed, innovative approaches to problem-solving.

A shifting landscape

At Canvas8, we support businesses by helping them understand audiences through two lenses. One of these is culture – the way we are impacted by the environment around us, and the other is behavioural science – the way we are programmed as human beings.

The move against the status quo is one of the major cultural shifts we are living through today. It is the reason behind the rise of consciously 'ugly' fashion, ultra-relatable micro-influencers and the backlash to clean eating. Arguably, it's also the reason Trump became POTUS and Brits voted for Brexit. And it is a major contributor to growing brand promiscuity. With 91% of global consumers having no qualms about 'cheating' on their favourite brand, loyalty is a fading notion.

> "With people increasingly frustrated with the status quo, it's clear-headed innovation that's helping brands thrive"

If you break this down into its building blocks, the pushback is fundamentally a human response to frustration, anxiety and fatigue. Unhappy with the ways things are, people are opting for unknown unknowns over known unknowns, gambling on uncertainty over risk. The results are largely chaotic. As we've seen politically, they can also be extreme. They are polarising and jolting. But they are also dynamic, fluid, and suggestible – making them rich areas of opportunity for brands who can provide order amidst the chaos.

Take Gillette's #MeToo campaign critiquing toxic masculinity. The clip racked up four million views on YouTube on the day of its release, winning the brand praise in global headlines and no doubt making its shareholders proud. Still, it polarised responses and weakened brand credibility. More often than not, when established brands find

themselves scrambling for relevance, it's because they've overlooked their audience. It means customers' frustrations with the market and industry have moved on, while they have not.

As the dip in big-brand loyalty and longevity shows, having deep pockets is simply no substitute for having your finger on the pulse of culture. So what can established brands learn from today's unicorns?

Rediscover your North Star

First, brands can rediscover their North Star. That means identifying what they stand for, and the human frustrations their business solves. Today's challenger brands are born out of frustration. It's solution-based finance that's taken fintech brand Transferwise from a start-up to a 'unicorn' with four million customers transferring US $4bn a month. And for heritage brands like The New York Times, building genuine people-centred solutions means that sales follow; their quality journalism has driven digital subscriptions up by 19% in the age of fake news.

Respond to customers to serve shareholders

Secondly, brands can understand that great responsiveness now means responding to the customer to serve the shareholder. It means putting the customer, not the shareholder, first. Having the courage to make tough calls

– to be brave and focused, but not reckless. Nike faced fierce backlash after featuring quarterback Colin Kaepernick in its anniversary campaign, with #BoycottNike trending on Twitter, people burning their trainers on YouTube, Trump denouncing the campaign as a "terrible message" (a surefire sign of a great campaign) and their stock price dropping nearly 4%. Since then, Nike has seen its value increase by almost US $6bn and had a 33% increase in online sales. Today, protecting shareholder interests increasingly is about listening to your customer, and having the agility to pivot, meeting their changing cultural expectations.

Be human

Finally, the beating heart of great brand responsiveness is being human. With two thirds of consumers worldwide shopping based on their values, it's no longer enough for brands to think about marketing to people rather than genuinely connecting with them. Often, that means demonstrating emotional intelligence and deep empathy – being inherently human. Earlier this year, dozens of companies stepped up to support deeply affected federal employees amidst America's longest-ever government shutdown. Banking giants Chase and Wells Fargo reversed overdraft fees. Kraft opened pop-ups allowing people to stock up on free food. The gestures were surprising and genuinely emotionally impactful, cutting through political partisanship with unprecedented human generosity.

Today's successful brands are redefining responsiveness by acting on people's frustrations with clear-headed innovative solutions. It's an attractive approach that treats people as more than revenue lines. And that is what consumers are drawn to. Brands who listen to their audience, are clear in their business beliefs, and can seamlessly align the two.

About Canvas8

Canvas8 helps businesses understand people and make better strategic decisions. Combining behavioural science with cultural insight, they inspire innovation in some of the world's leading brands, agencies and organisations.

CANVAS8

The Latest Consumer Trends You Need to Know About

Shedding light on the rapid evolution of media consumption

ANDREW O'CONNELL
Managing Director UK, Dynata

The digital landscape continues to change at an accelerating rate. With the relentlessly ongoing evolution of mobile technologies, digital tools and platforms, consumers' behaviour, usage, and attitudes also adapt and change. But in what way? Consumers are still watching television, reading newspapers and magazines, listening to the radio, searching online and using social media. Which means, we need to understand how consumers are consuming media before we can design relevant surveys that engage them.

For this reason at Dynata we have begun tracking trends to shed light on media consumption. We believe that quality is imperative throughout the research process but is essential at the outset, as the foundation for the process as it unfolds. We focus on the keystone that leads to a quality outcome: the individuals who are providing the survey responses. Better data about individuals leads to better data from individuals, which in turn translates into better insights and decisions. Having invested in ensuring that our data is of the highest quality, Dynata would like to share key consumer trends that will help you design better research, realise more comprehensive data sets, and obtain new insights to launch the most effective marketing campaigns.

Device use trends
Looking at device preference when taking surveys online gives an indication as to which devices consumers are most active on. For example, participants in the UK were much more likely than those from other countries to use their tablet (23% vs 15% rest of world) and also less likely to use their PC or laptop (55% vs 67% rest of world). Somewhat unsurprisingly the use

> "Participants in the UK were **much more likely than** those from other countries to use their tablets"

of smartphones was dramatically higher among younger participants, 34% of participants completed surveys on smartphones in the UK, however this jumps to 54% for the 18-24 age group. This online device behaviour gives a strong indication of the device preference for online activity among consumers, highlighting the need for mobile friendly strategies, not just in research surveys, but in all aspects of marketing and advertising.

Media consumption trends
The media landscape is in a state of flux with VoD and online news disrupting the traditional

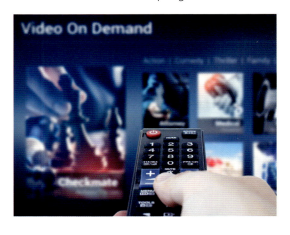

scene. In the UK for example TV makes up 47% of the media diet, online 39%, radio 13% and print just 2%. Focusing specifically on TV shows the impact of new technology by age, unsurprisingly indicating that millennials lead the way in VoD and streamed TV whereas the baby boomer generation are still more likely to be watching broadcast TV. Understanding trends in media consumption is extremely important to marketers and advertisers as they work to identify the best channels to invest in.

Trust and privacy
When interacting with consumers, trust and privacy are paramount. Living in a post-GDPR world means we are communicating with

> "The media landscape
> is in a state of flux with VoD
> and online news disrupting
> the traditional scene"

an enlightened audience who are more suspicious than ever of how their data is being handled. This was reflected in our findings, with 81% of UK respondents agreeing that consumers have lost control over how personal information is collected and used by companies. However, the picture is not totally bleak, 85% of UK respondents agreed that they would be more willing to share their data with businesses if they were more transparent about how they were going to use it, and that

respondents are willing to share their data if there is a clear benefit for them. What does that mean for marketers and advertisers? Well it's clear that consumers value honesty, and post GDPR businesses can't afford not to be honest, so it's time to make this a priority.

Conclusion

By tracking consumer trends as described – across device use, media consumption, privacy, culture, and the other areas mentioned above – our goal is to help researchers, marketers and advertisers create better studies and have a deeper understanding of the many nuances that bear on consumers thanks to a plethora of devices, new technologies, and the issues that they raise.

About Dynata

Dynata is one of the world's leading providers of first-party data contributed by people who opt-in to member-based panels. With a reach that encompasses over 60 million people globally and an extensive library of individual profile attributes collected through surveys, Dynata is the cornerstone for precise, trustworthy quality data. Dynata serves nearly 6,000 market research agencies, media and advertising agencies, consulting and investment firms as well as healthcare and corporate customers.

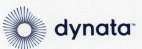

Appendix

Research and Results Overview 2019

Superbrands Expert Councils

Qualifying Brands

Research and Results Overview 2019

Results and Relevancy Highlights

STEPHEN CHELIOTIS
Chief Executive, TCBA
& Chairman, Superbrands UK

Providing a snapshot of brand sentiment in the UK since 1995, the Superbrands results reflect the changing perceptions of British consumers, professionals and experts on major brands operating in the country.

Just shy of 3,200 brands were evaluated in this year's surveys, almost evenly split between consumer and business-to-business brands. The former survey featured 1,596 brands across 78 different categories, which ranged from 'Automotive Products' to 'Vitamins and Supplements', and the latter 1,586 brands across 63 categories, covering everything from 'Accountancy and Business Services' to 'Waste Management and Recycling'.

Unusually for an industry award, brands do not pay or apply to be considered, the reason being that in order to provide a broad review of the market and identify the strongest brands in each category, all the key players in each sector need to be evaluated and voted on.

The business-to-business brands were assessed by an independent and voluntary expert council of 24 senior business-to-business marketing leaders and 2,500 UK business professionals, all with purchasing or managerial responsibility within their businesses.

A nationally representative sample of 2,500 UK adults – reflecting the breadth of opinion across the whole country – voted on the consumer brands. As a secondary quality control mechanism, our objective and voluntary Consumer Superbrands expert council also voted on these brands. Any brands lowly rated by the experts are effectively vetoed from attaining Consumer Superbrand status.

The rationale of two audiences voting on brands is simple, to ensure that any brand deemed a Superbrand is positively viewed both in terms of the output of its brand and marketing activity by the relevant experts evaluating brands in this context, and how that activity and the overall brand proposition lands and is perceived by prospective buyers.

While all voters are asked to bear in mind the same three core criteria that must be inherent in a Superbrand, namely quality, reliability and distinction, the reality of a sentiment survey is that an individual's perception will be impacted by a number of factors, including everything each brand says and does (or doesn't say and do) both in the short and long term.

Clearly a brand's ranking 'range' and, more importantly perhaps, position within their category, will typically be determined by major factors, such as awareness, physical and mental availability, market size and share, as well as the customer experience. Fundamental changes against these metrics tend to be slow and examples of brands deviating significantly from their 'range' tend to be less common. Large deviations can be a leading indicator of the start of long-term brand decline or growth.

More commonly a brand's ranking will move up and down within its typical range, with these shifts often reflecting shorter-term factors such as current brand activity, from the latest marketing campaign to new product developments, the commentary around that brand from third-party observers and influencers – including positive and negative press coverage – along with share of voice at the time of the research and any external market or competitor activity.

If analysing the results at an individual brand level therefore, both a short and longer-term view of the detail is essential, alongside a focus on performance relative to category peers rather than brands from very different sectors. Nevertheless individuals, in particular the press, unsurprisingly often focus on the overall winners or top 20.

Turning our attention to those top 20s, the results of both the Consumer and Business Superbrands surveys reflect a notable medium-term underlying consistency with leading brands tending to remain within their ranges, notwithstanding some 'within-range' short-term variability.

Nineteen of the top 20 Business Superbrands have featured in the top 20 on multiple occasions over the last five years; 16 of the brands featured in the top group last year, while three of the four 'new entries' are simply bouncing back up toward the top end of their range this year and re-entering the leading group. Johnson & Johnson and FedEx are back in after a temporary one-year absence – when they were marginally outside the top 20, in 24th and 22nd place respectively – while the Royal Mail is back in after a two-year absence, in which it placed 21st on both occasions. Only the surprise entry of Screwfix is genuinely a fundamental shift. This year the fast-growing multi-channel supplier of trade tools, plumbing, electrical, bathrooms and kitchens broke out of its typical range in the mid-30s to mid-40s – in the previous four years it placed 40th, 34th, 45th and 44th – so it will be interesting to see if the brand falls back into that zone or maintains its new higher range.

Seventeen of the Consumer Superbrands top 20 have also featured in the top 20 over the last five years more than once, while 11 of this year's top 20 were present in the previous year.

Many of the 'new entries', as with the Business Superbrands, simply placed towards the bottom end of their longer-term range last year and have edged back up again to re-enter the leading pack. British Airways, Dyson, Kellogg's and Mercedes-Benz all returned after a one-year break for instance.

This overall consistency in the survey is reflective of how brand perception and positions do tend to shift slowly over time. Reflecting this underlying consistency, as is typical every year, in the vast majority of cases the category leaders and order of brands within categories remains fairly constant. Of the 63 B2B categories only 15 had new leaders while one new category was added. Similarly of the 78 consumer categories only 15 were topped by a different brand from last year, while there were three new categories. In terms of the overall results the leading brand in both Consumer Superbrands and Business Superbrands remains the same as 2018, headed by LEGO and Apple respectively.

An additional data point, introduced last year for the first time in the Consumer Superbrands survey, is the relevancy index, which in addition to longer-term trends within the core survey can be a useful indicator of future potential brand growth or decline. Consumers are asked whether they believe an individual brand has gained or lost relevance to people today, compared with the past. This reduces the impact of longer-term goodwill on a brand's scores, and focuses consumers' minds on current use and importance of each brand to them. This index surfaces quite a different set of brands. Established titans like FMCG brands Coca-Cola or Gillette are replaced by rising disruptive brands, such as Netflix and Purplebricks. Unsurprisingly many technology, or technology enabled, brands make the top 20 for relevance. Other interesting shifts in consumer behaviour and sentiment are evident in this index, for example the rise of the discount retailers Lidl and Aldi, and increasing concern about the rise of cancer reflected in the increasing relevance of the cancer charities. Conversely those brands toward the bottom of the relevancy list may have troubled times ahead, many indeed having already suffered fundamental business problems, including retailers HMV, Carpetright, Oddbins, Mothercare and House of Fraser.

For those working at a given brand, we would encourage you to look deeper and wider at the results over the longer-term to understand the trends and what the results mean at an individual brand level – any individual brand analysis of the Superbrands results requires at least a medium-term view and a category specific focus to look at fundamental shifts in brand equity.

As ever we hope you find the top line results interesting and reflective of a broad church of opinion and nationwide sentiment – undoubtedly, they will not match your own personal perceptions neatly, after all none of us is a perfect match for the mythical 'average consumer'.

	Consumer Superbrands Top 10	Business Superbrands Top 10
1	LEGO	Apple
2	Apple	Microsoft
3	Gillette	Emirates
4	Rolex	British Airways
5	British Airways	Samsung
6	Coca-Cola	PayPal
7	Andrex	BP
8	Mastercard	Mastercard
9	Visa	Google
10	Dyson	Visa

	Brands	Gaining Relevancy	Losing Relevancy	NET
1	Amazon	73%	8%	65%
2	Aldi	68%	13%	56%
3	Macmillan Cancer Support	66%	11%	55%
4	Netflix	65%	11%	53%
5	Google	64%	12%	52%
6	Lidl	66%	14%	52%
7	PayPal	66%	15%	51%
8	LEGO	63%	13%	50%
9	Samsung	63%	14%	49%
10	YouTube	61%	13%	49%
11	Visa	61%	13%	48%
12	Heathrow	59%	11%	48%
13	Purplebricks	58%	11%	47%
14	Cancer Research UK	60%	15%	45%
15	Oral-B	58%	13%	45%
16	Apple	62%	17%	44%
17	Dyson	59%	15%	44%
18	TripAdvisor	59%	16%	43%
19	Nike	57%	14%	43%
20	Disney	57%	14%	43%

Superbrands Expert Councils

Over the years the Superbrands Expert Councils have read like a Who's Who of B2B and B2C marketing across the spectrum from brand marketing to PR and design, and 2019 exemplifies this.

It's an enormous privilege to call on the experience and knowledge of such exceptional panels. In an era blighted by fake news and populism, Superbrands at least continues to value expertise, and our selection process weaves together this expert view with a relevant consumer and business view to arrive at the list of brands we showcase here. We could not do it without the council members and their generosity in giving their time to celebrate the brands who have excelled this year.

ROB ALEXANDER (B)

Partner
Headland

Rob has had a 20-year career in advertising at TBWA\ and J Walter Thompson, encompassing strategy work for Shell, Vodafone, HSBC, Apple and the 2001 General Election for the Labour Party. Three years ago, Rob moved into the world of corporate and financial communications as a Partner at Brunswick, where he led the global campaign planning team. In September 2018 he joined Headland as a Partner to help lead campaign strategy and planning.

ALEX BIGG (B)

CEO
MHP Communications

With over 20 years' experience spanning public affairs, issues management, communications and campaign strategy, Alex heads up MHP, one of the UK's leading Public Relations consultancies. In addition, Alex serves as a board member of the Public Relations and Communications Association (PRCA) and sits on the UK management board of the Engine Group.

ANDREW BLOCH (C)

Founder & Managing Partner
FRANK
@AndrewBloch

Andrew is responsible for the day-to-day running of Frank, one of the industry's most decorated PR agencies and responsible for some of its most famous campaigns. Andrew has acted as official spokesperson for Lord Sugar for nearly 20 years. He is listed in the PR Week Power Book – The Definitive Guide To The Most Influential People in PR and is ranked as the most influential PR person on Twitter. He is also a founding mentor of the School of Communication Arts.

DARREN BOLTON (B)

Executive Creative Director
OgilvyOne Business

With over 20 years' experience in B2B and consumer marketing, Darren has helped generate successful integrated campaigns for many global brands. He is responsible for all creative work that comes out of the agency. His team are an in-house creative department of more than 30 talented experts. Their skills span all areas of the marketing mix, from copy, design and multimedia to UX and digital design and build.

ED BOLTON (C)

Creative Director
BrandCap
@TalkBrandCap

Ed has spent his working life creating compelling brands at Interbrand and Fitch, and currently heads up all things creative at BrandCap – a business consultancy that combines commercial acumen with creative, entrepreneurial brand thinking to transform the performance of organisations everywhere.

CATHERINE BOROWSKI (C)

Founder & Artistic Director
PRODUCE UK
@catinsky

Catherine is a practising artist and placemaking specialist with more than 16 years' event industry experience. She created PRODUCE UK as an artistic event-making and placemaking agency and has built a network of cultural programmers, conceptual artists, producers, digital strategists, designers and creatives that specialise in media and creative brand experiences. Catherine has a diverse work portfolio including Argent LLP and the London Design Festival, as well as Hyundai, adidas, British Land, Campari and Discovery Channel.

REBECCA BRENNAN (C)

Managing Director
Cubo

With over 20 years of agency experience, spanning digital start-ups to well-known networks, Rebecca's career has been spent at agencies including Mindshare, Ogilvy Interactive, OgilvyOne, Iris and MRM McCann. She has worked with some of the world's best-known brands such as Sony, adidas, Unilever, Amex and British Airways, to mention just a few. Rebecca is passionate about Behavioural Change and how brands are built through people, not just communications.

EMMA BROCK (C)

Founding Partner
Brock & Wilson
@emmabrock

Emma has experience in global advertising and brand design agencies, working on brands such as Nestlé, Diageo, Coca-Cola, McDonald's and Unilever. This diverse experience has led Emma to the belief that when it comes to branding, it only works if it all works. She knows how to build strong iconic (and award winning) brands and now runs her own brand design agency, helping brands realise their full potential.

VICKY BULLEN (C)

CEO
Coley Porter Bell

Vicky has been in her current role since 2005 and has led work for many of the world's largest brands including Unilever, Pernod Ricard and Tesco, delivering brand strategy and architecture, brand identities and experiences, naming and innovation. She is particularly interested in how learnings from neuroscience can be applied to branding to deliver results. Vicky sits on the Ogilvy UK Board, is a DBA Director and a member of the Marketing Society and WACL.

HUGH CAMERON (C)

Chairman
PHD UK

Hugh is part of PHD's UK leadership team who, over the last seven years, have received a sweep of marketing and media industry awards including Media Week Agency of the Year 2016 and, for four consecutive years, being one of The Sunday Times Best Companies To Work For. Hugh is an instinctive challenger and believes that if you are not challenging something you don't have a strategy or perhaps a future. This challenger behaviour has been central to PHD's success.

JACKIE COOPER (C)

Senior Advisor
Edelman

Jackie has over 30 years entrepreneurial experience in brand creative, business and personality strategy. She works across a portfolio of global clients including Unilever, F1 and JUST Water alongside building Edelman's offer with UEG in Europe. Jackie has led Edelman at Cannes, hosting events with Jamie Oliver, Will Smith, Mario Testino and most recently Ellen Pompeo. She is also a Board Advisor for Jamie Oliver Holdings and on the think tank for Kidzania.

CLAIRE COOTES (C)

Managing Director
LIDA

Claire has over 15 years of experience managing global client relationships at top digital direct agencies including OgilvyOne and Iris. In 2013 she joined LIDA, part of the M&C Saatchi Group, to lead the O2 business and was appointed Managing Director in 2017. She now has day-to-day responsibility for the effective running of the business, driving the agency's culture and vision as well as expanding LIDA's offering for its clients.

KATE COX (B)

CEO
Bray Leino

With 20 years' experience under her belt, Kate steers the creative communications agency, Bray Leino, to consistently rank among the top B2B agencies in the world, counting a number of B2B Superbrands among its clients. Kate leads a diverse team of specialists to focus on one aim; to drive brand and business success through delivering commercially creative work, which has resulted in an incredible client retention rate.

KIRSTY DAWE (B)

Co-Founder & Director
Really B2B
@kirstydawe1

Kirsty is passionate about Really B2B's ethos as the 'Real Results Agency' and its expertise in delivering measurable, data driven B2B campaigns for clients as diverse as Booking.com, Nespresso, Office Depot and American Express. Kirsty is a regular speaker at key B2B events and has a particular interest in ABM and educating on best practice in this area. She sits on the DMA B2B Council and is a regular trainer for the IDM.

CHRISTIAN DUBREUIL (C)

Managing Director
EMEA Ad & Audience
Dynata

Chris has been in the data insights industry for over 20 years and is the Managing Director EMEA, Ad & Audience of Dynata – the leading global digital data collection business. In addition, Chris serves as a board member for the Market Research Society's Company Partner think tank, helping to drive thought leadership in the industry. A frequent speaker and data industry commentator, Chris is fascinated by how people interact with brands in the digital space.

STEVE DYER (B)

Managing Director
Oil the Wheels

Steve has a unique blend of client-side industry knowledge with over 30 years' B2B agency know-how. He understands industrial / manufacturing decision makers and how to motivate them, because he used to be one! His industrial strength approach to brand marketing has fuelled a recent agency rebrand: Oil the Wheels. A strategic communications marketer, he's a Fellow of the CIM and IDM and has held senior positions on various B2B committees within the DMA.

JAMES FARMER (B)

Publisher & Founder
B2B Marketing

James is passionate about the B2B sector. He is a huge advocate of client-side, vendor and agency space taking centre stage, all geared around customer experience. His personal and business drivers are to continue to enhance the reputation and deliverability of creative commercial thinking within the B2B marketing sector; all to support business growth.

CAROLINE FOSTER KENNY (C)

CEO EMEA
IPG Mediabrands

Caroline has over 25 years of global client leadership and business experience across multiple verticals, spanning all marketing communications. A strategic leader, who is wholly focused on client growth and service, Caroline is driving transformation across the Mediabrands business. Prior to joining Mediabrands, Caroline was Global Chief Client Officer at MEC and worked for the WPP group for 15 years.

STEVE GLADDIS (C)

Chief Strategy Officer
MediaCom London

Steve is a member of the leadership team of MediaCom, the UK's biggest media planning and buying agency. He is responsible for the quality of the agency's communication planning work, across clients including Direct Line Group, Mars, Sky, Tesco, The Coca-Cola Company and Universal Pictures. He has worked with brands of all shapes and sizes for the last 24 years, and has been awarded for his work at the Cannes Lions and the global Festival Of Media.

IAN HAWORTH (B)

Chief Creative Officer, EMEA
Wunderman

Ian's rise in advertising has seen him go from tea boy to being creative lead at Saatchi & Saatchi Wellington (NZ), Tequila London and Global Chief Creative Officer at Rapp. Now at Wunderman, Ian heads up the creative output for the whole of EMEA. He has won over 100 awards, sat on the juries of all major contests (D&AD, Cannes Lions, the DMAs) and has helped raise the creative standard as well as nurtured fresh talent across the agency.

VANELLA JACKSON (C)

Global CEO
Hall & Partners

Vanella has always been passionate about branding and communications. She spent 20 years working in some of the UK's best advertising agencies, including BBH, AMV/BBDO and JWT, prior to her current role overseeing Hall & Partners. This strategic brand consultancy is powered by data and insight, with a reputation for pioneering new thinking to inspire the industry. Its award-winning initiative, The Hub, creates a new vision for insight in this new, fast-moving, digital business world.

NICK JEFFERSON (B)

Partner
Monticello

A partner with the advisory firm, Monticello, Nick is a strategy consultant with particular expertise in the space where brand meets culture. A former CEO of two creative agencies, he is an Englishman who speaks Spanish and French and works all over the world. Nick writes for both the Marketing Society and the Huffington Post as well as sitting on the Governing Body of The BRIT School.

ROB KAVANAGH (C)

Executive Creative Director
OLIVER UK
@robkav

Starting his creative career two decades ago at Ogilvy in New Zealand, Rob moved to London in 2001 and has copywritten his way around London's seminal brand response agencies – journeying through the likes of HTW, Craik Jones, Partners Andrews Aldridge and Proximity. Since joining OLIVER as ECD in April 2017, he has led award-winning campaigns across a variety of key brands. Despite living in the home of football all this time, he still favours the oval ball.

STEVE KEMISH (B)

Managing Partner
Junction

Steve is a multi-award-winning marketer and public speaker who has worked in digital marketing since 1997. He has had experience client-side, helped grow a leading email service provider, consulted to numerous clients on digital strategy, and helped build one of the most respected and awarded B2B marketing agencies in the UK. He is also an IDM tutor, a member of the IDM Digital Council, and a guest lecturer at various British universities.

OWEN LEE (C)

Chief Creative Officer
FCB Inferno

Owen has spent his career creating advertising for brands such as Mercedes-Benz, BMW, the UK Government, Tango and First Direct among many others. Since becoming Chief Creative Officer at FCB Inferno, the agency has won the Grand Prix at Cannes two years running. Previously, he ran his own advertising agency, Farm Communications. Before being on the Superbrands Council he sat on the CoolBrand Leaders Council for six years, when he was younger and cooler.

MARK LETHBRIDGE (B)

CEO
Gravity Global

Specialising in brand development, Mark is the Founder and CEO of Gravity Global, a specialist B2B marketing and communications agency, which represents global brands. Mark is also the past President of MAGNET that acts for more than 800 brands worldwide, setting best practice in global marketing and communications across 42 agency locations. Prior to this, Mark founded and was CEO of the AGA Group – a communications group focused on B2B and brand development.

NICK LIDDELL (C)

Director of Consulting
The Clearing

Nick leads the consulting team at The Clearing, an award-winning independent brand consultancy in London. With over 19 years' experience, Nick has worked with global business and consumer brands from Amex, Guinness and Prada to McLaren and the AELTC. Nick is a regular conference speaker, media contributor and has just published his second book, Wild Thinking.

AVRA LORRIMER (C)

Managing Director
Hill + Knowlton Strategies
@AvrainLondon

Throughout her career, Avra has worked on many of the world's best-known and most beloved brands. She has experience across a diverse array of sectors including FMCG, travel and automotive. An American expat residing in North London, Avra lives with her husband and daughter. In her free time she reads, occasionally blogs and is an aspiring voice-over artist.

MICK MAHONEY (C)

**Partner
& Chief Creative Officer**
Harbour

Mick has been rewarded by every major festival with over 150 awards including Grand Prix at both Cannes and One Show and numerous Golds and Silvers at Cannes, British Arrows and D&AD. He has created famous campaigns for brands such as Nike, British Airways, Boots, Vodafone, Johnnie Walker and Stella Artois. His career has spanned London's best creative agencies from BBH to Ogilvy. This year he launched Harbour, an independent communications consultancy.

CLAIRE MASON (B)

Founder & CEO
Man Bites Dog

Claire is an entrepreneur, author and founder of Man Bites Dog – a multi-award-winning thought leadership consultancy with global reach. With 20 years of experience leading global strategic marketing and thought leadership programmes, Claire creates signature global campaigns for the world's smartest organisations. Specialising in technology, professional and financial services, Claire is also the leader of the Gender Say Gap® initiative to increase the visibility of expert women in business.

AMY McCULLOCH (C)

**Co-Founder
& Managing Director**
eight&four

Amy is Founder and MD of Creative and Media agency eight&four. The eight&four ethos is 'Talk Less. Say More' and firmly believes that brands should cut through content pollution, not add to it. The agency's mission therefore, is to provide audiences with quality and meaningful experiences.

STEPHEN MEADE (B)

Chief Executive
McCann Enterprise

Stephen is CEO and Founder of McCann Enterprise, a corporate and B2B specialist agency within McCann Worldgroup, and recently voted 'Best B2B Marketing Agency' by the RAR. Prior to setting up McCann Enterprise, Stephen was European and UK Head of Planning for McCann. He joined McCann from Springpoint, where he was Managing Director, having previously spent some 15 years at both Publicis and HHCL, Campaign's Agency of the Decade in 2000.

VIKKI MITCHELL (B)

Director, Corporate Practice
KANTAR

Vikki is a specialist in branding and positioning, corporate reputation and creative development research. She regularly partners with multi-national and challenger brands to understand how to maintain their corporate reputation during a crisis, and how to optimise their communication materials, track their brand and understand the evolution of the customer journey. Vikki sits on the BIG Group board and is a frequent speaker at B2B events.

ROB MORRICE (B)

CEO
Stein IAS

Under Rob's guidance, Stein IAS has become a truly global B2B agency force. Named Business Marketing Association's B2B Agency of the Year five times, it has collected numerous global B2B awards since its inception in 2013. With locations across North America, EMEA and APAC, Stein IAS works with brands including Oracle, HSBC, Merck, Ingredion, Trelleborg, Marshalls, Tetra Pak and Weight Watchers.

NICK MORRIS (C)

Founding Partner
Canvas8

In 2008 Nick founded Canvas8 to challenge the formica world of market research. Canvas8 is a behavioural insight practice that helps businesses, brands and organisations understand people so they can do what they do best. Canvas8 has helped the Bill and Melinda Gates Foundation understand the science of influence, Weber Shandwick become Global PR agency of the year, Nike plan for the World Cup and the Euros, Google pivot and the British Government prepare for life post Brexit.

RICHARD MOSS (C)

Chief Executive
Good Relations

Richard is Chief Executive of Good Relations, one of the UK's leading PR and content agencies. Starting his career in FMCG marketing, managing the Andrex, Carlsberg and Mr Kipling brands, he moved into the public relations industry to pursue his passion for more authentic communication solutions. Today his agency's proposition is centred around 'Contagious Truthtelling' with clients including Subway®, Lidl, B&Q and Airbus.

JAMES MURPHY (C)

Founder & CEO
adam&eveDDB

James co-founded adam&eve in 2008, merging with DDB in 2012. It's the Gunn Report's most awarded agency ever, has won Top UK Agency at Cannes for the last four years and has won the IPA Effectiveness Grand Prix an unprecedented three times in a row. AdAge named it International Agency of the Year 2015 and 2017, and it has been Campaign's Agency of the Year in 2010 and from 2014 to 2017. James is Chairman of the Advertising Association.

MICHAEL MURPHY (B)

Senior Partner
Michael Murphy & Ltd

Michael has had a long career in public relations. Five years ago he established his own advisory firm, Michael Murphy & Ltd, which provides non-executive and advisory services around the world to a range of marketing and communications consultancies and agencies as well as firms in other sectors. He also mentors and advises a number of senior business leaders and is Vice Chair of Governors at London Metropolitan University.

THOM NEWTON (C)

CEO & Managing Partner
Conran Design Group

Thom is a progressive leader with over 20 years' experience in the design industry. In his current role, he has led the agency during the most dynamic period of growth in its 60-year history – through the development of the in-house studio model (Studio by Conran Design Group), the naming and packaging offering and expansion into the US. Conran is part of the Havas network and the Vivendi group of companies. Thom is a member of the Havas UK Board.

TIM PERKINS (C)

Deputy Group Chairman
Design Bridge

Tim has over 30 years experience of international brand design and has been an integral part of the Design Bridge team for 25 years. Now one of the most successful and respected brand design agencies, Design Bridge has a reputation for delivering award winning work across a broad range of clients such as Diageo, Unilever, AkzoNobel, Mondelēz and Fortnum & Mason. Tim is a champion of long-term relationships built upon bold creativity, simplicity and honesty.

REBECCA PRICE (B)

Partner
Frank Bright & Abel

Rebecca is a brand strategist and communications specialist. She has a knack for finding what matters and expressing it well, and knows that the right creative expression is about so much more than design alone. She is Co-Founder and Partner of creative consultancy Frank, Bright & Abel.

JULIAN PULLAN (C)

Vice Chairman
& President International
Jack Morton Worldwide

Julian is Vice Chairman and President International of brand experience agency, Jack Morton Worldwide. Rated among the top global brand experience agencies, Jack Morton Worldwide integrates live and online experiences, digital and social media, and branded environments that engage consumers, business partners and employees for leading brands everywhere.

SANDY PUREWAL (B)

Founder
Superfied

Sandy has over 20 years of sales, marketing and PR experience, advising B2B brands from global blue chips to disruptive startups. He co-founded Octopus Group (now Superfied) and has spearheaded its award-winning Brand to Sales proposition combining comms, creative and technology to accelerate demand. Sandy's experience includes working with Vodafone, Cisco, Accenture, Travelex and Adecco on both local and international programmes. Sandy has been a PRCA Council Member and is in the PR Week Powerbook.

DAVE ROBERTS (B)

Creative Partner
Superunion

Dave is the multi-award-winning Creative Partner at Superunion, with a passion to bridge the gap between creativity and strategy. With his wealth of experience, he has developed some of the world's most revered brands including Nespresso, Investec, Nokia, Samsung, HSBC, Molton Brown and Kew Gardens. At the heart, Dave is committed to helping clients accomplish authentic business strategies and finding ways to turn them into meaningful and highly crafted creative solutions.

TOM ROBERTS (C)

CEO
Tribal Worldwide London

Tom leads Tribal Worldwide London, part of the Tribal DDB Worldwide network, held by marketing services giant Omnicom, as CEO. Tom has responsibility for the agency's strategic direction, expanding client relationships, and managing the executive team. Tom heads up both large-scale national and international projects, most recently leading the team that designed the multi-award-winning digital connected customer journey for Volkswagen UK. He is also a member of the DDB UK Executive Board.

GLENN ROBERTSON (B)

Owner & Managing Director
Purechannels

Glenn is one of the UK's leading experts in channel marketing and Owner of award-winning channel agency, Purechannels. Entrepreneur, marketer and inventor, Glenn's client experience spans major global brands, SMBs and funded start-ups. He leads the Purechannels team to continually pursue excellence in everything they do, creating a difference through three core principles: niche expertise, stunning creative and client satisfaction.

GARY ROBINSON (C)

Creative Partner
Studio of Art and Commerce

At Studio of Art and Commerce, Gary has helped create a successful series of mini documentaries for Walgreens Boots Alliance as well as the first advertising campaign for BrewDog, the successful crowdfunded brewery. He was previously ECD of FCB Inferno where, in his four years, he oversaw the most creatively awarded years in the agency's history.

SUSANNA SIMPSON (B)

Founder
Limelight
@susannasimpson

Limelight gives talented, ambitious businesses and people the recognition they deserve. Its major skill lies in building business credibility through thought leadership programmes for corporates, private businesses and individuals. Working predominantly in the B2B sector, Limelight delivers reputation driven growth for businesses including Axicom and Gallup and its personal branding programme, The Brand You, raises the profiles of respected business leaders and entrepreneurs.

MARTA SWANNIE (C)

Digital Creative Director
Superunion

Marta is a Creative Director at Superunion, with a particular focus on innovation. She has created brand identities, products and experiences for some of the world's most exciting companies, including PlayStation, Red Bull, Orange, Tate, National Gallery, British Airways and IAG's new airline LEVEL. She is a regular juror at industry events, from the Cannes Lion festival to this year's D&AD New Blood awards.

EMMA THOMPSON (C)

Chair, Consumer Marketing
Weber Shandwick

Emma has spent the last 20 years advising the world's best known brands and companies in public relations, brand strategy and consumer engagement. She has launched brands, products, services and campaigns for everyone from Coca-Cola to easyJet, Microsoft to Virgin. She now heads up Consumer Marketing at the world's leading PR and engagement agency, Weber Shandwick and remains a hands-on strategic lead for clients such as Kellogg's, Pearson, Centrica and Virgin Atlantic.

ALAN VANDERMOLEN (B)

President, International
WE Communications
@AlanVanderMolen

Alan runs WE Communications businesses outside of the US. He designed the agency's Brands in Motion and Stories in Motion studies, which now form the backbone of the agency's point of view and approach to client assignments. Alan also spearheaded the launch of PLUS, a WE-led, antinetwork group of global, independent specialist agencies helping brands shake the shackles of mundane, holding company 'solutions'.

GUY WIEYNK (C)

CEO
Publicis UK & Western Europe
Global Lead
Sapient Inside

Over the past three years, Guy has led the transformation of Publicis UK's broad client offering and seen some of the agency's biggest wins from the last decade including Morrisons, Heineken and the International Olympics Committee. He also leads Sapient Inside – the collaborative offering between Publicis Communications and Publicis Sapient. Prior to this, Guy spent 17 years at AKQA where he built the agency globally, trebling its revenue and winning over 300 major awards for his work.

DYLAN WILLIAMS (C)

Partner & Chief Strategy Officer
Droga5 London

Dylan came to prominence in 1998 upon appointment as BBH's youngest company director. A move to Mother in 2004 culminated in Campaign voting him the industry's Number One Strategist and Mother its Agency of The Decade. After two years as Global CSO at Publicis Worldwide, he joined Droga5 London as CSO and Partner in 2016. The agency has since doubled in revenue. Dylan sits on Facebook's Client Council and Tech City Advisory Board at 10 Downing Street.

DAVID WILLAN (B)

**Co-Founder
& Former Chairman**
Circle Research (now Savanta)

David has spent a lifetime in B2B research. Having co-founded BPRI and sold this business to WPP, he became Chairman of Circle Research, which is now known as Savanta. David oversaw the sale of this business to Next 15 plc.

MATT WILLIFER (C)

Chief Strategy Officer
WCRS
Partner
Engine

Matt's career combines classic brand planning with cutting-edge digital expertise. He joined BMP DBB from Oxford University in 1995. As Head of Strategy at M&C Saatchi, he won the inaugural APG Global Strategy Agency Of The Year Award. Following that, he spent a two-year stint as CEO of a games developer. Now, as part of the senior management team at WCRS, Matt oversees the agency's strategic output across brand, advertising, digital, social, and everything in-between.

PROF. ALAN WILSON PHD (B)

Professor of Marketing
University of Strathclyde
@ProfAlanWilson

Alan is a Professor of Marketing at the University of Strathclyde Business School. Before joining the University, he was a senior consultant at a London-based marketing consultancy. He is the author of several business books and has written numerous articles on corporate reputation, customer experience management and branding. He is also a Fellow of both the Chartered Institute of Marketing and the Market Research Society.

QUALIFYING BRANDS

The brands listed here have all qualified for the status of Business (B) or Consumer (C) Superbrand in 2019 by scoring highly with the Business or Consumer Expert Council, and the Consumer or Business Professional audiences. Where brands perform strongly with both Business and Consumer voters, it is possible for them to qualify as both a Business and a Consumer Superbrand.

Brand	
3M	B
7-Up	C
AA	C
ABB	B
ABP (Associated British Ports)	B
ABSOLUT VODKA	C
ABTA	B
Acas (Advisory, Conciliation & Arbitration Service)	B
Accenture	B
Access Self Storage	B
Acer	B
Actimel	C
Activia	C
adam&eveDDB	B
Adecco	B
adidas	C
Adobe	B
ADT	B
Aegon	B
Aer Lingus	B
AIG	B
AIM	B
Air France	B
Air Products	B
Airbus	B
AKQA	B
AkzoNobel	B
Aldi	C
Alfa Romeo	C
Allen & Overy	B
Allianz	B
Alpen	C
Alstom	B
Alton Towers	C
Always	C
Amazon	C
Ambre Solaire	C
AMD	B
American Airlines	B C
American Express	B C
American Express Travel	B
Amey	B
AMV BBDO	B
Anchor	C
Andrex	C
Anglo American	B
Aon	B
Apple	B C
Aptamil	C
Aquafresh	C
Arcadis	B
ArcelorMittal	B
Arco	B
Argos	C
Ariel	C
Arm	B
Arriva	B
Arsenal FC	C
Arup	B
ASDA	C
Ashridge Executive Education	B
Aston Business School	B
AstraZeneca	B
Atkins	B
Audi	C
Aunt Bessie's	C
Auto Trader	C
Autodesk	B
Autoglass®	B C
Avery	B
Avis	C
Aviva	B C
AXA	B C
Axis Security	B
B&Q	C
Babcock	B
Bacardi	C
BAE Systems	B
Baileys	C
Bain & Company	B
Bakers	C
Balfour Beatty	B
Bank of America Merrill Lynch	B
Bank of Scotland	B
Barclaycard	B C
Barclays	B C
BASF	B
Basildon Bond	B
Baxter	B
Bayer	B
BBC	C
BBC Children in Need	C
BBH	B
BCG (Boston Consulting Group)	B
BDA (British Dental Association)	B
Beck's	C
Beechams	C
Ben & Jerry's	C
Benylin	C
Bertolli	C
BHP	B
Bibby Line	B
BIC	B C
Biffa	B
Big Yellow	B
Birds Eye	C
Bisto	C
BLACK+DECKER	B C
Bloomberg	B
Bloomsbury Professional	B
BMA (British Medical Association)	B
BMW	C
BNP Paribas	B
BNP Paribas Real Estate	B
BOC	B
Bodyform	C
Boeing	B
Bold	C
Bombardier	B
Bombay Sapphire	C
Bonjela	C
Booker	B
Booking.com	C
Boots	C
Bosch	B C
Bose	B
Bovril	C
BP	B C
BPP Professional Education	B
Brakes	B
Brandon Hire	B
Branston	C
Braun	C
Bristol-Myers Squibb	B
British Airways	B C
British Chambers of Commerce (BCC)	B
British Council	B
British Gas	C
British Gas Business Energy	B
British Gypsum	B
British Heart Foundation	C
British Land	B
British Red Cross	C
Britvic	C
Brother	B
Brunswick	B
BSI	B
BT	B C
BT Sport	C
Budweiser	C
Buildbase	B
Bulmers	C
Bunzl	B
Bupa	B C
Bureau Veritas	B
Burger King	C
Buxton	C
Cadbury	C
Caffè Nero	C
Calor	B
CALPOL	C
Cambridge Judge Business School	B
Campbell's	C
Canary Wharf Group	B
Cancer Research UK	C
Canon	B C
Capgemini	B
Capita	B
Capital FM	C
Captain Morgan	C
Cargill	B
Carling	C
Carlsberg	C
Carphone Warehouse	C
Carte D'Or	C
Carter Jonas	B
Cass Business School	B
Castrol	B
Cat	B
Cathay Pacific	B C
Cathedral City	C
CBI	B
CBRE	B
CEMEX	B
Center Parcs	C
Centrum	C
Cesar	C
Channel 4	C
Chelsea FC	C
Chessington World of Adventures	C
Chevron	B
Chubb - Insurance category	B
Chubb - Security category	B
Churchill	C
CIMA (Chartered Institute of Management Accountants)	B
CIPD	B
Cisco	B
Citi	B
City & Guilds	B
Clarks	C
Classic FM	C
Clear Channel	B
Clearasil	C
Clifford Chance	B
CMI (Chartered Management Institute)	B
Coca-Cola	C
Coca-Cola London Eye	C
Colgate	C
Colman's	C
Comfort	C
comparethemarket.com	C
Compass Group	B
Continental	C
Converse	C
Co-operatives UK	B
Cornetto	C
Corona	C
Corsodyl	C
Costa	C
Costain	B
Cosworth	B
Country Life	C
Courvoisier	C
Cow & Gate	C
Cranfield School of Management	B
Cravendale	C
Crayola	C
Credit Suisse	B
Crowdcube	B
Crown Trade	B
Crowne Plaza	B C
Cummins	B
Cunard	C
Cuprinol	C
Currys	C
Cushelle	C
DAF	B
Daily Mail	C
Dairylea	C
Danone	C
David Lloyd Clubs	C
De La Rue	B
De Vere	B
Debenhams	C
Dell	B C
Dell EMC	B
Deloitte	B
Deloitte Real Estate	B
Delta	B
Dettol	C
Deutsche Bank	B
DeWALT	B
DHL	B
Digital Cinema Media (DCM)	B
Digitas	B
Direct Line	B C
Disney	C
Disney Channel	C
Dolmio	C
Domestos	C
Domino's Pizza	C
Doritos	C
Douwe Egberts	C
Dove	C
Dow	B
DPD	B
Dr Pepper	C
Dreams	C
Dropbox	B
DS Smith	B
Dulux	C
Dulux Trade	B
Dun & Bradstreet	B
DuPont	B
Duracell	C
Durex	C
Durham University Business School	B
Dyson	B C
E.ON	B
E45	C
Early Learning Centre	C
easyJet	B C
eBay	C
Echo Falls	C
Eddie Stobart	B
Edelman	B
Eden Project	C
EDF Energy	B C
Edwardian Hotels London	B
EE	C
Elastoplast	C
Elsevier	B
Embraer	B
Emerson	B
Emirates	B C
Epson	B
Equifax	B
Equiniti	B
Equinix	B
Ericsson	B
Etihad	B C
Euronext	B
Europcar	C
Eurostar	B C
Eurotunnel	B
Eversheds Sutherland	B
evian	C
ExCeL London	B
Expedia	C
Experian	B
ExxonMobil	B
EY	B
Facebook	C
Fairtrade Foundation	B
Fairy	C
Fanta	C
Farley's	C
Febreze	C
FedEx	B
Felix	C
Ferrero Rocher	C
Filofax	B
Financial Times	C
Finastra	B
First	B
Fisher-Price	C
Fitbit	C
Fitch Group	B
Flash	C
Flora	C
Flymo	C
Foot Locker	C
Ford	C
Forrester	B
Foster's	C
Fred Perry	C
Freeview	C
Freightliner	B
freuds	B
FSC (Forest Stewardship Council)	B
FTSE Russell	B
Fujitsu	B
G4S	B
Galaxy	C
Gallup	B
Garnier	C
Gartner	B
Gatwick Airport	C
Gatwick Express	B
Gaviscon	C
GE	B
Gillette	C
GKN	B
GlaxoSmithKline (GSK)	B
Glencore	B
Glenfiddich	C
Globalstar	B
GoDaddy	B
Goldman Sachs	B
Google	B C
Gordon's	C
Gourmet	C
Graham	B
Grant Thornton	B
Great Ormond Street Hospital Charity	C
Great Portland Estates	B
Green & Black's	C
Green Flag	C
Greggs	C
Grey London	B
Grosvenor	B
Groupon	C
Guinness	C
Gumtree	C
H&M	C
Häagen-Dazs	C
Halfords	C
Halfords Autocentre	C
Halifax	C
Hall & Partners	B
Halliburton	B
Hallmark	C
Halls	C
Hamleys	C
Hanson	B
Hapag-Lloyd	B
Hardys	C
Haribo	B C
Hartley's	C
Haymarket	B
Hays	C
Head & Shoulders	C
Heart	C
Heathrow	B
Heathrow Express	B
Heineken	C
Heinz	C
Hellmann's	C
Help for Heroes	C
Henkel	B
Henley Business School	B
Herbal Essences	C
Hermes	B
Hertz	C
Hewlett Packard Enterprise	B
Highland Spring	C
Hilti	B
Hilton Food Group	B
Hilton Hotels & Resorts	B C
Hiscox	B
Hitachi	B
Holiday Inn	B C
Holland & Barrett	C
Honeywell	B
Hoover	C
Hornby	C
Hotels.com	C
Hotpoint	C
House of Fraser	C
Hovis	C
Howden	B
Howdens Joinery	B
Hozelock	C
HP	B C
HP Sauce	C
HSBC	B C
HSS Hire	B
Huawei	B
Huggies® Wipes	C
Iams	C
IBM	B
ICC Birmingham	B
Iceland	C
IKEA	C
Imperial College Business School	B
Imperial Leather	C
Informa	B
Infosys	B
Ingersoll Rand	B
Initial	B
Inmarsat	B
innocent	C
Instagram	C
Intel	B
Intelsat	B
International Paper	B
Interserve	B
Investec	B
Investors in People	B
IoD (Institute of Directors)	B
Ipsos MORI	B
Iron Mountain	B
Irwin Mitchell	B
ISS	B
ITV	C
ITV Media	B
IVECO	B
J.P. Morgan	B
J2O	C
Jack Daniel's	C
Jacob's	C
Jacob's Creek	C
Jaguar	C
Jameson	C
Jammie Dodgers	C
JCB	B
JCDecaux	B
JD Sports	C
Jewson	B
Jiffy	B
Jim Beam	C
JLL	B
John Deere	B
John Frieda	C
John Lewis & Partners	C
John West	C
Johnnie Walker	C
Johnson & Johnson	B
Johnson Controls	B
Johnson Matthey (JM)	B
Johnson Service Group	B
JOHNSON'S	C
Johnstone's Trade	B
Jordans	C
JUST EAT	C
JWT London	B
Kaspersky Lab	C
Kellogg's	C
Kenco	C
Kenwood - Household Appliances category	C
KETTLE Chips	C
Kew Gardens	C
Keyline	B
KFC	C
Kier Group	B
KIMBERLY-CLARK PROFESSIONAL	B
Kindle	C

Please note that this list reflects the brands as presented in the Superbrands research voting process; brands may subsequently have been altered or entirely rebranded, while others may no longer be sold or operational.

Brand	Qualifier
Kingsmill	C
Kingspan Group	B
KitKat	C
Kleenex	C
KLM	B
Knight Frank	B
Knorr	C
KPMG	B
Krispy Kreme	C
Kronenbourg 1664	C
Kuehne + Nagel	B
Kwik Fit	C
Lacoste	C
Ladbrokes	C
Ladybird	C
Laing O'Rourke	B
Lambert Smith Hampton	B
Land Rover	C
Landsec	B
lastminute.com	C
Le Creuset	C
Lea & Perrins	C
learndirect	B
Leeds University Business School	B
Legal & General	C
LEGO	C
LEGOLAND	C
LEGOLAND Discovery Centre	C
Lemsip	C
Lenor	C
Lenovo	B C
Leo Burnett London	B
LEVC	B
LexisNexis	B
Lexmark	B
Lexus	C
Leyland Trade	B
Leyland Trucks	B
LG	B C
Lidl	C
Lilly	B
Lindt	C
LinkedIn	B
Linklaters	B
Listerine	C
Liverpool FC	C
Lloyd's	B
Lloyds Bank	B C
Lockheed Martin	B
Logitech	B
London Business School	B
London Metal Exchange	B
London School of Economics and Political Science (LSE)	B
London Stock Exchange Group	B
Loomis	B
L'Oreal Elvive	C
Lucozade	C
Lufthansa	B
Lurpak	C
Lynx	C
Maclaren	C
Macmillan Cancer Support	C
Madame Tussauds	C
Maersk Line	B
Magnet Trade	B
Magnum	C
Makita	B
Maltesers	C
Mamas & Papas	C
Manchester Airport	C
Manchester Central	B
Manchester City FC	C
Manchester United	C
Manpower	B
Marie Curie	C
Marks & Spencer	C
Marmite	C
Marriott Hotels & Resorts	B C
Mars	C
Marsh	B
Marshalls	B
Martini	C
Marvel	C
Massey Ferguson	B
Mastercard	B C
Maynards Bassetts	C
McAfee	B
McCain	C
McCann London	B
McCoy's	C
McDonald's	C
McKinsey & Company	B
McLaren	B
McVitie's	C
MediaCom	B
Menzies Aviation	B
Menzies Distribution	B
Mercedes-Benz	C
Mercer	B
Mercure	B
Michael Page	B
Microsoft	B C
Miele	C
Mindshare	B
MINI	C
Mintel	B
Miracle-Gro	C
Mitie	B
Mitsubishi Electric	B
Moleskine	B
Molton Brown	C
MoneySuperMarket	C
Monster	B
Moody's	B
MORE TH>N	C
Morgan Stanley	B
Morrisons	C
Mother London	B
Mothercare	C
Mr Kipling	C
Mr Muscle	C
Mr Sheen	C
Müller	C
Murphy	C
Nando's	C
National Express	B C
National Grid	B
National Trust	C
Nationwide	C
NatWest	B C
NEC - Technology category	
NEC - Conference & Event Venues category	B
Nescafé	C
Nespresso	C
Nestlé Cereals	C
Nestlé Professional	B
Netflix	C
NETGEAR	B
Neutrogena	C
Next	C
NFU	B
NFU Mutual	B
Niceday	B
Nicorette	C
Nielsen	B
Night Nurse	C
Nike	C
Nikon	C
Nintendo	C
Nivea	C
Nokia	B
Norton	C
Novartis	B
Novotel	B
npower	B C
NSPCC	C
Nurofen	C
Nutella	C
NVIDIA	B
O2	C
Oasis	C
ODEON	C
Office Depot	B
Ogilvy	B
Olay	C
Olympia London	B
Olympus	B
Omega	C
Optrex	C
Oracle	B
Oral-B	C
Ordnance Survey (OS)	B
OSRAM	B
Otis	B
Oxfam	C
Oxford Black n' Red	B
OXO	C
P&O Cruises	C
P&O Ferries	C
P&O Ferrymasters	B
Paddy Power	C
Pampers	C
Panadol	C
Panasonic	B C
Pandora	C
Pantene	C
Paper Mate	B
Parcelforce Worldwide	B
Park Inn by Radisson	B
Park Plaza	B
PARKER	B
Parker	B
PAXO	C
PayPal	B C
PayPoint	B
PC World	C
Pearl & Dean	B
Pedigree	C
Pepsi	C
Perrier	C
Persil	C
Petrofac	B
Pfizer	B
PG Tips	C
Philadelphia	C
Philips	B C
PHS Group	B
Pickfords	B
Pilkington	B
PILOT	B
PIMM'S	C
Piriton	C
Pitney Bowes	B
Pizza Hut	C
PizzaExpress	C
Play-Doh	C
PlayStation	C
Plumbase	B
Plusnet	B
Polypipe	B
Portakabin	B
Post Office	C
Post-it	B
Pot Noodle	C
Premier Inn	B C
Pret	C
Primark	C
Princess Cruises	C
Pringles	C
Prudential	B C
Publicis London	B
Puma	C
Purina	C
Purplebricks	C
PwC	B
PYREX	C
Qatar Airways	B C
Quaker Oats	C
Qualcomm	B
Quality Street	C
RAC	C
Rackspace	B
Radisson Hotels	B C
Radox	C
Ramada	B
Red Bull	C
Redland	B
Reebok	C
REED	B
Reed Exhibitions	B
Regus	B
Rennie	C
Rentokil	B
Rexel	B
RIBA (The Royal Institute of British Architects)	B
Ribena	C
Ricoh	B
Ricoh Arena	B
RICS	B
Right Guard	C
Rightmove	C
Rio Tinto	B
River Island	C
Robertson's	C
Robinsons	C
Roche	B
Rolex	C
Rolls-Royce	B
Rotary	C
Rothschild & Co	B
Rowntree's	C
Royal Albert Hall	C
Royal Bank of Scotland	B
Royal Caribbean International	C
Royal Doulton	C
Royal London	B
Royal Mail	B C
RS Components	B
RSA	B
RSPCA	C
Ryman	B
Ryvita	C
S&P Global	B
S.Pellegrino	C
Saatchi & Saatchi	B
Safestore	B
Sage	B
Sainsbury's	C
Saint-Gobain	B
Salesforce	B
Samsung	B C
San Miguel	C
Sanatogen	C
Sandals Resorts	C
SanDisk	B
Sandvik	B
Sanofi	B
Santander	B C
SAP	B
SapientRazorfish	B
Sarson's	C
SAS	B
Savills	B
Savlon	C
Scalextric	C
Scania	B
Schindler	B
Schneider Electric	B
Schwartz	C
Schwarzkopf	C
Schweppes	C
Scottish and Southern Electricity Networks	B
Scottish Hydro Electric Transmission	B
Scottish Widows	B
ScottishPower	B C
Screwfix	B C
SEA LIFE Centres	C
SEGRO	B
Selco	B
Selfridges	C
Sensodyne	C
Serco	B
Seven Seas	C
Sharp	B
Sharwood's	C
Sheba	C
Shell	B C
Sheraton	B
Shredded Wheat	C
Shred-it	B
Siemens	B C
Siemens Healthineers	B
Silentnight Beds	C
Silver Cross	C
Silver Spoon	C
Simple	C
Singapore Airlines	B C
Sir Robert McAlpine	B
Skanska	B
Sky	B
Sky Media	B
Skype	B
Slaughter and May	B
Slumberland	C
SmartWater	B
Smeg	C
Smirnoff	C
Smith & Nephew	B
Smiths Group	B
Smurfit Kappa	B
Snap-on	B
Sodexo	B
Sofitel	B
Sony	C
Sony Professional	B
Sophos	B
Southern Comfort	C
Specsavers	C
Speedy	B
Spotify	C
Sprite	C
SSE Enterprise	B
STABILO	C
STAEDTLER	B
Stagecoach	B
STANLEY	B
Starbucks	C
Stella Artois	C
STIHL	B
Stobart Group	B
Strepsils	C
Strongbow	C
Strutt & Parker	B
Subway	C
Sudafed	C
Sudocrem	C
Superdrug	C
Superdry	C
Sure	C
SurveyMonkey	B
Swarovski	C
Swissport	B
Symantec	B
Tabasco	C
TAG Heuer	C
TalkTalk	B
TalkTalk Business	B
Tampax	C
Tarmac	B
Tata Communications	B
Tata Consultancy Services (TCS)	B
Tate & Lyle	B
Tate & Lyle Cane Sugar	C
Taylors of Harrogate	C
Ted Baker	C
TEMPUR	C
Tesco	B C
Tetley	C
Tetra Pak	B
Texaco	C
Texas Instruments	B
Thales	B
The Baltic Exchange	B
The Body Shop	C
The Daily Telegraph	C
The Famous Grouse	C
The Guardian	C
The Institute of Financial Accountants (IFA)	B
The Law Society	B
The National Lottery	C
The Open University Business School	B
The Soil Association	B
The Sun	C
The Times	C
Thomas Cook	C
Thomson Reuters	B
Thorn	B
Thorntons	C
Thorpe Park	C
thyssenkrupp	B
Ticketmaster	C
Tipp-Ex	B
Tissot	C
tommee tippee®	C
TomTom	C
TONI&GUY	C
Toolstation	B
Topman	C
Topshop	C
Toshiba	B C
Total	B
Totaljobs.com	B
Toyota	C
Travelodge	B C
Travis Perkins	B
TRESemmé	C
TripAdvisor	C
trivago	C
Tropicana	C
TSB	B
TUI	C
Twinings	C
Twitter	C
Typhoo	C
Tyrrells	C
UK Mail	B
UK Power Networks	B
Uncle Ben's	C
Unipart	B
Unisys	B
United	B
University of Edinburgh Business School	B
University of Glasgow Adam Smith Business School	B
UPS	B
Vaillant	B
Vanish	C
Vaseline	C
Veet	C
Vent-Axia	B
Veolia	B
Vicks	C
Viking	B
Viking Cruises	C
Virgin Atlantic	B C
Virgin Holidays	C
Virgin Media	B
Virgin Media Business	B
Virgin Mobile	C
Virgin Trains	B C
Visa	B C
VMware	B
Vodafone	C
Volkswagen	C
Volvic	C
Volvo	C
Volvo CE	B
Waitrose & Partners	C
Walkers	C
Wall's	C
Wall's Ice Cream	C
Warburtons	C
WARC	B
Warwick Castle	C
Waterford	C
Waterstones	C
WBS (Warwick Business School)	B
WD-40	C
Weber Shandwick	B
Wedgwood	C
Weetabix	C
Western Union	B
Western Union Business Solutions	B
Westfield	B
WeTransfer	B
WeWork	B
WhatsApp	C
Whiskas	C
WHSmith	B C
Wickes	C
Wikipedia	C
Wilkinson Sword	C
William Hill	C
Willis Towers Watson	B
Willmott Dixon	B
Wincanton	B
Wolseley	B
Woolmark	B
Workspace	B
Worldpay	B
Wrigley's	C
Xbox	C
Xerox	B
Yakult	C
Yale	B
Yodel	B
Yorkshire Tea	C
YouGov	B
YouTube	C
Zara	C
Zenith	B
Zoopla	C
Zopa	B
Zurich	B C

Key

B - Business Superbrands Qualifier

C - Consumer Superbrands Qualifier